SEEING LIGHT
IN THE DARKNESS

A Story of Surviving Affliction with Laughter and Grace

JEFFREY C. SMITH
WITH JOHN AREHART

*"Whoever follows me will never walk in darkness,
but will have the light of life."*

- John 8:12b

*"…it's not easy living with any disability, but in your book, you
seem to guide the reader past the 'physical' and into a deeper
understanding of who God is in the midst of every challenge."*

Joni Eareckson Tada,
Founder, CEO of Joni and Friends

*For my wife, Devon – in my eyes, God's angel
and the fulfillment of my highest dream.*

TABLE OF CONTENTS

ACKNOWLEDGEMENTS

I'd like to acknowledge and thank the following people for helping me realize my dream of writing this book, a dream I have had for decades:

Carl Roesler, for assisting with the photographs; Laura Roesler, for always encouraging me I could write and write well; Telma Roesler, for researching numerous Bible verses, and Mark Roesler, as God's instrument for softening my heart so that I could receive His free gift of salvation through Jesus Christ.

Scott Saari, who takes time from his work to drive me around the country to engagements and laughs at my jokes, even when the humor falls short.

John Arehart, who had a vision for how I could move beyond my fears and self-limiting attitudes and become more the man that God had intended me to be.

I applaud Mike Stenberg, of VAS Graphic Design, for creating my Amazing Jeffo promotional materials, and for designing a book cover that reflects my ham-bone nature. In addition, I want to express my heartfelt gratitude for the numerous daytime, late night, weekend, and holiday phone conferences to get the formatting just right.

Eric Anderson, for all his assistance providing and creating essential materials for the continuing development of Amazing Jeffo.

I am grateful to all those whose friendships have never tarnished over time, the kind of friends who are there at the hospital checking on my well-being barely after I've arrived; who have patted my shoulder when I needed it and whacked me on the head when I needed that as well, and everything in between: Don and Laurie, Mark, Scott P., Kathy, Craig, and Tom.

To my siblings and their spouses: Dave and his wife Linda, Steve, Mike and his wife Mollie, and Dana and her husband Steve: my gratitude for treating me simply and solely as a brother (or brother-in-law), with all of the positives and negatives that come with it.

My utmost respect and appreciation to my dad, whose wisdom and advice helped me spread my wings and launch from the nest.

Finally I'd like to thank the two most influential and loving women in my life: my mom and my wife, Devon. I'm indebted to my mom for her years of nurturing and teaching, her impeccable memory of the events of my early childhood, and her foresight knowing before anyone else that God had placed me on earth for a purpose.

And to my beautiful Devon, whose insight, wit, judgment, and assistance is only surpassed by the unconditional love she gives me each day. I will love and honor you all the days of my life.

Without God's grace and sustenance, I wouldn't be here today. I thank Him above all.

INTRODUCTION

I remember meeting Jeff for the first time in the foyer of our church over a decade ago. He stood next to a wall, and I was introduced to him. He extended his hand, and I shook it. I knew those hands immediately—they were twisted and misaligned like my grandmother's. But unlike my grandmother, whose rheumatoid arthritis kept her virtually indoors all the time, here was a person who was not only outside but in the limelight. Jeff told me he was a magician. I looked him up and down—the hands, the cane, the eyes—and I knew I'd get to know this guy better. Little did I know how much better and how much fun we would have becoming friends and business associates.

First and foremost, Jeff and I are friends. Years before we finally decided to start DATS, we had spent many hours together in prayer groups, Bible studies, and WWII discussions. As we learned more about each other, I suspected Jeff could speak effectively to a wider audience than his magic shows offered; they typically were for Cub-Scout-aged children. The life lessons he sprinkled throughout his shows were too good for kids only. I saw him doing more— offering life lessons to adults in large auditoriums. I saw Jeff's story as inspirational and worthy of a large audience; he, being in the trenches of self-employment, hadn't been able to lift his eyes and see how far he could go since he was too busy chasing daily business opportunities. In these dealings as Amazing Jeffo, he had a great deal of self-confidence, but I saw potential for him to shift arenas into the realm of inspirational speaking. The opportunity came when Jeff received a call from a school district asking for a combination program—a magic show with a speech given by Jeff Smith, not Amazing Jeffo. This request was the beginning of our business partnership: DATS (Disability Awareness Training Seminars).

Jeff and I started writing, and writing, and rewriting. I introduced Jeff to coffee at our 6:30 a.m. sessions. We wrote the entire script for the presentation. We researched disability statistics and wrote more. During these hours of give-and-take, we learned about each other's working style, which would lay the groundwork for taking on the more ambitious project of writing this book. We practiced our presentation (not nearly enough in hindsight), took a deep breath, and went to do our first DATS presentation. More presentations followed.

The partnership works because we complement each other. Jeff has an attention to detail that I could never approach, and I'm the "visionary" in his words—the one who dreams of his being on Oprah one day and on the New York Times Best Seller list. Maybe that dream isn't so farfetched after all. Who would have thought a man with a severe stutter, no eyesight, and debilitating rheumatoid arthritis would be an accomplished magician with over 3,000 shows performed? I quit betting against Jeff a long time ago. The man is a winner. It's been a pleasure to be part of the ride.

– John Arehart

PROLOGUE

As the applause begins, adrenaline courses through me, and at that moment, I am no longer disabled. The pain of arthritis is gone, the embarrassment of my ileostomy has disappeared, and my stutter has vanished. "Good evening, Ladies and Gentlemen! I am the Amazing Jeffo, a magician who happens to be blind…long time, no see!"

After the performance, as my driver leaves the university heading to the next show, I reflect how grateful I am and how amazed I am to be here despite doctors' predictions I wouldn't live past age 13. Much like the Israelites in the desert, God has been leading me through a rocky, perilous, sometimes overwhelming landscape, where I would come to know and trust Him and experience His amazing power to transform.

As we accelerate onto the freeway, pictures flash in my mind like an old silent movie, with ever-increasing speed. I settle back into my seat and let contrasting images of my life wash over me: grand hotels and medicinal-smelling hospital rooms; running around outside with buddies and the feeling of warm, wet plaster hardening around my leg; joyous family parties where time seemed to fly and lonely hospital stays lasting months; reading superhero comics before bed and struggling to learn braille with twisted fingers…and then, one day, watching a B-movie that, unbeknownst to me, would foreshadow the direction in which God would lead me.

Let the show begin….

Chapter 1

Intestinal Fortitude or "The Week from Hell"

M y first five-and-a-half years of life were typical in every way, but that changed suddenly one evening in the early spring of 1961. My mom had just fed my siblings and me before taking a quick shower with plans to leave us with a babysitter.

"Mama," I said faintly, entering the bathroom.

"What is it, Jeffrey? I'm trying to get ready," my mom said through the shower's spray. She looked out from the curtain and saw my stricken face.

"What's wrong, honey?"

"I went icky poo in my pants," I said.

"Accidents happen," she reassured. "We'll clean it up, and I'll take your temperature."

She dried off and put me in the shower. After I was clean,

Martha and Alyce Bumgarner as toddlers with Nonnie Helen. The two women who were my greatest helps; it wouldn't happen, of course, for another 24 years.

I said, "I feel fine now, Mama, but I had a stomachache before." Shortly afterward, I announced, "I need to go again," and soiled my pants seconds later. While cleaning me up, my mom noticed

17

blood in the diarrhea. But the shower raised my spirits. "I feel good now, Mama."

"I don't think we should go out," she said to my dad. But he assured her they weren't going anywhere far. The babysitter and he convinced my mom everything would be fine.

Alyce Bumgarner, a 1957 nursing school graduate, and my soon- to-be personal white-clad angel of mercy.

When they returned home later that night, they were instantly overwhelmed with a sick odor. My mother was irritated.

"Why didn't you call me?" she snapped at the babysitter.

"I didn't want to disturb your evening. Jeff's been going all night. I used everything I could find in the linen closet," she exclaimed. Every stitch of underwear, sheets, blankets, and pajamas in the house was either soaking in the basement washtub or lying on the floor. "I feel fine, Mama," I said, trying to defuse the alarm.

The next morning (Sunday), my mom called Dr. Harold Flanagan, our family pediatrician, who said to call back first thing in the morning. I refused to eat because I figured out eating made me go in my pants. Diarrhea continued throughout Sunday night, and Monday was a nightmare. Barely after daybreak, we called Dr. Flanagan. He squeezed us into a packed appointment schedule for early afternoon.

While waiting for the appointment, my mom began the monumental task of washing all my "accidents" from the night before. Between one of the wash loads, she called my Aunt Alyce, a registered nurse. "Alyce, can you look at Jeffrey? I don't know what's going on." Alyce agreed and took off for our house.

"Please Jeff, you have to eat something!" my mom encouraged. I had a small bowl of rice. Minutes later, I was in the bathroom. "Just stay right there. I'll be right back, Jeff. Your Aunt Alyce is here." *No way am I going to leave this toilet*, I thought. I overheard my mom showing Alyce a sample of the dirty linen. "I have seen this before, Martha, but not in someone Jeffrey's age," Alyce said. "I don't want to alarm you, but this looks like ulcerative colitis."

The bouts of diarrhea continued throughout the morning. In less than forty-eight hours, I had transformed from a healthy five-year-old to a pale, gaunt, listless child.

Dr. Flanagan listened intently to the details of the severe and frequent diarrhea. After a thorough examination including a hemoglobin count, Dr. Flanagan said, "Mrs. Smith, I don't think we should wait on this thing. Jeffrey needs to be hospitalized as soon as possible for blood transfusions. His hemoglobin is dangerously low.

My mom's father (my Papa Charlie) and her mother (my Nonnie Helen) out on the town in the late forties.

That evening, I was admitted to St. Joseph's Hospital to begin a series of tests. My parents canceled hosting Easter dinner the following Sunday. I stayed in the hospital the entire week, and on Easter I was lonely. My parents visited me in the morning, but when they left I felt glum, mostly because I couldn't hunt for my Easter basket of chocolate eggs, suckers, and jelly beans.

My parents were barely gonewhen I was surprised by guests. My mom's parents—Charlie and Helen Bumgarner—spent the afternoon with me. Nonnie Helen and Papa Charlie—not realizing the status of my volatile digestive tract—were loaded with Easter candy, fruit, and a big stuffed animal. Their goodies were banned, but their presence more than made up for the "candy-free zone" of my hospital room. They kept me from dwelling on being away from my family that day. I didn't know this would be the last time I'd ever see my Nonnie Helen.

"Mrs. Smith, we've decided exploratory surgery is necessary on Jeffrey," Dr. Flanagan announced. "I've scheduled it for tomorrow morning." Despite St. Joseph's strict policies on visiting hours, Dr. Flanagan arranged for my parents to stay with me the night before surgery. "I did this for you, Mrs. Smith, because I fear Jeff might have cancer, and I want you and Mr. Smith to spend as much time with him as possible." With tears in her eyes, my mom hung up the phone, trying to absorb this latest news.

She realized she hadn't spoken with her mom, Helen, since their visit to me on Easter. She called her. "Hello?" my grandmother answered weakly.

"Mom, is everything all right?"

"Yes, Martha," she sighed. Her responses were detached, but my mom thought it was because of my illness. "I need to wash my hair, Martha, and do the laundry." My mom was alarmed because normally Nonnie Helen had these things finished by early morning. "I don't like how you sound, Mom. I'm getting someone over there."

She immediately called Aunt Alyce.

"Alyce, you need to check on Mom right now. I know this is terrible timing, but I don't like how Mom sounds, and I don't have a car!"

"I'm on my way," Alyce exclaimed with rising fear. My aunt had just returned from her honeymoon and was in the midst of opening wedding gifts with friends and family. She ran out the door, apologizing to her guests as she left.

Twenty minutes later, Alyce called my mom, hysterical. "I can't get into the house! I got a ladder from the neighbor, looked through the window, and saw Mom lying unconscious on the floor!" My mom called my father, who was an insurance agent in the Lloyd F. Smith Insurance Agency started by his father in 1933. Lots of times, he'd be on sales calls, but fortunately this time he was at his desk.

He met my panicked aunt. "I'll try to knock in the door," he said. Alyce looked at the massive oak door with uncertainty. He took a run at it with his powerfully built frame. They heard a sharp crack, but the door stood firm. He hit it again, but the door remained intact. Grunting in disgust, my father ran at the door with everything he could muster. The solid oak door, frame, and plaster came crashing in. They rushed into the house, and Alyce started CPR. My dad called the police who sent an ambulance. Miraculously, my grandmother responded to the CPR. She weakly asked, "Lloyd...Alyce, what are you doing here? I need to get up... get my chores done." Alyce smiled, wiping away tears.

"Mom, we're taking you to the hospital."

Papa Lloyd started the Lloyd F. Smith Insurance Agency in 1933, now in its fourth generation.

Papa Charlie, former professional dancer, whose love of classical music, jazz and showbiz I inherited.

My dad's father, Papa Lloyd, drove my mom to Miller Hospital where Nonnie Helen lay in the ICU. Our neighbor watched my siblings David, Dana, and Stephen. At the hospital, my mom was stopped by a business representative. "We first need to verify your current insurance information."

Astounded and irritated, my mom took off for the elevator, shouting back, "I guarantee you'll get paid! In the meantime, my mom is likely dying!"

She found my grandmother in an oxygen tent fighting a severe case of pneumonia. Once assured her mother was stable, my mom tracked down her father, Charlie, with the help of his secretary. "Get here right away, Dad," she said. "I think Mom's dying."

Nonnie Helen held her own through Tuesday, the day of my surgery. Very early that morning, my mom approached my grandmother's bed. She wanted to give my grandma the best chance of fighting the pneumonia. She knew her mother had already been very upset about my condition. "Good news, Mom," she fibbed. "The doctors found out the problem with Jeff. They removed a little polyp that was causing all the bleeding. He's all right." One tear came out of my Nonnie's eye. She smiled and fell back unconscious.

At nearly 2 a.m. that morning, while my parents and grandpa were anxiously waiting for news about my grandmother, a grim- faced physician approached Papa Charlie. "Charlie, I'm sorry, but Helen didn't make it." Papa Charlie gasped and collapsed on the floor. My grandfather was immediately taken to the ICU, the very same unit where his wife had just died. Doctors feared my grandpa had contracted the same Friedlander's pneumonia that had just killed his wife. My parents reeled. Throughout the next few days, everyone's nerves were raw as doctors repeatedly alerted the family of my grandfather's impending death. He did pull through but not until recuperating in the hospital for three months. Numbly, my parents tried to digest the death of my grandmother and my grandfather battling for his life.

With my grandfather stabilized for the moment, my parents decided to go home for a couple of hours of sleep before returning for my 7 a.m. surgery.

"Lloyd, I'm losing my whole family!" my mom said as they drove back to the hospital the next morning. They arrived looking haggard, but after the surgery they were rewarded with the news that I did not have cancer. The doctors discovered I had a large diverticulum, which is a pouch in the intestines filled with infection. They removed it and hoped they had solved the problem.

"No matter what it costs, we want our son kept in 24-hour intensive care," my dad said, knowing this level of care would make it possible for them to leave me and attend the funeral and care for my grandfather in the days thereafter. My parents and Aunt Alyce rushed off to attend Nonnie Helen's funeral.

Doctors kept me in the hospital for several additional days, fearing I might have contracted the Friedlander's pneumonia from my grandmother.

Years later, my mom said, "Those were the worst days of my life."

"...you may have had to suffer grief in all kinds of trials..."
1 Peter 1:6

"When you're going through hell, keep on going."
–Winston Churchill

CHAPTER 2

PEERING INTO A FUTURE
OF UNCERTAINTY

After a week, I returned home and soon began bleeding again. "We've exhausted our options, Mrs. Smith," said Dr. Flanagan, "Jeff is a sick, sick child." He and Dr. Bernstein, a leader in pediatric proctology, were assuming based on my symptoms and test results that I had an intestinal infection. They concluded it couldn't be ulcerative colitis because I simply didn't fit the profile. I was much too young. They put me on Asulphadine and a strict, modified diet with low roughage. Naturally, I focused on the parts of the diet that denied my taste buds—no cranberries (my favorite), no grape juice (my favorite), no black olives (my favorite), no dairy ice cream (my favorite), and on and on went the list. My mother now had to prepare a special diet for me; every meal was custom. Even with the special diet and medication, I still battled a spastic, explosive bowel to the tune of as much as 28-30 bouts of diarrhea daily. I should have applied to the NASA program as the first self-powered child in space.

Me on the right, already starting my thankless career of bugging to death my big brother Dave. But he stopped short of completely strangling me, realizing it would all be caught on film.

While my guts were trying their best to turn me inside out, I began limping the fall prior to kindergarten. My mom noticed my limping one day while I was playing with my brother. "Why are you limping?" she asked. Upon closer examination she saw that my left index finger joint had swelled to the size of a walnut, and my knee was swelling noticeably. "I don't know," I said.

"Does it hurt?" she asked.

"No."

I wanted to return to playtime more than I wanted to acknowledge the discomfort. My mom wasn't willing to take to heart my casual appraisal that everything was fine. She was already in a hypersensitive state of concern given what had exploded onto the scene earlier that year of 1961. Without hesitating, she called Doctor Flanagan about my swollen joints. She felt reassured knowing Dr. Flanagan was my doctor and also the president of the Minnesota Society of Pediatrics. Anguishing memories flooded her thoughts while waiting to connect with the doctor. She couldn't help thinking about the circumstances surrounding the onset of my ulcerative colitis.

"Mrs. Smith, tell me about Jeffrey." After relaying details of my inflamed knee and finger to the doctor, an appointment was scheduled the next day. After many tests, all inconclusive, Doctor Flanagan said, "We think an infection in Jeff's G.I. tract is resulting in his knee inflammation. It's our best guess at this point." Flanagan prescribed aspirin to cool down my over-heated knee. The medication helped, but every morning I'd wake with the knee just as swollen as before. I had been a robust child the first five years of my life, but in less than a year I'd become a shadow of myself. My left knee continued to swell; the leg also began to curl up, and I could no longer straighten it all the way.

My mom arranged another appointment with our trusted Dr. Flanagan. He epitomized the ideal of a pediatric physician: kind, knowledgeable, and friendly. He involved me in the conversations instead of directing everything at my mom. He'd wrap his arm around our shoulders to soften the blows as he delivered bad news, which was becoming all-too frequent. After exams and blood work, he'd say, "Jeff, why don't you go out to the play area while I chat with your mom?" Amidst my play, I'd wonder what they would be talking about.

Flanagan would talk to my mom as a friend as he shared examination and test results. During one of these discussions, he said, "In all my years of practice, I've never seen a little boy with intestinal diarrhea symptoms to this degree...and now this knee inflammation...I don't know what to make of it, Martha!"

Fortunately I was an October baby, so my illness didn't interfere with my schooling yet. Finally, the doctors in the Twin Cities threw their hands up and said their treatments weren't working. Dr. Flanagan told my mom, "We want to admit Jeffrey for an extensive testing and studying program at either the Mayo Clinic or the University of Minnesota." Alyce, my mom's only sibling, interned as a Mayo nurse and strongly recommended this famous institute. She thought, right or wrong, that I would get more personal attention there, rather than being seen more as a number at the U of M.

The Mayo Clinic is located in Rochester, Minnesota, which was 90 miles south of our home. I was scheduled for five days of testing. These days included lots of scary exams, cold x-ray tables, painful needles, irritating enemas, nauseating drinks, and upset stomachs. "Come on, now!" demanded the x-ray tech. "The doctor wants you to drink this so we can get a picture of your stomach." I was tired of the constant invasive testing. I rolled away from her and dug in my heels. "I drank that stuff before. It makes me want to throw up!"

"Ginger, could you come in here?" asked the frustrated x-ray tech. "See what you can do."

Moments later, I felt a gentle hand on my shoulder. "Jeff, I know this stuff tastes yucky. But it's really going to help us figure out how to make your tummy feel better. Will you drink half of it for me, please?" Ginger implored. "If you drink it, I'll see if I can get a piece of candy afterwards to get the icky taste out of your mouth."

Her soft voice and gentle touch gave me just enough encouragement to swallow down the chalky, thick barium. Of course, the promise of candy didn't hurt either.

It was during this battery of tests that I would be officially diagnosed with rheumatoid arthritis and ulcerative colitis. This would begin a concurrent and ongoing battle with these diseases that would stretch to decades.

Later, my mom said it seemed that I was taking all the procedures in stride, but in reality I was just an expert at keeping a cool exterior. However, this facade would soon shatter as a result of my stress, and I would face my most disabling disability— stuttering. My speech difficulty began about the same time I acquired colitis and RA (rheumatoid arthritis) at between five and six years old. Stuttering was having a snowball effect in that the stuttering was making me more nervous, and the nervousness was making me stutter more. Routinely people thought they were helping me by trying to complete what I was trying to say, which only stuck pins in my deflating ego. Even if that person was accurately finishing my thought, it annoyed me, and I'd respond, "No—what I was going to say was...." Then I'd come up with a new ending to what I had begun just to show them in my passive- aggressive way that I was a master of my own thoughts. For example, I'd try telling a little friend:

"I ate so many sausages, I had to g-g-go...t-t—to-o th-th-th...."
"To the bathroom," chimed in the friend.

"No! Go to the kitchen and tell my mom to buy some more," I fibbed. In retrospect, this kind of mental gymnastics forced me to develop my vocabulary and become more spontaneous, both important tools on stage today.

My first day in Rochester, I was in line with a group of bowel illness patients who were literally ten times my age. I was dressed in a snazzy red sports coat with a black and red tie. The patient in front of me turned around, looked at me and said to my parents, "Excuse me, is this young fellow your son?"

My mom smiled, "Yes, he is."

"I was standing here in line, all nervous about my upcoming tests when I noticed your son. I said to myself, 'If this little guy is standing here in line all by himself, holding it together, there is no reason that I can't do it.'" They all had a good laugh, and he went back in line.

While in Rochester, we stayed at the historic Kahler hotel. I remember being impressed by its old-world charm and all its ornate appointments. It seemed to me to be its own little city, having a coffee shop, cocktail lounge, formal and informal restaurant, gift shop (including toys and comics), barbershop, and more. The hotel appeared all the larger from the perspective of a little guy like me.

27

This is why it seemed so out of place to me that doctor's orders called for giving me daily enemas right in our lovely hotel room.

After the first day of testing at Mayo, we returned to the hotel. My dad thought it would lighten my spirit if he pretended I was one of his drinking buddies. "Say Jeff, how's about you and I get ourselves a couple of cocktails in the lounge?" I first looked at my mom, who looked disapproving, but I smiled at this outrageous suggestion and said:

"Ok, sounds good."

We walked into the lounge, and I thought we were going to sit at one of the tables when my dad announced, "Let me help you up on one of these bar stools." This was starting to be fun. "What will you have, Jimmy Slicks?" asked my dad (this was one of his many nicknames for me, that also included James Q. Jefferson and Jimmy Johnson, just to mention a few).

"A kiddy cocktail," I said, the only supposed "big guy" drink I knew.

"Lloyd," my mom questioned. "Martha, please, it's cocktail hour."

"Hey, young man, where can I get a snazzy blazer like that?" the bartender asked.

"Ask my mom," I said. He smiled and turned to other customers. We started in on our drinks. My dad had his customary Old Crow bourbon and water; Mom just had water since she was pregnant and feeling a little queasy with the flu; and I had my kiddy cocktail "neat."

Suddenly, my mom said, "Excuse me, Lloyd, I'll be right back." She got up and frantically looked for the ladies room outside of the lounge. She made it to the entrance and became violently ill, messing up her lovely matching outfit and making a mess all over the lobby carpet. In addition to being mortified by publically vomiting, my mom was equally aghast at her appearance of coming out of a lounge as a drunken pregnant woman. Next, an elderly female hotel guest approached her. Afraid, my mom thought she was going to be lambasted for public intoxication, but instead the kind woman said:

"Can I help you, dear?" She escorted my mom to a chair.

"Thanks," my mom said, sitting down. She added,

"I want to assure you, ma'am, I haven't been drinking. I have the flu." The elderly woman smiled and said,

"Are you with someone I can help you find?"

"Yes, my six-year-old son and husband Lloyd are in the lounge." The woman smiled and said, "Wait here, and I'll look for them."

After finding us in the lounge, we retrieved my mother and took her to our room. My dad arranged for a hotel nurse who would take care of my mom the next day. My dad was faced with the unfamiliar responsibility of taking me to my next day's appointments. After another grueling day of poking and probing, it was time for a consultation with the overseeing physician, Dr. Bianchi, who had jet-black hair, arresting good looks, and wore pointy black shoes. My dad, having noticed how positively I had responded to his amusing suggestion of cocktails, thought it would be equally fun for me to play a little joke on the doctor. So right before the visit, still wearing my stylish red blazer, we went to the elaborate underground subway system complete with shopping kiosks where we stopped at a cigar shop. "My son likes the premium cigars—Harvester, if you've got it. Make that two, his tastes are impeccable," said my dad to the amused clerk. We grabbed our cigars and made our way back to our appointment with Dr. Bianchi.

He greeted us warmly, "Sit down and make yourselves comfortable," he said, pointing to the two chairs in his office. Before the doctor could begin telling us of the test results, my dad gave me a cue that we had prearranged, and I pulled the two cigars out from my inside breast pocket and said, "Would you like to try one? They're very smooth."

The doctor laughed, took the cigar and said, "I'll smoke it later, if you don't mind."

"Sure," I said. And he launched into the results of the tests: they broke the news to me that I had rheumatoid arthritis and ulcerative colitis.

I went home, and I continued on medication and a strict diet of low fiber and no dairy. I was sure the doctor's printed orders read, "Take by mouth: yucky tasting stuff."

About this time I was enrolled in kindergarten. My mother went to the school in advance and met with the principal, nurse, and my teacher to give them a heads-up on my condition. The first few days of kindergarten, as expected, were a little scary but exciting and without incident. But one day early in the school year while I sat in Mrs. Avery's kindergarten class (I had been suffering with severe abdominal cramps that morning) as I raised my hand to ask to go to the bathroom, I lost control and soiled myself while sitting at the desk. As the odor wafted over the classroom, I heard comments begin.

"Phew!"

"Who cut the cheese?" "Yuck?"

"Who did it?"

"Children, we don't talk that way in class," said Mrs. Avery sternly. After a moment, she added, "Someone please open the window." I would have been comforted knowing that Pumba, the warthog, laments in the Lion King ditty *Hakuna Matata*, "I'm a sensitive soul, though I seem thick-skinned. And it hurt that my friends never stood downwind."

My abdominal cramping had stopped, which gave me relief for the moment. I quickly said to Mrs. Avery, "Can I go to the bathroom?"

She took me out in the hallway and said with an exasperated tone, "Jeff, didn't I tell you that whenever you have to use the bathroom, just get up and excuse yourself without asking permission?" She didn't understand how sudden and explosive these attacks could be. Mrs. Avery escorted me to the nurse's restroom. While there, she was joined by the nurse and together they tried to maintain their composure as they peeled off my soiled clothing. In spite of their attempts to spare me from embarrassment, I was well aware of their visceral reactions to the odor as they choked and coughed. I saw their faces wrinkle up as they couldn't help but inhale the overwhelming odor of disease. My mom had left a change of clothes with the nurse in case of emergency. When I returned to the classroom, I tried to act as if nothing had happened in spite of wearing a fresh outfit of clothes, but my classmates provided me with plenty of snickers, whispers, and exaggerated expressions that would heighten my embarrassment throughout the day and the rest of the month. The never-ending barbs only added to my anxiety about my condition, and my stuttering increased. My inability to speak fluently was shattering my self-image. Tremendous frustration arose not being able to articulate ideas and answer questions in a normal response time. The "accident" was my first of many in Mrs. Avery's class that month; my condition worsened, and I was pulled from her class later that fall.

Here began the acute self-consciousness and awareness that I was 'different' which would follow me for years.

My mom and dad with her sister, Alyce, and husband Sheridan. Aunt Alyce, a nurse, and Uncle Sheridan provided invaluable advice, support, and assistance to my parents and to me throughout my illnesses.

"Turn, O Lord, and deliver me: save me because of your unfailing love." Psalm 6:4

"Do not free a camel of the burden of his hump; you may be freeing him from being a camel." –G.K. Chesterton

CHAPTER 3

WHAT NOW! OR "NOW WHAT?"

Test results and information about my condition were being shared between doctors in the Twin Cities and the Mayo Clinic. With my colitis symptoms worsening, it was back to St. Joseph's Hospital and another round of tests and treatments. After days of inconclusive tests and ineffective treatments, all the while experiencing uncontrollable diarrhea and being fed intravenously, doctors decided there was no other option than more exploratory surgery. They successfully removed a length of diseased intestine.

All of these negative circumstances gave me a sense of uncertainty. Strangely, however, instead of these events totally overwhelming me, they actually provided me an opportunity to take back a degree of control through humor. Around this time, I had started seeing things on TV talking about a spy named James Bond. My parents explained to me what a spy does. *Cool!* I thought.

During one of my Mayo clinic visits, my dad and I stopped at a newspaper kiosk that had paperback books. I saw that one of the books had a picture of James Bond on the cover standing next to a provocatively dressed woman. The woman, of course, held no interest to someone six years old. But the determined look on James Bond's face and the gun he toted really grabbed my curiosity. "Dad, can I get this book?" I could hardly read, but I thought maybe I could find someone to read it to me.

He picked up the book, saw the easy-looking woman, and said, "Uh…I don't think so." But I didn't need a James Bond book to assume the role of a secret agent.

While doctors were preparing for my latest exploratory surgery, one of my greatest accomplishments of stealth to date was breaching the security of the nurses' station during what was supposed to be naptime. I carefully poked my head out of the hospital room and looked furtively left and right. Crawling down the hall, I waited for just the right moment. Then, when no one was looking, I scampered under the long nurses charting table unbeknownst to anyone. As one of the nurses removed a chart from the opening in the center of the table, there was room for me to pop my head up and say, "Hi!" She shrieked, and the metal chart clattered to the floor. The rest of the nurses laughed. The head nurse said, smiling, "Very funny, this is nap time—back...to... your...room." I always seemed to be able to make the staff smile. This in return made me smile, which I know boosted my spirits.

One of the things that wiped that smile off my face was hospital Jell-O. It was standard fare for hospital meals as much as silverware and napkins. (Since familiarity breeds contempt, I did not eat Jell-O again for twenty years.) They always served it in a bowl of one-inch cubes that were harder than Jell-O has a right to be. It wouldn't have been so bad if they allowed me to use it as part of a craft project, but instead they expected me to eat it. I wondered just how resilient these cubes were. To test this, I threw one at the wall. It didn't bounce back to me as I had hoped, but lay intact on the floor. "What is this Jell-O doing over here?" the nurse noticed as she was clearing my dishes.

"It musta' fallen off my spoon," I said.

For as much as I despised Jell-O as a kid, ironically, today I sometimes incorporate it into my preschool magic show. "Good morning, boys and girls. I am Amazing Jeffo, not to be confused with Amazing Jell-O because I'm not that wiggly!" This line always gets lots of giggles from the kids since silliness is their preferred form of humor. While I'm packing up after the show as the kids are leaving the auditorium, they call out, "Goodbye, Amazing Jell-O!" I pretend to be annoyed, and they giggle all the more. I came around full circle with Jell-O when I was around thirty years old. At the annual Christmas dinner my parents routinely hosted, my mom served a festive holiday salad. "Mom, this is delicious. What's all in here?" I asked with a mouth full of Jell-O.

"Basically, it's Jell-O with strawberries, wine, and whipped cream." I was converted. I am now a recovering Jelloholic, at least around Christmas.

Jell-O aside, while I was in the hospital, doctors removed more diseased intestines.

The surgery initially gave my worn-out intestinal tract a break—enough of a break that it fooled the junior partner filling in for Dr. Flanagan, who was out of town. "Jeff, what would you think about me sending you home today?"

"I guess I'd like that," I answered with uncertainty because I still didn't feel "right."

The next morning, my parents received a call from Dr. Flanagan.

"I'm very sorry, Mrs. Smith. There's been a terrible mistake. Jeffrey should have never been discharged so soon. He needs to be readmitted."

I was having lunch while watching my favorite kids show, *Lunch with Casey*, when Mom broke the news.

"I'm so sorry, Jeffrey, Dr. Flanagan said we need to bring you back to the hospital for more tests."

After being discharged a second time, it wasn't more than a week or so later that my symptoms returned in full force. Between the hospital stay and recovery at home, I was gone from kindergarten for about six weeks.

The Twin Cities doctors were perplexed. They didn't know why the attacks on my G.I. tract were continuing, but figured they had to have missed something. Even more exploratory surgery was recommended. But this time doctors agreed I needed to be admitted to St. Mary's, the largest private hospital in the world at that time. It was founded by the Franciscan Sisters in 1889 as a response to a tornado that ravaged the greater Rochester area. Ever since, it has had a working relationship with the Mayo Clinic, which was founded in 1883. My parents decided rather than commuting daily between St. Paul and Rochester, approximately 90 miles, my dad would set up my mom at the Kahler hotel in Rochester, a short walk from St. Mary's. They also arranged for my paternal grandmother to move into our home and assist my dad with my siblings, enabling him to continue his business.

We were introduced to Dr. Hugh B. Lynn, the chief of St. Mary's pediatric surgery department. Lynn headed up a team of staff and visiting surgeons, both national and international. Usually following a day of tests, my mom would meet with this group to go over results and discuss options. At one of these meetings, a Swedish doctor stood up and boldly addressed the group:

"In Sweden, we have different attitudes and approaches than doctors from your country. Here, in this country, your doctors prefer a conservative approach. In Sweden, we understand the conservative approach, but in your son's situation, this is only going to delay the inevitable. His colitis is wearing down his body, and I believe an aggressive approach to this disease must be taken as soon as possible. Otherwise, his disease will eventually kill him," he said in his thick accent.

Alarmed, my mom asked, "Doctor, what could or would be done for Jeffrey if he were in Sweden?"

"We would go ahead and perform an ileostomy."

"We don't understand, doctor," my dad broke in, "What's an ileostomy?"

"An ileostomy is a surgical procedure that removes the bowel, and large intestines to the area of the ilium, high up in the G.I.tract," he said.

This opinion obviously put my parents in a quandary. They had been comfortable and trusting of the expert medical opinion of doctors in the Twin Cities, yet they wanted me to have the best chance of survival. They took the middle ground by giving permission to continue current treatment and hope that tests would eventually lead us to a solution with which they, and I, would feel comfortable.

This approach was problematic because of the lack of comparative cases of other children my age with my degree of colitis. Also, without the diagnostic tools common today, such as MRIs and CTs, definitive diagnosis was more reliant on educated guesses and deductive reasoning to determine treatment. Eventually doctors decided on a plan of action. They called in my parents and announced, "We believe the best approach at this point for successful results for Jeffrey's condition can only be accomplished by performing a colectomy." A colectomy involves removing the colon. A procedure best done by a surgeon while asleep—meaning I'd be asleep, not the surgeon.

Gratefully, I was too young to understand all the details or risks of my condition and relied on the reassurances of my parents and the comforting smiles of the staff for solace.

"Trust in the Lord with all your heart and lean not on your own under-standing..." Proverbs 3:5

"Remember, men need laughter sometimes more than food."
–Anna Fellows Johnston

CHAPTER 4

NOW APPEARING FOR A LIMITED TIME ONLY?

The surgical team anticipated I would be at St. Mary's for around 10 days. With a day or two devoted to building me up with blood transfusions (my favorite…Not!), I had a chance to begin working the crowd, in the form of charming the hospital staff. I always had a comfort level with adults because my parents took my oldest brother Dave and me to most of their social events. They'd plop us right in the middle of the party, and we'd just interact. I quickly learned you can get more with honey than vinegar. We were well behaved and had good vocabularies for our tender ages. My precociousness was charming to many. I didn't really see myself as a funny guy but developed my sense of humor to receive positive feedback. I unconsciously discovered that levity and positive thinking build on each other. Humor was helping me to view life more positively. Conversely, focusing on the positive helped me to see the laughter and enjoyment in each day. How overwhelming can a challenge be if we can laugh in the midst of it?

"Laughter is the greatest weapon we have and we, as humans, use it the least," said Mark Twain. My sense of humor also served as a coping mechanism to emotionally shield me from the teasing and chiding of children from the mishaps revolving around my "accidents."

One of my first successful attempts to work the crowd came when I charmed one of the aides, who on a nightly basis, wheeled a cart from room to room dispensing water, tea, coffee, or light snacks. "Can I ride along with you in your cart?" I asked with great anticipation.

She didn't understand. "I can just curl up inside your cart and, if you don't want anyone to see me down there, I'll just close its curtain. I promise I won't fall out."

"OK, but just for a little bit," she said as she shook her head incredulously. As she moved from room to room, I periodically peeked out from underneath and said "hi!" to the patients if they seemed friendly. They were likewise charmed and appeared to take it all in as a value-added service of the hospital. I gave a whole new meaning to the phrase, "Coffee, tea, or me!"

The following afternoon, surgery was performed. As the surgical team had anticipated, a colectomy was proven to be a necessity once they opened me up because the colitis had spread throughout my colon. Colon and bowel surgeries typically are performed in the afternoon because they're considered "dirty" surgeries. Operating later in the day reduces the chance of infecting subsequent patients. Dr. Lynn confidently said to my parents, "Father, mother, we believe that Jeffrey should have no further difficulty in this area."

"Thank you, Doctor. This is such a burden off our shoulders," my mom said while my dad nodded.

"In about a week or so, Jeffrey will be back home," said the smiling doctor.

However, after a week in recovery with nurses regularly checking my vitals, the staff and Dr. Lynn were more than concerned. My postsurgical temperature was not coming down, my white blood cell count was going up, and I was listless. My mom became aware something wasn't right even before my vital signs indicated it. The day before I was to be discharged, my mom came to see me during the afternoon. She sat with me for several hours and observed my behavior: listless and silent. She went to the nurses' station and said, "I'm not trying to butt in, but I feel there's something not right with Jeff."

"We have already made this observation and have charted it," said the head nurse sympathetically.

After visiting hours, my mom went to the desk again and asked, "Please stay in communication with me back at the hotel." Returning to the Kahler hotel, she packed her things to get ready for my dad's arrival the next morning to take us home.

At 6 a.m. the phone rang. My mom knew before answering that it was going to be Dr. Lynn. "Mother Smith, this is Dr. Lynn. I'm sorry, but we can't release Jeffrey. We've had him in X-ray all night long trying to determine what's wrong. You had best get hold of Father Smith and tell him he should come down here. Jeffrey's in trouble. Please come to the hospital immediately."

Upon arrival, she found about a half-dozen specialists outside my hospital door waiting for her. They encircled her, and one of them said, "Mrs. Smith, we want you to go into Jeff's room, smile, and act as if everything is all right. He's quitting the fight. Everything in him is starting to shut down. He's not responding. He's just staring at his drainage catheter."

My mom put on her best face, marched into my room, and tried to get me going. "Look at me, Jeff," she urged. I just kept looking at the catheter. I wouldn't acknowledge her presence at all. She became frightened but didn't want me to know how frightened she was. After failing repeatedly to get me to communicate with her, she began to say silent prayers beseeching God. While in prayer for many minutes, she suddenly noticed a peaceful, joyful smile come upon my face. "Jeff? What are you smiling about?" I turned my head, finally acknowledging her presence, and responded:

"Mama, I just saw the most beautiful man and he smiled at me." Not expecting such a response from a seven year old, my mom was trying to analyze what I had said.

"Tell me, Jeffrey, what he looks like."

"He has a long white dress on and long hair and a shine around him, and he smiled at me, Mama." At that very moment, my mom thought God had come to take me then and there. Her heart was pounding as her prayers continued:

"Lord, don't take him." The door burst open and orderlies came through with a gurney.

"We're taking him down to X-ray again. Dr. Lynn wants you to stay right here. He will call you." She sat in my darkened room, terrified, and prayed.

After nearly an hour, the phone rang. "Hello," she said.

"We found it!" Dr. Lynn said. "Several adhesions have developed in the healing process. They've entangled themselves around Jeffrey's colon, kidneys, and some abdominal organs."

Dr. Lynn began prepping me for emergency surgery that morning. My dad arrived and joined my mom, and they accompanied me to surgery as far as the nuns would allow.

When the surgical team opened me up, they discovered an advancing infection from a strangulated intestine. They removed an infected section of colon and kept me under sedation until their exhaustive search for any additional infection was complete. Once again Dr. Lynn met my parents after surgery. "Mother, Father, I think we got it and just in time," he said. Relieved, my parents let out a long sigh.

Instead of my vision being a harbinger of death, it was telling me everything was going to be ok. As my mom explained to me years later, "I knew God gave you back to me instead of taking you from me. He answered a mother's prayer."

"Thank you," my mother said to Dr. Lynn. After several days of recovery, we drove home with relief and high hopes. But these hopes would again be dashed when my RA took a turn for the worse.

"O Lord, you brought me up from the grave, you spared me from going down into the pit." Psalm 30:3

"Smooth seas do not make skillful sailors." – African Proverb

CHAPTER 5

BODY TRACTION OR "WHAT'S A NICE KID LIKE YOU DOING WITH A JOINT LIKE THIS?"

After 30 days in St. Mary's, I was more than ready for a change of scenery, but St. Joseph's Hospital wasn't exactly what I had in mind. My arthritis erupted, causing my knee to swell to the size of a cantaloupe. The pain and constriction in my knee made it almost impossible to walk. A year earlier, I had been referred to Dr. Frank Babb, a stern-looking Englishman with round, wire-rimmed glasses and an innovator in the field of orthopedic surgery. He founded St. Anthony Orthopedic Clinic in St. Paul, Minnesota.

Arriving back home, we made an appointment to see Dr. Babb. He had already casted me two or three times over the course of the last year (unfortunately not for a Hollywood movie, but for my repeatedly constricting knee). Each of these times, I'd be anesthetized, and my knee would be forcibly straightened, then put in a cast. I'd awake from my comfortable drug-induced slumber, and as the anesthesia wore off, my knee would throb. Eventually the pain would subside as my knee adjusted to being straight. I'd be in a cast for about a month, but each time the cast was removed, my knee would return to its former position: a 45-degree flexion.

Between these castings, physical therapy was prescribed which consisted of my dad dropping me off at St. Joseph's Hospital three times a week for sessions lasting three hours in the morning throughout third grade. The physical therapist and my parents thought spending mornings in PT and the balance of the day at school sounded like a sensible plan—but no one had asked me.

As we arrived at school following my first session of therapy, my mom said, "I packed a bag lunch in case you missed the hot lunch."

I didn't mind so much the novelty of having a bag lunch at school; since, after all, this had been the daily fare I had enjoyed in front of the TV with my old buddy Casey Jones in earlier times. Though what I hadn't anticipated was eating alone in the lunchroom. The unintentional segregation from my fellow students left me with an overwhelming sense of isolation. I broke down in tears. "What's the matter Jeffrey? Is your arthritis hurting?" enquired a sympathetic lunch lady.

"Yes," I sobbed, too embarrassed and confused with emotion to explain my feelings.

"Let me get your teacher."

Shortly thereafter my teacher appeared with a classmate pulling alongside him her desk chair.

"We don't have a wheelchair, but Jimmy can roll you around on my desk chair," Mrs. P. explained.

As we entered the classroom I was overcome by myriad comments: "Neato!"

"I get to push him next!"

"No fair! I knew Jeff first," rang out the voices.

No breaking of bread, nor the most crowded of lunchrooms, could ever have done as much to give me a sense of belonging and rally my spirit. I felt even more special when a few kids commented, "It must be nice going to school only in the afternoon, huh, Jeff?"

Friendship certainly wasn't a component of my physical therapy. Over the years, the treatment of RA has greatly improved. But in the early 60's, they actually used brute strength to straighten arthritic joints. M-m-m…That felt good…Not!! I saw my physical therapist as the embodiment of pure evil, undoubtedly because I needed a channel for my anger and frustration. After soaking me in a very hot thera- peutic tub to loosen muscles and ligaments, which also weakened me to a point where I'd be begging them to take me out of it before the

25-minute timer was up, my therapist would strap me face down on a table and hook heavy weight bags on the back of my heel for about a half hour. The procedure had minimal effect, not only because of the relentlessness of RA, but also because of my efforts to relieve the painful stretching by lifting my rear end against the belt holding me down, which countered its therapeutic intent.

Months after completing my physical therapy, my family was out for dinner at a club that was sponsoring a bingo night; I suddenly realized the bingo caller was my evil therapist. I pointed her out to my mom as I gasped, "Mom! Look! It's that devil lady!" "Jeffrey!" said my mom, "That's very rude. That's Helen. She's a very nice lady."

"She's evil!" I insisted.

My mom assumed a pleasant countenance while painfully squeezing my arm and said with an exaggerated smile, "People are just trying to help you. I don't want to hear any more of that from you."

I knew I had no chance of winning bingo as long as my therapist was calling out the numbers. Neither winning at bingo nor succeeding at physical therapy was in the cards.

My physical therapy was discontinued once Dr. Babb realized its futility. "Jeffrey, I've given this problem knee a lot of thought and decided I have no other choice but to put your leg in traction." Hearing the word "traction" conjured up images of a tractor. *They're going to put me into a tractor? How's that going to help?* I was once again admitted to St. Joseph's Hospital. Spending all that time prostrate, I could have used a concept like "frequent flier" points, but in my case "frequent lie-er" points. My first few days in the hospital were devoted to measurements, x-rays, and blood transfusions, which left me with a lot of idle time.

St. Joseph's staff was made up of nuns who were also licensed nurses. Although some people erroneously stereotype nuns as stern and stodgy, I found them anything but. Stunts and pranks were the order of the day. Practical joking in the hospital was, for me, a passive-aggressive way to rebel. I overturned the apple cart whenever possible, launched paper airplanes off the sun deck of the hospital's roof, disappeared during mandatory naptime (eventually being found hiding in playroom cabinetry), and raced down the hall in my wheelchair. I pretended my small wheelchair was an Italian sports car—slim, aerodynamic, and highly maneuverable. I could lock up one or both of my wheels by slamming down the hand breaks to either make a hairpin turn or stop on a dime if a nurse gave me "the look." The main drag of the pediatric wing provided perfect racing conditions: lengthy and on an incline; my fingers were the pistons, my muscles were the cylinders that revved my motor and got me up and going. Any patient I challenged on the pediatric floor was summarily beaten—I retired undefeated. My little hands were strong. Arthritis hadn't yet affected them with the exception of that initial finger, which my mom first noticed was swollen as I played with my brother Dave three summers earlier.

Racing wheelchairs wasn't enough to satisfy or occupy my restless nature, so I decided to shoot hospital booties up the in- house mail vacuum tube. My ammo depot was a canvas cart transporting dirty laundry on its way to be washed.

"Hey mister, can I ride in your thing?" I asked the orderly. "Are you kidding? It's full of dirty clothes!" said the laundry attendant.

I waited until he stopped to collect more laundry, then grabbed some booties conveniently perched on top of the pile, stuffed them in my bathrobe pockets, and went on my way. I only wish I could have seen the expression on the nurse's face who opened the tube on the next floor. You might ask, "Where were the nurses while you were perpetrating this?" Strangely enough, standing right there with me, finding it all-so amusing (talk about team building). I became such a fixture at the nurses' station, they allowed me on occasion to answer the incoming intercom requests. I'd respond to the buzz of the intercom with the authoritative voice of a six-year-old, "Can I help you?" Although I'd typically stutter in a situation like this, I didn't because I was so exhilarated by their confidence in me.

Once I got into a lot of trouble by taking apart my TV set during mandatory naptime. I used a small tool kit purchased during my just completed Mayo/St. Mary's junket. The mini toolkit was one of the pieces that I considered essential, and I slipped it into the suitcase my mom packed for me. The toolkit had all that a five- year-old handyman could possibly need—screwdriver with interchangeable bits, poker, punch, and a wrench. Getting out of bed, I removed the back of the TV, pulled out some tubes and cables along with unscrewing some other "pieces" (I don't know what they were). A nurse happened to come in and said, "You took the TV apart."

"I was trying to get a better picture," I answered.

"You better get this thing back together before naptime is over or else..."

I stuttered "O-Okay." Not knowing whose wrath would be greater, my parents or the nun, fear fueled my inspiration, and I quickly put the TV back together in complete working order. Back in those days, hospital's TVs were an a la carte item: two dollars a day (wheeled in on a "carte"). Later, as weeks progressed after surgically hooking me up to body traction, my father, always tight with a dollar, was outraged by what he called a daily "usury" fee and negotiated to buy his own 19-inch Zenith TV for my personal use and had it delivered to my room.

TV's must have inspired naughtiness in me. I always preferred a private room, probably to command all the attention from adults.

Overcrowding once necessitated getting a little roommate, much to my displeasure. To show my annoyance, I changed my TV viewing habits from children's shows like *Captain Kangaroo* and *Dave Lee's Popeye and Pete* to news broadcasts and programs like *As the World Turns* and *The Guiding Light*.

"You can't really like soap operas," asked my roommate's mom incredulously.

"Oh, sure! I don't watch kid stuff," I lied.

Just because I have multiple disabilities doesn't mean I can't also sometimes be a jerk.

Except for those times when I'd get in trouble, daytime activities kept my spirits relatively high. But the nights were long. When my parents' schedule allowed only a daytime visit, at night I paced to the end of the long hallway and back. Each end had a large picture window, one facing the mural identifying by name the New York Tea Company building. The other window framed the majestic Minnesota State Capitol. When the spotlights shone, the golden sculpture of a chariot with a team of galloping horses at the base of the dome magically glowed.

But when an evening visit was in order, I'd sometimes worry too. When dinner was over, I'd lie there wondering, without warrant, whether my mom and dad would come, dreading the thought of being alone. Straining to identify every clip-clop from the hallway, I'd think, *That sounds like my dad's feet, but those don't sound like my mom's steps*, or vice-versa. Since I was but one of many children in that ward, I went through a rollercoaster of emotions every night until the clip-clops stopped at my doorway.

I didn't care that frustrated hospital staff once took my call button away after I continually rang it, seeking adult playmates— because it made me eligible for the "no-bell" prize! My charms and offbeat silliness regularly bailed me out of trouble. Combined with my parents' training in politeness and manners, I was saved from severe discipline, even allowing me to get privileges other children would not receive, such as having tea and crackers with the head nurse of the pediatric ward in her office. One privilege came as a direct result of my courage under fire. Since it often took four people to hold me still enough for an IV insertion, I made the head nurse (the mother superior) promise that if I was a good boy when the IV transfusions were completed, I'd be allowed to have buttered crackers and tea with her in her office. So as it turned out, I had my IV taken out at midnight and then reminded Mother Superior of her agreement. "A promise is a promise," I said. She acquiesced. After downing many saltines, I said, "I think I would like one more cracker, please."

"You've had enough. It's now time for bed," she said smiling. I believe everyone except for me was looking forward to having me encased in body traction for their respective reasons. Dr. Babb wanted to add to his success story portfolio and fulfill his Hippocratic Oath. My parents were hopeful that traction would eventually return their son to a more normal existence. The hospital staff was grateful for the chance to regroup from my ongoing pranks.

The three-month plan was to incrementally turn screws attached to wires elevating my leg and straighten it out over the course of time. I can't really tell you about the process of being put into full- body traction because I was anesthetized at the time, but I woke up amazed to see this Rube Goldberg contraption around me. It obviously did not come from a kit. In the operating room, doctors assembled a combination of wood, wire, plaster, cotton, and screws. Ta-Da! I was fully casted in plaster up to my chest except for my right leg. This would turn out to be my longest hospital internment—from mid-November 1964 to mid-February 1965.

As with any kid, parents are the center of their universe. Even if few words were spoken, Mom and Dad's hospital visits were the sparkling pinnacle of my day. Naturally, I wanted their shiny presence to illume my little world for as long as possible. When either my dad or my mom began fidgeting or glancing at their watches I knew time with them was nearing its end. Desperately, I'd begin conjuring up any form of small talk to postpone the inevitable.

"Mom? Could you read me a story before you go? How about *The Three Musketeers*?"

"*The Three Musketeers*?! That would take weeks!" I tried a new tactic. "Dad? How's the dog?"

"He's just fine," chuckled my dad. "Mom? Do you wear a girdle?"

"Do you even know what a girdle is, young man?" questioned my mom.

"Um-m, no, not really," I answered sheepishly. "But I heard about 'em on TV!"

"I think it's time we tuck you in. Visiting hours are over; we'll be back tomorrow night," Mom said reassuringly.

These were emotionally difficult moments amidst the uncertainty surrounding me. Pulling pranks and interacting with staff were my tools to keep from worry, and to fill the seemingly endless days.

"…With the Lord a day is like a thousand years, and a thousand years are like a day." 2 Peter 3:8

"Laughter gives us distance. It allows us to step back from an event, deal with it and then move on." – Bob Newhart

Chapter 6

The Beatles or "He Loves You, Yeah, Yeah, Yeah"

As a coping mechanism to deal with the monotony of being bed-ridden, I continued to use mischief and manipulation to amuse myself. I was never aware of the tradition of having a cast signed until a nurse asked if she could. This appealed to me because it sounded kind of "naughty," messing up a white cast and all. I encouraged other staff to do likewise. In the process of their leaning over to leave me with their John Hancock, my eyes were drawn to their big open pockets that were filled with all types of interesting items. I needed to check out these goodies. With the popularity of the new James Bond movies, I felt like a secret agent as I surreptitiously lifted items from inviting pockets. When nurses bent down, I would slyly steal pens, pencils, rulers, and even eyeglasses, slipping them under my sheet and later ditching them in my drawer when the coast was clear. Finally, one of the nurses caught on and made me confess my nefarious actions, curtailing any possibility of conducting a flea market. She informed the other nurses of the where-abouts of their belongings. Soon there was a steady stream of nurses rummaging through my drawer exclaiming, "Yes, this is mine, and so is this…so you had it, you dickens!"

Where the hospital staff ever got the idea that they would have a respite from my pranks just because I was in body traction, I'll never know. I think, generally, the nurses and staff found me to be a breath of fresh air. Instead of focusing exclusively on my illness, I saw my hospital stays as opportunities for playtime. Accomplishing my goal sometimes required manipulation. I could attempt to justify my behavior by saying

I was trying to control my out-of-control health. One way or the other, I relished persuading nurses and staff to act outrageously.

One morning a nurse came into my room and slid her hand into a pocket of her freshly starched uniform. As she reached into her pocket, I heard the sound of starched fabric separating from itself, similar to painter's tape being peeled away from a wall. I don't know why, but my auditory receptors were pleased with this odd sound, so much that I wanted to hear it on a regular basis. From that point on, I had nurses report to my room at the start of their shifts and allow me to open up their pockets and separate their cuffs, pleats, and collars from the rest of their uniform.

As I lay there and the weeks passed, I noticed what appeared to me as a loosening in my cast. The plaster surrounds seemed to be moving away from my skin and becoming oversized. Of course, in reality, my ulcerative colitis was steadily making me lose weight. Eventually, I could fit my entire arm into the cast and scratch anywhere I needed to.

Knowing that I would be in the hospital for the long haul, I wanted my room to reflect my personality and tastes. The room became awash with funny get well cards, stuffed animals, toys, plants, flowers, and pictures of the Beatles, compliments of visitors and items I purchased from the candy striper cart. These young, pink-and-white clad female volunteers visited rooms rolling a cart loaded with toys, crafts, colored pencils, magazines, even comics and paperback books. I don't know if it was all the cool merchandise or the candy striper herself with a certain *je ne sais quoi* that came from wearing that great-looking outfit that so lifted my spirits whenever she visited. I would only discover the answer some 40 years later.

My parents, although financially well off, were frugal and gave me a very limited allowance each week to "waste on the cart." But my uncles, aunts, and parents' friends had no qualms indulging me. More than once, I had as much as $10 to blow on piles of trinkets from the cart (considering a ten spot went a long way back then).

I always preferred a private room to command the exclusive attention of adults and to have enough room for my growing collection of stuff, a natural result of long-term hospitalizations. One day my parents walked in and saw me paging through a paperback book about the Beatles. (The Beatles gave me a hopeful focal point; their next album, song, TV appearance, or magazine article helped give me something to look forward to.) The book had cute stories about them and glossed over their wild lifestyle. My parents who had heard about their antics in the news said, "Jeff, John Lennon said they're more popular than Jesus."

"John would never say that!" I retorted. All my parents could do was shrug.

I was living vicariously through the Beatles. The nurse supervisor had a phonograph in her office and wheeled it into my room so I could play my two Beatles albums and several 45s over and over again. Once the three-minute song was over, I pushed the call button and asked, "Could you send the nurse in here to turn my record over?"

When the weary nurse arrived, she asked, "Jeff, wouldn't you be more interested in hearing the long play album? I think those songs are the best." The anticipation of the release of the next album kept me going in more ways than I realized. (But what I hadn't realized at the time was that my true anticipation of a future was in Jesus Christ.)

My Beatles fascination coincided with the current dance step—the "twist." I unintentionally learned its intricacies as I watched *American Bandstand* Saturday mornings, primarily to hear Beatle songs. Despite being self-conscious about my physical awkwardness, I couldn't resist the limelight when invited by my parents to play a Beatles record and demonstrate my dance acumen to their guests. Out of respect for my beloved singing group, I took my twisting very seriously. With a furrowed brow and an expression of steely-eyed determination, my arms churned away as I alternately pivoted each heel while squatting and rising in time to the beat. American Bandstand, here I come! Despite my parents' request to continue my public exhibitions, my interest waned. Every time I'd display my talent, my routine was interrupted by stifled adult giggling. "We're not laughing at you—it's the intense look on your face!" chimed my parents while their guests nodded, barely holding back tears of mirth.

When I heard my grandma was going on a cruise to England, the home of the Beatles, I called her and asked, "When you go, Grandma, make sure you stop at Liverpool. Knock on the Beatles' door and ask them for an autographed picture, especially John Lennon. If you can't get a picture of all of them, just get John. Pay for it if you have to."

"I'll do my best," said my Grandma.

When she returned six weeks later, my first question to her was "Did you meet them? Did you get me an autographed picture?"

"I'm sorry, Jeffrey. They were out of town," she said. I believed her when she added, "I went to their house, knocked on their door, and the butler told me they weren't home."

I thought to myself, *Shoot! I bet I just missed them.* As a substitute, she handed me an oversized postcard with a picture of a bobby holding girls back as the Beatles ran by.

I had three other near-misses as it pertains to the Fab Four. The first had to do with them coming to Bloomington, MN, as part of their 1965 tour. The father of my best friend was friends with one of the facilities personnel at Metropolitan Stadium, site of their upcoming performance. One day our phone rang. "Jeff!" my friend said excitedly, "My dad got us two tickets to see the Beatles!" I couldn't believe it. My dream to actually see them in person was coming true. I shared the great news with my mom and dad. One man's treasure is another man's garbage.

"Your father and I have to talk about it first." "What's there to talk about?" I asked incredulously.

"There's going to be thousands of crazy fans screaming and pushing."

"But, Mom! Ricky said that we're going to be sitting inside a press box," I explained.

"Well, maybe, but I can't promise you anything, Jeffrey, before your father and I talk."

"Maybe" in our house usually ended up meaning "No." Sure enough, they nixed the concert for reasons of safety. Only a fellow Beatlemaniac could truly sympathize and understand my grief.

The second "near miss" came following the news I received when Ricky called, "Jeff, my dad talked to his friend at the stadium and guess what?"

"What?" I stuttered with anticipation.

51

"The Beatles are going to call you before the show from backstage!"

"Holy Cow!! I don't believe it!"

Unfortunately, my mom and dad hadn't coordinated our family vacation plans with the Beatles' concert scheduler. I never really enjoyed family vacations because so much of it revolved around physical activities. So I was thrilled when I heard my parents decided instead I would stay with my Aunt Alyce and Uncle Sheridan. *How convenient,* I thought. *I'll be around for the Beatles' phone call.* I called up Ricky and gave him my aunt and uncle's phone number.

Papa Charlie's artistic labor of love, creating and painting ceramic figurines of the Beatles and constructing a stage complete with mics and red leather skirting. My youngest brother, Mike, broke this, too.

The big day arrived: August 21, 1965. I'd been listening to all the reports on local top 40's radio stations about the Beatles' arrival. But that night, my (up until then) favorite aunt announced, "Jeff, go brush your teeth and comb your hair. We're all going out to Shakey's Pizza."

"Oh, I'm sorry, Aunt Alyce. I'm going to have to stay here for when the Beatles call," I said matter-of-factly. "We can't leave you here. We're responsible for you."

"I'll be fine." They weren't convinced by my pleas, and once again, the rules of history won out: two against one, no chance. Angrily I went with them and loudly demonstrated the silent treatment.

"What did the Beatles say to you, Jeff?" Ricky asked me the next morning on the phone.

"I had to go to the stupid pizza place."

"Really?! My dad was told they were for sure going to call you." I had a vague sense of satisfaction years later when I heard Shakey's Pizza had gone out of business.

The third "near miss" relating to the Beatles was only realized years later. I happened to own the first recording of their music on VJ records. The Beatles played second billing to an English folk singer named Frank Ifield. "With the Beatles" was typed in very small letters down in the corner of the album cover. I sold it years later for quick cash, maybe $2 at a used record store. Recently, it was listed at $25,000.

"Prosperity is not without many fears and distastes, and adversity is not without comforts and hopes." – Francis Bacon

If I didn't wear a lift in my left shoe, I'd have to change my name to Eileen.

CHAPTER 7

THE BLOODY TRUTH
AND MONSTERS

Today, caffeine from coffee is my chosen morning stimulant rather than the frigid metal of a bedpan, but I would gladly suffer the shock of cold steel any day over the embarrassment and irritation resulting from uncontrollable colitis.

While the primary concern of my orthopedic doctors was the arthritis and corresponding full-body traction, I still continued to pass whole blood. During my stay in traction Dr. Harold Flannigan retired, and he was replaced by another member of his team, Dr. John Gallagan, who went by "Bud." He was a sweet soul whose office was in St. Paul, a compassionate doctor who today reminds me of Marcus Welby.

Dr. Gallagan regularly scheduled blood transfusions to keep my hemoglobin up, particularly during this time in traction because the rate at which I was losing blood was at dangerous levels. After determining that another transfusion was necessary, he said, "Jeff, I'm sorry, but I'm just going to have to do it."

I, being a big fan of Saturday night professional wrestling, piped up and said, "Could we try Geritol instead?" Geritol was a cure-all product that was hawked every week by the big name wrestlers whom I idolized, namely Verne Gagne, my favorite. At that time, Geritol contained a high level of alcohol, a level no longer allowed by the FDA in over-the-counter remedies. No wonder some little old ladies did handstands after taking their "medicine"!

Dr. Gallagan gently replied, "I don't think so, Jeff." He later said to my mom, "Martha, it broke my heart seeing that pleading look on Jeff's face when he asked me about Geritol."

I thought Geritol would have been a perfect alternative to those dreaded blood transfusions. I hated the long needles in my little arm. Nurses would too regularly come in and change the transfusion line because a vein had collapsed or deteriorated. Other times the nurses would have to change the line because it was plugged. They would squeeze it, and the result would be searing pain shooting up my arm. I loathed the smell of alcohol, the pinch of my skin, and the ever-probing needles trying to find my veins. I started to imagine the IV cart looking like some kind of atomically-mutated mosquito, a creature right out of the 1950s B-horror movies I'd watch so often because they'd happen to follow my favorite children's show, *Lunch with Casey.*

I'd really like the formula of these "B" sci-fi monster movies. The scripts all included a pretty girl, who was intelligent, but still expected to serve coffee to the men and, most importantly, could belt out an ear-splitting scream. The movie makers all used ordinary animals, fish, or insects as the star, blowing them up to gigantic proportions through trick photography. As blatant as the editorial comments were about the dangers of nuclear proliferation, it went totally over my head. I just liked the giant, mutated creatures.

I was distracted one afternoon when Mel Jass, the movie matinee host, was announcing today's upcoming feature. I thought he said, "So let's begin today's big movie, *Portrait of a Lobster*, starring Vic Morrow." *Great!* I thought, anticipating the appearance of a gigantic, atomically-mutated crustacean.

I sat through this boring movie with nothing but a bunch of talking heads. I kept wondering, *When and how are they going to introduce the giant lobster?* I'd occasionally spot a window behind the actors who were droning on and on about something. *Finally!* I thought. *Just watch! A giant claw is going to come smashing through the window, pinch a guy by the neck and drag him out, screaming.* I eventually heard the real title of the movie about 10 minutes before the stupid thing was over. What Mel had actually said was Portrait of a Mobster. "*Portrait of a Mobster*!!" I bellowed. *I might as well have taken a stinkin' nap!* I thought.

Years later my excitable nature regarding monsters was validated. In the mid 70's, *Saturday Night Live*, hosted by Robert Klein, reenacted this cheesy genre with a skit about a giant, mutated lobster eating New York.

"He will yet fill your mouth with laughter and your lips with shouts of joy." Job 8:21

"Once you find laughter, no matter how painful your situation might be, you can survive it." – Bill Cosby

CHAPTER 8

DIFFERENT BEDSIDE MANNERS OR "TO EACH HIS OWN"

Thank God for Dr. Gallagan who was sensitive to my fears and tried whenever possible to do what he could to soften the hard truths about my disease. Compassion wasn't something Dr. Gallagan put on like a white doctor's coat to be discarded at the end of the day; he was true to this ideal always.

Once at a parish fundraiser that my parents and Dr. Gallagan attended, my mom along with several other guests were politely listening to Mrs. Anderson (we'll call her), who said, "You wouldn't believe what I have gone through. You all know about my son John who broke his leg, now believe it or not, he needs another operation on that same leg to reset it! My Johnny was in that cast for six weeks! Now he'll be in another one for six more weeks! His crutches are always in the way. And the plastic wrap we have gone through...You can't imagine how difficult it is for him to shower. I don't know if I can take it anymore. He's been so impatient with me! I'm so tired of taking him to the doctor. You can't believe the problem we've had getting him in the car. I feel like my world is on the edge of collapse. I just don't know what to do..."

My mom bit her lip thinking, *good grief, you want to hear a story*...but to my mother's surprise, Dr. Gallagan piped up and said, "Mrs. Anderson, if you want to hear something tragic, talk to this lady about her son." Putting his arm around my mother's shoulder, he added, "He is a very sick little boy with a lot of problems and your son is going to be okay." Mom had to hold back tears. In just a few sympathetic words, he had released years of frustration. He gave my mom much-needed validation and encouragement.

My dad had been in his own world trying to be a successful insurance agent; in1968 he sold more auto insurance than any other independent agent in Minnesota. We needed every bit of his earning power because, ironically, I was uninsurable. He was spending thousands of dollars out of pocket each month for my medical care, which he never let on to until years later.

"From everyone who has been given much, much will be demanded." Luke 12:48

His insurance savvy ultimately paid off when he negotiated to have me join a group policy with stiff, yet manageable, premiums. Although my dad found the financial strain difficult to deal with, the emotional strain of my physical challenges caused him to escape more and more into his business and drinking. "Where's dad?" I'd ask more and more often at the dinner table as I plainly noticed the unoccupied chair.

"He's working late tonight," my mom routinely explained, leaving out any gory details.

My dad, Lloyd Smith, fulfilling his military obligation as golf-pro and part-time weight lifter at Camp Atterbury, Indiana, 1953.

Oblivious to the harm my dad was doing to his own body, he had definite views about me attaining good health. He believed to a great degree that one becomes healthy from the outside in. Always well-tanned himself, he frequently encouraged me to "get your kisser in the sun." He also thought he could restore my health by feeding me a steady diet of milkshakes, vitamins, and iron-rich food, much to my mom's dismay. He worked out constantly, which he began doing in earnest in 1944, when he, along with a few dedicated souls, (Charles Atlas among them), lifted weights and built up their bodies decades before the physical fitness boom blossomed in the 1970s. My earliest memories of my dad are with Dave and me taking turns lying on his back while he performed his morning push-ups. "How many can you do, Dad? Can we both be on your back at the same time?" we asked, thinking there was no limit to his strength.

Money had been used in my dad's family as a means to show affection and, in his way of thinking, another "therapy" for wellness. It was common during his upbringing for his relatives to pass out dollar bills to the children. This practice was continued by aunts and uncles to my siblings and me (once again to my mom's dismay).

Once while my parents walked alongside my gurney en route to surgery, my dad addressed me by one of my many nicknames, "Jimmy Slicks—there's going to be a 10 dollar bill waiting for you afterward if you don't give the surgeons too hard a time." Money was his incentive for me to make it through surgery.

My mom jumped in and said, "Lloyd! Jeff doesn't need that money for heaven sakes! What are you going to do if he really gets sick?"

In my drug-induced state, I muttered, "Well, now wait a minute, Mom..."

Once when I was in traction, my dad thought to impress the nurse by turning me into a strapping, hairy-chested lad. He said to me, "We need to get some hair on your chest. Here, let me help..." He began ripping off handfuls of his own chest hair and sprinkling them on my bare chest right above the plaster line. He pressed the button for the nurse and waited to show off my new robust health. The nurse didn't know what to make of it. She looked at my mom with a look that said *is this guy nuts?* My dad's humor escaped her. He sneezed and suddenly my anemic state returned. As pleasant a thought as it might have been that renewed health was just a matter of borrowing a little chest hair, I knew it wouldn't stop the unrelenting effects of colitis.

I could tell my parents must have been anticipating that my medical conditions would accompany me for the remainder of my life because of the types of advice they began dispensing. They were becoming used to the readjustments and modifications that were becoming a larger part of my life. As physical challenges mounted, my dad often said, "Jeff, with all the time you spend recovering, use your brain and think about something you can invent that will make you money." My mom was also free with advice about careers that disabilities wouldn't impinge on.

"Jeff, with your artistic talents, even if you end up in a wheelchair, you could be an architect." As I was going blind, she suggested, "Jeff, even if you go blind, you could be a psychologist."

My parents, especially my mother, viewed physical challenges as "what's the next step?" or as a problem to be solved. Her pragmatic approach relied greatly on a philosophy of not treating me differently than my siblings. This included not allowing me to use my disabilities to my advantage. "Mom! Can you give me a ride up the hill to the bus stop? My arthritis hurts too much." Tough as it was on her, she knew that the best thing for the medication to take effect and allow me to limber up was to make me walk the block to the bus stop. "There's no such thing in our family as *can't*," she'd remind me.

Treating me like any other of her children was demonstrated during non-school days as well as the lazy days of summer vacation. Without school, I wasn't forced to get out of bed at a certain time. Therefore, I'd give in to the soreness and aches typical of an arthritic in the morning and lay there until noon or later. "Jeffrey!" my mom would yell up the stairway. "It's eight o'clock. Come on down. I made some nice oatmeal for you," she'd say with a lilt in her voice.

When I hadn't come down, she'd try again, her irritation evident. "I'm not kidding, Jeffrey! It's 8:45. Your oatmeal is going to be ruined if you don't get down here right now! And I'm not going to make a new batch either!"

"OK, I'm getting up!" I'd yell back just to silence her. My mom would get involved in something, and 60 minutes later I'd hear, "That's it! It's 9:45! I'm going to the grocery store. I'm leaving your oatmeal covered in the oven. I've had it!"

Typically, as long as I was sitting or, even better, lying down, I was for the most part pain-free. This is why it was difficult to be on time even when oatmeal, my favorite, was beckoning. Finally, at noon I'd realize I couldn't stay in bed all day. I'd crawl out, slowly make my way to the bathroom, and eventually, painstakingly, head downstairs for breakfast.

The habit of staying late in bed those mornings gave rise to the creation of a new breakfast dish–oatmeal a la fork and knife! By the time I'd get downstairs, between the effects of air and oven heat, the oatmeal would have transformed into a type of rubber. I'd just throw a lot of milk on it and start cutting. Over time I developed a taste for oatloaf. It tastes just as good. You just have to chew longer.

"As parents feel for their children, God feels for those who fear him."
– Psalm 103:13, MSG

"Laugh and your life will be lengthened for this is the great secret of long life." –Og Mandino

CHAPTER 9

CHRISTMAS IN THE HOSPITAL OR "NO CHIMNEY REQUIRED"

Being a frequent visitor to the hospital, it's not surprising that my nearly three months in traction overlapped with December 25, 1964. However, I wasn't completely disappointed spending the greatest of kid holidays in the hospital. Christmas was huge to my mom. Eleven months of the year, she was a no "monkey business" disciplinarian. But this time of year, the kid in her came out.

Her father, my Papa Charlie, was someone who really went overboard celebrating the season. I'm told he'd climb up on their roof shortly after my mom and her sister Alyce went to bed. He'd rattle sleigh bells and stomp around with heavy boots, doing his best imitation of reindeer to pump up the excitement level of two little girls almost to their breaking point, so it was natural that she wanted us kids to also experience the same kind of excitement.

My mom festooned the hospital room with all the trappings of Christmas: greeting cards perched and hung on display, window decals bearing images of the season, a lighted, miniature tree, my Christmas stocking from home, and garlands strewn about. Christmas morning was magical.

Mom received permission to leave her large collection of wrapped packages in Mother Superior's office. I don't know how the nurses snuck all that stuff in my room while I had visions of sugar plums dancing in my head (I've always been a very light sleeper); the nurses must have used magic. I imagine they spoke not a word but went straight to their work and filled all the stockings of this little twerp.

"Every good and perfect gift is from above, coming down from the Father of the heavenly lights..." – James 1:17

"Time always seems long to the child who is waiting—for Christmas, for next summer, for becoming a grownup: long also when he surrenders his whole soul to each moment of a happy day."
– Dag Hammarskjold

CHAPTER 10

FROM THE FRYING PAN INTO THE FIRE OR "FOR NOTHING WILL BE IMPOSSIBLE WITH GOD"
(LUKE 1:34-37)

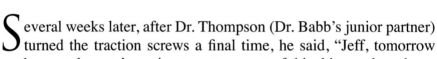

Several weeks later, after Dr. Thompson (Dr. Babb's junior partner) turned the traction screws a final time, he said, "Jeff, tomorrow or the next day, we're going to get you out of this thing and send you home. How does that sound?"

"Great!" I said. But I felt ambivalent because I would miss the newfound friends and attention that came with my long-term hospitalization. Overall, I enjoyed my hospital stays. I had fun. Being one of five siblings with an overtaxed mother and a father consumed with his business, I could never expect this kind of attention at home. Once my healing was underway and the pain of the procedures had passed, the attention that the hospital staff gave me was welcome.

My mom and dad were there visiting me when Dr. Babb invited them to watch the process of releasing me from my plaster encasement. *I can't wait to bend my knee again*, I thought. Once the body cast was removed and I bent my knee for the first time in months, I thought, *Ohhh, that feels good! It's great to be free!*

My mood instantly changed when I heard the doctor say, "We're going to have Jeff wear a half-cast at night, wrapped with elastic bandages." Before I went back into the casting room, I bent my knee as many times as possible.

Afterwards, Dad said to Dr. Babb, "I've got some special plans for Jeff when he gets home." Smiling, he continued, "I'm going to beef up this scrawny little kid with a steady of diet of meat and potatoes."

Mom cringed with embarrassment hearing my dad tell Dr. Babb how he was going to cure me, but I could understand where Dad was coming from: he had built himself up from a thin, 100 pound four-teen-year-old to a 264 pound muscle mass bearing a 48-inch chest, 19-inch biceps, and an 18 ½-inch neck.

"Lloyd, I'll tell you the truth," he interrupted. "Jeff is in bad shape. If he were my son, I'd take him from here directly to Mayo. I wouldn't even bother going home." My dad silently took in the news. We packed my belongings, said goodbye to all my new friends and headed home. The quiet drive home left each of us pondering where we stood. I was excited about reacquainting with my siblings and anticipating the familiarity of home life. Mom wrestled with a feeling of uncertainty, and Dad felt unsettled because a renowned physician had shot down his plan to rejuvenate my health. We all had a lot to consider.

As much as we all wanted to return to normalcy, the next day the sky fell in. My dad was at the office, and my mom was at home helping me adjust and become comfortable. On the radio and TV, bliz-zard news alerts were interrupting regular programming throughout the morning. By noon, whiteout conditions blanketed the metro area, and I'd had at least a dozen bloody stool discharges. My clothes and bedding were soiled and my mom just couldn't keep up. A spirit of discouragement gripped my mom and me as tightly as my writhing bowels. Finally, after another blood-filled bowel movement, my mom called my dad. She spoke into the receiver in tears, "Lloyd, if you don't hire a twenty-four-hour nurse or take him right now to the hos-pital, I'm not going to be responsible for Jeff's death." Dad left work immediately, put chains on the car, helped bundle me up, and got me in the car. Leaving the city was no problem, but as we got further down Highway 52, things became dire.

"Lloyd, what's going on?" asked Mom.

"Looks like the road is closed," my dad said looking at the squad cars in the middle of the road.

"Jeff looks terrible, Lloyd. What are we going to do?"

"I'll talk to them." My dad got out of the car and faced the stinging wind and snow of a Minnesota blizzard.

"Hello, officer," my dad said.

"Sorry, sir, this road is closed. It's impassable."

"Officer, we need to get to the Mayo Clinic immediately. My son is bleeding badly."

"Where is he?" asked the police officer. Dad pointed to the back seat of the car. The officer walked to the car. My mom rolled down her window and pleaded,

"We need to get him to the hospital. Can you help us?" Suddenly a snowplow appeared. The cop waved him down, and a quick conversation ensued. My dad got back in the car. "They're going to give us an escort down," said Dad. Mom took a deep breath, and we were slowly but methodically moving again down the highway—snowplow and squad car with flashing lights leading the way for the remaining 40 miles to Rochester. They led us right up to the Rochester exit and waved goodbye. My mom prayed a silent thank you to the Lord for getting us there safely.

"Hear my cry, oh God; Listen to my prayer. From the ends of the earth I call to You, I call as my heart grows faint; lead me to the rock that is higher than I." Psalm 61:1-2

"Life is like a game of cards. The hand that is dealt you represents determinism; the way you play it is free will." —Jawaharal Nehru

CHAPTER 11

No Other Choice or "My Very First Bag of Tricks"

O nce we arrived, Dr. Lynn immediately started blood transfusions to get me stabilized. He wanted my parents to talk with a team of European surgical specialists, some of whom had made their recommendations for my treatment a year earlier: an ileostomy. My parents had hesitated at that point to give approval for such drastic surgery. They were concerned with the finality of the procedure.

"If we give doctors permission to totally remove Jeffrey's bowel, colon, and most of his intestines, we have nothing to fall back on," mulled my mom. (In those days, there was no such thing as a bowel transplant.) The next day, my mom and dad sat in the enormous gallery where hundreds of people sit, row after row, waiting to see specialists or waiting for one of their loved ones to finish an exam. The doctors called them in. The topic of this meeting turned out to be exactly what my parents had expected.

Once introductions were complete, the same blonde Swedish surgeon repeated what he had said a year earlier, "Your little boy's colitis is wearing down his body, and I believe an aggressive approach to this disease must be taken right now. Otherwise, his disease will kill him." This time my parents didn't hesitate.

"All right. I'm assuming an ileostomy is our last option?" asked my mom.

"Yes. It is the best approach considering your son's condition," reassured the lead surgeon. Then, in what sounded to my mother as a confrontational tone, the same doctor asked:

"Do you feed Jeffrey a lot of protein?"

"Yes, I do. I feed my kids a lot of meat and cheese. Is there something wrong with that?" my mother said apprehensively.

"On the contrary, Mrs. Smith. We have never seen a seven-year-old with such muscle development. We feel it has only helped him recover from the surgeries he has had thus far and will help him recover from the ileostomy."

"It's how my mother raised me and how I've raised my kids," my mom said with increasing confidence. (My parents' families believed that it was important to buy the best food for their children, even if it meant sacrificing in other areas; my parents often had weekly grocery bills of $300. None of my siblings were fat, just very sturdy.)

"Please continue this diet, Mrs. Smith," the doctor urged, "it will help Jeffrey with what we feel is the only treatment we have left for him."

I still remember how sensitive and encouraging the doctors were to my situation. They were well aware that what they were proposing was quite a bellyful, no pun intended, to a child my age. In fact, I later learned I was the second youngest patient in Mayo history at that time to receive an ileostomy. After sparing me some of the details of the procedure, such as having to remove my entire bowel, large colon, rectum, anus, and part of my small intestines, all unsalvageable from the effects of ulcerative colitis, they explained that when I awoke there would be one inch or so of small intestines called a "stoma" protruding out of my stomach to the right of my belly button. They kept me calm by talking about it in lighter terms, which also helped me feel comfortable with it.

"Some people, Jeffrey, have given a name to their stoma," a physician explained. Big Red, Stanley Stoma, and Tiny Toot were some of the names he mentioned. "Are you interested in naming it, Jeff?"

"How 'bout Cyclops?" I said immediately. "Cyclops? Why Cyclops?"

"Because he's only got one eye!" This seemed a natural name for it considering I was a big fan of the Hercules movies where he regularly battled a Cyclops.

In spite of the encouragement from the doctors, I didn't want them to take my stuttering as a lack of intelligence. Early on, I got into

68

answering questions by making wild guesses. Strangely, I seemed able to ace the odds in some situations. For example, when I was about to get my ileostomy, a doctor from Kentucky was part of the surgical team. Being a playful type, he asked, "Do you know where I'm from?"

"Kentucky," I answered.

"Did someone tell him?" he asked as he looked around the room, totally amazed that I knew. It was just a lucky guess but I wanted to play it up big…a foreshadowing of the theatrics of Amazing Jeffo.

"I watch *Daniel Boone* on TV. I know he's from Kentucky, and you sound like him," I fibbed. The doctor narrowed his eyes because Fess Parker, the actor who played Daniel Boone, wasn't from Kentucky but simply had a generic Southern accent. Incidents like this bolstered my self-confidence and offset feelings of inadequacy stemming from my stuttering and other physical differences.

The international team of surgeons and physicians was extremely supportive. Once surgeons had spent time both reassuring and explaining to me all the changes that could be expected after an ileostomy, one of which included wearing and maintaining an elimination bag, they asked me if I had any questions. I responded with one of my greatest concerns at that time in my life, "Will I still be able to become a millionaire?"

"Bob Hope and Red Skeleton had ileostomies," responded a doctor. "Do you think they're rich?" asked another. "I think so," I said.

Here I am today, 48 years later, and doggone it if those doctors didn't mislead me. I'm still not a millionaire! Nonetheless, I can honestly say that I am rich with friends, family, and experiences, none of which I'd trade for a million bucks. The richness of this support was sustained by an inexhaustible might.

"Because of the Lord's great love we are not consumed, for His compassions never fail. They are new every morning; great is your faithfulness." Lamentations 3:22-23

My stoma lives by its own code of the road: "Let's rumble." A rebel without a pause.

CHAPTER 12

SURGERY OR "SONNY'S GOT A BRAND NEW BAG!"

Doctors couldn't have prepped me any better physically and psychologically for my life-changing ileostomy procedure. Part of the prep was their attitude that since I'd be the one with the ileostomy, I should be the one taking care of it.

"Your mom can't be with you all the time, Jeff, so you might as well start taking care of it right from the get-go," they said, while my mom nodded eagerly in agreement.

One of the factors that kept my mind off the impending surgery was the time and effort I spent ingratiating myself to the St. Mary's pediatric staff. In essence, I had become the mascot of the staff at St. Joseph's Hospital back in the Twin Cities; in contrast, I found the St. Mary's staff friendly but not as easily succumbing to my charms. *A tough nut just needs more time to crack,* I thought. My upcoming surgery and recovery would afford me all the time I needed.

My D-Day arrived the following afternoon. I never became used to the unnerving steps of surgical preparation; especially the injection that reduced the amount of anesthetic needed but caused an intensely dry mouth and thirst. Lawrence of Arabia had nothing on me! I ramped up the charm, and from my gurney choked out, "D'you think I could have just a little water?"

"You're not supposed to have anything by mouth before an operation," the nurse said, sympathetically.

"But I'm so thirsty!" I gasped.

Whether it was due to the pitiful expression on my face or the raspy appeal in my voice, the nurse said, "Well, maybe it would be all right to let you suck on a wet washcloth."

Miniscule as they were, the drops of water were ambrosia. Even greater than water drunk from a squirt gun, in my 7-year-old mind.

My Aunt Alyce, the nurse, sat with my parents in the waiting room for what surgeons expected would be a four to five hour procedure. After several hours of waiting, the double doors to the surgical hallway crashed open.

"Mr. and Mrs. Smith?" asked a tall, rigid-looking nurse with the sternest expression imaginable.

"Yes, is everything all right?" asked my mom. "Come with me," said the nurse.

My dad and my aunt stood up and began walking toward her, but the nurse pointed to my aunt and said, "You stay here."

"It's okay ma'am; she's my sister and an RN at Miller Hospital," said my mom.

"She can't come in," responded the nurse.

"Is there something wrong?" my mom asked, alarmed. "Come with me," the nurse said again mechanically, pointing to my parents. They walked through a long hallway and stopped at an elevator.

"Where are we going?" asked my mom as they entered the elevator. The nurse said nothing. Leaving the elevator, she led my parents down another hallway which was lined with windows that looked into operating theatres.

The nurse abruptly said, "Wait here." She disappeared through a door. A few minutes later, the doors burst open and the head of pathology, covered in surgical garb with only angry eyes visible, thrust a stainless steel specimen tray toward my mom. Using his forceps, he hoisted a bloody, fetid mass of indistinguishable tissue under my mom's nose that once had been a healthy bowel, rectum, and anus. She reeled; my father caught her before she hit the floor. "How in the world does a seven-year-old boy have such a diseased bowel?" spat the surgeon.

"Doctor, I have no idea," she said tearfully. The doctor's expression softened.

"I didn't mean to upset you. I'm sorry, but it's just that I've never in my career seen a bowel this diseased, and it's from such a little boy."

"Is my son all right?" my stunned mother asked.

"He's still on the table. He is holding his own," said the surgeon. My parents numbly took the elevator back to the waiting room. The image of my rotten intestines would haunt my mother's sleepless nights for days after the surgery.

Times like these tax our trust in God's promises. All we can do is cling to His word, even if we do not feel His presence. Sometimes, as AA says, "We must fake it to make it."

"But they who wait for the Lord shall renew their strength; they shall mount up with wings like eagles; they shall run and not be weary; they shall walk and not faint." Isaiah 40:31, ESV

CHAPTER 13

ON THE REBOUND OR "I HEAR THAT TRAIN A'COMIN'"

My emergency admittance to St. Mary's Hospital was not only due to blood loss but also alarming weight loss. At the pre-op physical I tipped the scales at 43 pounds, but no one knew my true weight because I was still in a full leg cast. In the two weeks following surgery, I gained ten pounds. Doctors and my parents were delighted. "If Jeffrey keeps gaining at this rate, we're going to have to roll him out of here!" said Dr. Lynn. Everyone laughed and silently hoped that I was on my way to good health at last.

After Cyclops had been installed and we had time to be properly introduced, I had lots of time on my hands. To relieve the boredom, I thought I'd play out my fascination with monsters, a subject often on my young mind. I took one of the spare elastic bandages, which were still being used to prevent my knee from curling up, and completely wrapped it around my head until I looked like a mummy. The next person to enter the room was a naive student nurse, unfamiliar with both my medical profile and prankster nature.

Seeing my head wrapped up, the Asian nursing student assumed I'd had brain surgery. Partly because I felt embarrassed and partly because I was getting hot under the bandages, I started unwinding them.

"Oh! Little boy! Don't do that! I'll get help!" she said with great alarm. Through my muffled speech, I tried to calm her down, but she ran out of the room screaming, "The brain surgery boy in 304 is unwrapping his bandages!"

The supervising nurse calmly reassured her that the pediatric ward did not have any brain surgery patients. The next day, after everything had calmed down, the shaken student nurse stopped by my room and said, "Naughty boy! You scare Suni! You no scare Suni anymore!"

To this day what Dr. Lynn said continues to bewilder me. I don't know how I could even begin to gain any weight with an ileostomy. The normal length of the intestinal tract is about 30 feet; doctors explained I was left with less than 12 feet. By all appearances, whenever I eat, food doesn't stay with me long enough to absorb the calories and nutrients.

Once doctors had explained to us it would take several weeks in the hospital to convalesce, my parents arranged for my grandmother to stay for this additional period of time with my four siblings back in the Twin Cities. With everything that my mom was dealing with, it was nice that my dad had the resources to continue housing her at the comfortable Kahler Hotel.

If my mom had ever had the opportunity to participate in the Miss America contest, she would have won the Miss Congeniality award every year, I'm sure. At the Kahler she made quick friends with a lady named Diane Awsumb, whose child was also being cared for at St. Mary's. They often had coffee and dinner with one another as they shared concerns about their children.

Like many children of my generation living in the Twin Cities, I was devoted to Casey Jones, a local children's TV legend. I watched his show, *Lunch with Casey*, every day without fail. I wanted my mom to prepare for me the same lunch fixings as Casey. My mom did her best to accommodate me, but his chow always looked more appetizing. His railroad engineering garb, which consisted of gray striped overalls, conductor cap, red neckerchief, and big old watch chain dangling out of his pocket, were familiar and reassuring symbols.

Roger Awsumb, a.k.a. "Casey Jones," was due to join his wife Diane to visit his son. My mom thought it would be the ultimate thrill for me to meet Casey, and Mrs. Awsumb said she would arrange it with her famous husband. Mom took every advantage of this opportunity by telling me in advance of Casey's arrival to build my anticipation to a state of frenzy.

Well, the big day arrived. Casey was preceded into the room by my mom, who heralded his entrance as if she was a part of the royal court announcing the King had arrived.

"Jeffrey," Mom said with a lilt, "Casey's here to see you." He came into my room and boomed, "Hello, Jeff."

His face looked like Casey and his voice sounded like Casey, but he sure didn't dress like Casey. This guy was decked out in a three-piece suit. The real Casey wore railroad garb, not CEO duds. Our eyes locked, and then I looked away.

My mom cleared her throat, "Say 'hello' to Casey Jones, Jeff," she said in a mock happiness, which clearly indicated to me she was enraged. But I had made up my mind. This guy was an imposter. I wasn't going to say "hello." Mom and Casey exchanged uncomfortable glances.

"Well, you get some rest, Jeff," said Casey. He smiled at my mom; she returned the smile, and he left. I could hear his animated voice as he visited another child on the floor next door followed by a burst of giggles and laughter.

My humiliated mother steeled her eyes on me and quietly said, "Never do that to someone again. Ever. He took time out of his personal schedule just to see you. You were rude." She then left the room.

Despite her reprimand, I still felt I was in the right, on behalf of kids everywhere, in protecting the integrity of the TV legend, the great engineer, Casey Jones.

"Children, obey your parents in everything, for this pleases the Lord." Colossians 3:20

"Wisdom comes by disillusionment." – George Santayana

CHAPTER 14

ILEOSTOMY FALLOUT OR "I'M TOTALLY BAGGED!"

The "solution" to my life-threatening ulcerative colitis had been an ileostomy. As invasive and physically altering as the ileostomy was, the greatest impact on my life wasn't the new way I went to the bathroom, but rather, the psychological effect it had on me.

When I returned to my second grade class following surgery, I asked the teacher to gather the kids so I could tell them about my ileostomy. I hoped she'd say yes; I had a need to feel accepted among my peers.

In spite of my classmates' fascination with my ileostomy story, as soon as the next school year rolled around I became closed-mouthed with what I felt had to be kept a secret. As I later transitioned into junior high school, which was filled with its own challenges of fitting in, my secret weighed heavily on me.

One day between classes a new friend stopped me and said, "Jeff, you won't believe what I just heard!"

"What's that?" I answered with uncertainty.

"It's so weird! Mark Adams told me you wear some kind of bag on your stomach. And get this! He said you poop into it. "

Feeling a hot flush of embarrassment wash over me, I stuttered, "I wear what?! A bag? Poop?! I don't know what he's talking about!" I lied, afraid of taking any chances of possibly losing this new friend.

The technology of the day used in the surgical procedure was far ahead of the technology surrounding the ileostomy appliance itself. Since I was the second-youngest patient to ever receive one at a time when practical solutions to living daily with an elimination bag had yet to be perfected, I, along with other pioneer patients, had to live with the fallout.

The present-day appliance makes living with an ileostomy more practical, even convenient. But in 1965 it was a completely different story. The "Robinson appliance," (commonly known as my bag), was attached to a plastic disc, or collar, by a rubber band. You've heard the expression "hanging on by a thread"? The same peril existed using the thin rubber band recommended by the manufacturer.

One of the defects of this design was the rubber band could break or slip off the disc at inopportune moments. The narrow margin of error also applied to the manner in which the plastic disc adhered to my abdomen. An elastic belt was the only thing that held the appliance onto my body. I often thought of myself as a guinea pig.

Another natural result of the appliance design was that when the ring pulled away from my body due to an inadvertent motion, volumes of methane gas escaped, far exceeding any amount that comes as a result of your garden-variety passing of gas. If that wasn't embarrassing enough, without a bowel, whose natural function includes reabsorbing fluid from fecal matter, my stool typically resembled diarrhea. This compounded the odor. When a gas leak occurred, this took ultimate acting on my part to deflect the suspicions of those nearby. It's a crying shame they don't have an Oscar category for this kind of role. I'd surely be unanimously voted the winner in this most bizarre category. My body of work in this area would be so superior compared to the common tooter, even greater than the difference of the acting prowess of Lawrence Olivier vs. Pee Wee Herman.

One of my greatest thespian opportunities arose later on in sixth grade while boarding the school bus. Well, I must have moved this way rather than that way as I boarded the bus, and sulfur from the very gates of hell wafted up and were trapped inside my parka. Unlike the normal situation where unfortunate souls are trailing someone who's backfired, those behind me were spared—for the moment. My coat had unintentionally created a sort of delayed-action fuse that would detonate a time-release stink bomb. As I sat there waiting, I realized this would be the crucible moment when I'd need to appear nonchalant while all the world around me was falling apart.

Kids sitting near me slowly began noticing the malodorous fumes. Systematically, row-by-row, they began to voice their protestations.

"Who farted!" "Don't look at me…"

"Man, who cut the cheese!"

"I think it's you, Jeff!" said the boy next to me who was getting the worst of it.

Being confronted with the truth called for reaching into my acting reservoir to a depth rarely drawn upon. *Yes! I must use emotion to be the most convincing!* I thought.

"Me? Yeah, right! It's obviously you!" I passionately retorted. The youthful innocence that characterized the occupants of the bus seconds earlier had started to transform into a classic mob mentality.

"The smell must be coming from Russell's bunny!" someone yelled.

"I gave my bunny a bath this morning!" Russell cried out in defense of his pet, hugging the bunny like a mother rabbit protecting her young. He had brought his bunny to school for show and tell.

"Throw it out the window!" somebody bellowed. "Yeah, yeah, yeah!" rang throughout.

"Don't make me stop this bus!" the driver yelled to no one in particular.

The bunny and I were both humiliated and were glad to be going home to our respective "hutches."

Looking back, these humiliating experiences off-set my bent toward a self-centered attitude, which was, in part, a natural result from the exceptional degree of adult attention I received.

"It was good for me to be afflicted so that I might learn your decrees." Psalm 119:71

How to Drive Your Parents and Siblings Crazy

Getting the ileostomy saved my life, but as I mentioned earlier, it caused its own unique challenges. Before the development of deodorizer tablets, which I consider the greatest invention of the

20th century, I have fond, if not downright perverse, memories of hearing my parents' choked voices echoing up the stairwell of our spacious house.

"Oh, my Lord! Jeffrey! Open the window! For the love of Mary! Open the window!"

Winter and the resulting frozen windows only magnified the problem. On at least one occasion, desperate attempts to air out the bathroom resulted in the window crank breaking off in the hand of a panicked parent or sibling. I admit having a twisted enjoyment over those times when I would use the toilet while my brothers lathered up in the boys communal shower. The quiet, sleepy routine of morning prep would suddenly be shattered by angry, unintelligible bellows from the shower. I'd chuckle to myself because I knew my brothers were trapped; their only option was to stay close to the floor and hold washcloths over their noses.

Another time, I thought it was a good idea to leave on the sink in the basement bathroom a plastic cup to rinse out my bag instead of trudging upstairs to use the bathroom. My dad had a mini gym in the basement. When my younger brother Steve and my dad were lifting weights, Dad took a break to refresh himself. I was in the kitchen and overheard Steve yell in a panic, "Dad! Jeff rinses out his bag with that cup!" My brother afterward told me when my dad understood what he had heard, he spat a stream of water out of his mouth all over the mirror in front of him, just like an old Three Stooges movie.

Years later, at a family and friends barbecue in the mid 90's, while standing at the hors d'oeuvres table with beverage in hand, I felt something land on my left shoe. *No! It couldn't be that!* I thought. I cautiously reached down and felt my upper pant leg, which had that perfect, crisp GQ look, not the familiar lump of my bag. Not moving a muscle, I casually said, "Say, mom? Do you mind coming over for a minute?

"Well, I'm kind of busy serving, Jeff. Is it important?" she asked.
"Oh-h…I think so…" I said with rising tension in my voice. "What is it?" she asked impatiently.

"My bag just fell off," I whispered. "Well, where is it?"

Where do you think? I thought, but instead responded, "Left foot." "Wait there. I'll get a container."

Feigning nonchalance, she quickly returned, bent down, lifted my pant leg, and placed the wayward bag into the plastic container. "Mike! Please be a dear and take this out to the garbage," she casually asked my brother.

"What is it?" Mike responded, thinking she might be making a hasty decision about throwing out one of her tasty offerings.

"Never mind. Just take it out, please."

I never checked back with Mike to find out if his curiosity got the best of him. Miraculously, nothing had spilled out, but I was now going commando, ileostomy style. After some makeshift adjustments involving a Ziploc sandwich bag, my brother Steve drove me back to my apartment where I kept my ileostomy supplies — never getting a chance to sink my teeth into Mom's baby back pork loin ribs. Until this unexpected turn of events, I would never have been described as a party pooper!

If I was fortunate enough to be at home for these kinds of mishaps, the blessing of a family's unconditional bond enabled me to deal with it and even enjoy the humor of it.

"But God will never forget the needy; the hope of the afflicted will never perish." Psalm 9:18, TNIV

Snub the Club – or Where's The Back Door?

Although I appreciated the extra attention that came with having special physical needs, my utmost desire was to fit in and feel like a regular kid, but my parents' decision to bring me to monthly ileostomy support groups ran contrary to that desire. The other members of this club were decades older than I. It seemed strange to me that a bunch of people would meet, have cookies and punch, win door prizes of ileostomy supplies, and discuss "defecating with dignity," in so many words. While watching yet another *Your Stoma is Your Friend* video, I whispered to my mom, "Can we go, now?"

"We can't go yet, Jeff. You might win a prize!"

"Gee, maybe I'll win the latest and greatest in elimination bags!" I whispered back.

My eight-year-old mind typically wandered during these meetings. I found it more interesting spending my time looking around and wondering, *Who's packing?* since attendees included both present and future ileostomy patients. I'd play my own version of "Where's Waldo?" Glancing at the different members, I'd think, *Hmmm...bag on the left or bag on the right?*

I think these support group meetings would have been more successful if they'd pointed out the advantages of having an ileostomy. One of these benefits is not needing to find reading material before visiting the restroom; your hands are already busy enough!

"A joyful heart is good medicine." – Proverbs 17:22, ESV

"You can't deny laughter; when it comes, it plops down in your favorite chair and stays as long as it wants." – Stephen King

Oh, the Versatility of the Humble Ileostomy Bag
In a pinch, a clean ileostomy bag can be used to:
- *carry your goldfish to the vet for its 6-month checkup.*
- *pipe frosting onto your cupcakes.*
- *substitute for helium balloons for your child's birthday party. (No helium necessary when following a chili and broccoli feed!)*
- *substitute as a flotation device at the annual Ileostomy Regatta.*
- *substitute for a missing soaker hose: just poke and soak!*
- *operate as a methane-powered predator drone for military special ops.*

Chapter 15

A Stiff Leg–and
A Stiffer Upper Lip

As I was growing up, my RA and other physical issues caused me a degree of physical and social isolation because I had limited opportunities to develop friendships with neighborhood kids and class-mates. Long-term hospitalization, homebound recovery, and three to four times weekly physical therapy sessions made me feel more like a visiting foreign exchange student than a native-born neighborhood kid. I was out of place. When I had a full leg brace made to prevent my left knee from re-curling following my months in traction, I feared being fodder for teasing in the neighborhood. Other children called me "Hop Along," "Peg Leg," etc. Once again, my defense was to use humor to redirect attention away from comments aimed at me.

A few years later, when my leg was made straight by surgically fusing my knee, I remember using the fusion to my unfair advantage against others. I'd win bets with unsuspecting kids who weren't familiar with my condition: I'd challenge the ones who always thought they were the best at everything. I would bet them I could hold my left leg out extended in front of me longer than they could hold out one of their legs. I never lost.

I wore a two-inch lift in my left shoe to offset the difference between my two legs that had resulted from surgery. When some of the kids noticed this thick shoe, they called me "Frankie," short for Frankenstein.

Most of the humor I used to brush off the teasing went over the heads of tormentors who were too slow to catch on.

"Why is your sole so big?" they'd ask.

"I'm a secret agent and keep weapons in there," I'd respond. However, humor could only go so far as an effective defense mechanism. After weeks of putting up with comments from a bully at school, I begged my mom to convince my older brother Dave to take on my antagonist. Dave, a fifth grader, reluctantly agreed to talk to the third-grade bully the next day.

"Thanks a lot, Mom," Dave said when he returned home. "I did what you asked me to do. I found out his mom just died! I felt like an idiot. I told him it's OK to tease Jeff."

"What?" my mom said.

"Well, he's worse off than Jeff," responded Dave.

"I know his mom dying is a terrible thing, but it's only making it worse for him by being mean to other kids," my mom explained. "OK, but I'm never, ever doing this again," he said, storming off.

Overall, being the object of teasing was a negative, but in the large scope of things it helped keep my ego in check. It also helped to hone my ability to think on my feet and give the appearance of being in control on the stage of life. Spontaneity has proven time and again to get the biggest laughs on the professional stage as well.

Robust Dave and Skinny Jeff just before my parents realized he'd been eating all my food. Actually, the real culprit was the residual effects of chronic colitis which had steadily robbed my body of nutrients, eventually making me the second-youngest in medical history to receive an ileostomy.

"Remember how the LORD your God led you all the way in the wilderness these forty years, to humble and test you in order to know what was in your heart, whether or not you would keep his commands." Deuteronomy 8:2

Joint without a Point or "A Cane is My Crutch"

The common approach among all my doctors was to proceed with my treatment one step at a time to avoid the unnecessary side effects that can come with using a more aggressive method. As a result, many times we saw my doctors' frustration and disappointment when a "safer" approach had failed. One of my orthopedic doctors, Dr. Thompson, once said, "Jeffrey, the Hippocratic Oath says we never want to hurt the patient or cause physical harm if it is avoidable. Surgery is a last alternative when all else fails."

My three months of traction had yielded only bedsores. The pain and curvature of my left knee soon returned and caused great discomfort and difficulty walking. My doctors sympathized with everything I had recently gone through and hoped they could delay resorting to what they knew to be my last option: a knee fusion. Dr. Babb explained, "We know a knee fusion is inevitable, but we want to wait until Jeff's left leg can grow a little more. Fusing the knee now will stunt growth in that leg, and he'll eventually have two different leg lengths, creating its own problems. We're hoping until that time to treat his knee with medication, therapy, and maybe have him use a cane."

"Old guys use canes," I protested. My parents must have appreciated my point of view and asked Babb if he would mind if we got a second opinion from doctors at the Mayo Clinic. "I want you to make the right decision for Jeffrey, Mr. and Mrs. Smith," Dr. Babb reassured them.

Their request for a second opinion conveniently coincided with my three-month check-up at Mayo, scheduled for the coming week. My heart sank when Mayo doctors convinced my parents that a cane would help prevent wear and tear on my knee. Challenging as it was on my psyche to begin using a cane at only eight years old, acquiring it was equally daunting. As instructed by doctors, we mailed the cane prescription to a medical supply house in Minneapolis.

Having arrived by special delivery, my mom opened the package to discover a far-too-long, shiny black cane with a brass lion's head affixed to its top. "What were they thinking?" complained my mom. We sent this dressy-looking cane back with a note reiterating the desired length and the need for it to have a support grip. Shortly, another special delivery arrived at our door. This time it was a wooden cane, the right length and grip, but with topless island women carved on its shaft.

"Can't we just cut it down to the right size?" I asked, thinking how funny this cane would look to my friends.

After mailing this inappropriate cane back, we then received a cane with the right length and support grip, but its handle could be unscrewed to reveal a hollow shaft containing three empty, corked vials.

"For Heaven's sake! This is for someone who wants to take the party with him."

"What do you mean, Mom?"

"It means that these vials are made for alcohol!"

To me, it looked like a cane that would be used by James Bond. "I can fill those tubes with milk and orange juice," I pleaded. "Are you kidding? They'll go sour!"

This cane, like the others, was returned. Maintaining her patience, my mom called the supply house and once again very deliberately went over the details of what my doctor had prescribed. This time the clerk understood, and I received a plain, adjustable metal cane with a proper support handle. Bo-o-or-ring!

I used the cane, along with physical therapy and medication, for fourteen months. After no improvement, it was then that my parents and doctors agreed time had run out. As my parents and I had done so many times before, we had to look ahead for better days.

"Be strong and take heart, all you who hope in the LORD." Psalm 31:24

"It's the possibility that keeps me going, not the guarantee." – Nicholas Sparks

Chapter 16

Knee Fusion or "The Straight Truth"

"To keep Jeff from needing a wheelchair permanently, I have no other choice than to surgically fuse his knee. It can't wait any longer, Mr. and Mrs. Smith. I'll admit Jeffrey to Midway Hospital tomorrow and schedule surgery first thing next week," said Dr. Babb. He turned back to me and said, "You're going to be better off with a fused knee, Jeff. Your leg will be permanently straight, but it will eliminate your pain and stabilize it." (In 1966, total knee replacements were in their infancy.)

The prospect of having a "peg leg" for the rest of my life was depressing, but the thought of having a lifetime of unendurable knee pain was horrific. I clung to the hope that surgery would ease my pain.

After surgery, I woke up wearing a heavy-duty plaster cast with three exposed pins at the knee and ankle joints. Their purpose was to ensure that there would be no movement in the knee area while the bottom of the femur fused with the top of the tibia. This would take two to three months. Once the anesthesia wore off, all of the surgical sawing, drilling and reattaching bone to bone resulted in the worst pain I had ever experienced to date. All the pain meds the nurses gave me were to no avail.

My mom was so desperate for me to have pain relief that when she happened to spot our next-door neighbor, a family physician on staff, she ran after him and pleaded for help. He came into my room and said, "Maybe we can adjust the pillows a little under your elevated leg,

Jeff." My mom thanked him as he left, but the repositioning brought me no relief.

Soon thereafter, Dr. Babb came in the room and immediately noticed my leg had been moved from his careful positioning.

"Who moved this cast?" he demanded.

"I'm so sorry, doctor. Jeffrey has been in such pain that when I saw my neighbor, who is a doctor here, I asked him for assistance. He suggested moving his leg to a more comfortable position."

Babb interrupted with a thunderous voice, "A wet cast should never be moved. He should know that!"

"I'm sorry," my mother repeated as Dr. Babb repositioned my cast.

He left the room, and I gritted my teeth for a couple of days until the pain subsided. After about ten days, I was discharged.

It was August of 1966; I would turn 10 years old at the end of October. Instead of anticipating the start of a new school year, I pondered missing more school.

I recovered at home in a wheelchair. Our three-story house, nice as it was, had no elevator, naturally. This meant I had to stay on the floor my father moved me to before he left for work.

The pain was manageable during the day, but at night it often kept me awake. One night, after great difficulty getting comfortable, my mom noticed I had finally drifted off. She was a firm believer in the healing effects that come from good sleep.

Raising five kids, my mom had many opportunities to display a temper, most often justifiably. Of course, as with most parents, outside the home, she was always a model of composure and diplomacy—though not this night. Our next-door neighbors had a challenging marriage that I often became unintentionally privy to because I was equipped with ears. Hysterical screams awoke me from my comfortable sleep, and as a result, I became aware of the throbbing pain in my knee. "I can't fall back to sleep with Mrs. Johnson screaming," I said.

Much to my surprise, my polite mother stormed down the steps, dialed Mrs. Johnson's number, and said, "I have a sick little boy just home from the hospital. He's in severe pain from doctors removing his knee. I just got him to sleep, and then we hear a shriek from over there that would wake up the dead!"

The novelty of hearing that tone of voice directed toward a neighbor was kind of entertaining and distracted me enough to forget the ache in my knee. I fell back to sleep.

My mom would have been just as upset had she realized during my recovery that a neighbor boy had taught me how to pop a wheelie in my wheelchair, cast and all.

Gratefully, I had that natural ability of a child to maintain equilibrium and take one day at a time in the face of uncertainty.

"I will be glad and rejoice in your love, for you saw my affliction and knew the anguish of my soul." Psalm 31:7

CHAPTER 17

HOMEBOUND TUTOR OR "GOING TO SCHOOL IN MY PAJAMAS"

Since my knee fusion and the recovery time at home overlapped with the beginning of fourth grade, the school district provided me with a homebound tutor, Mrs. Shackle. She was a retired elementary school teacher and epitomized your classic, conservative "little old lady," who, accordingly, drove a 1964 blue Ford Falcon.

Every visit, my mom set us up on the dining room table, and Mrs. Shackel enjoyed her morning cup of coffee prepared by my mom just as they both liked it: thick and super-charged.

Each tutoring session was the same: Mrs. Shackel and I worked two hours, had lunch, and worked two more hours. Without realizing it, I was learning and having fun too. We grew fond of each other.

She took me to her house that summer for lunch and a tour of her large garden, then shared photographs and stories about trips to Europe. I thanked her and thought that would be the last I'd see of her, but God had other plans for our future.

"There is surely a future hope for you, and your hope will not be cut off." Proverbs 23:18

"A teacher affects eternity; she can never tell where her influence stops." – Henry Brooks Adams

CHAPTER 18

FREE AT LAST OR "A CAST PARTY WITHOUT STARS"

S everal weeks of healing ensued and it was time to remove the cast. For days I had been wondering, *How are they going to separate the three spikes from the plaster, let alone my bones, without it hurting?*

My dad brought me to St. Joseph's where we were met by a physician's assistant who escorted us to the "cast room." We were joined there by Dr. Babb.

"Is it going to hurt?" I asked, seeking out the kindest face. The physician's tech reassured me that the cast would be cut off pain- free by use of a vibrating saw. Adjusting for a ten-year-old's vocabulary, I'm sure at the time I was thinking something along the line of *modern technology is truly a marvelous thing.*

How was I to know Dr. Babb relied on tried-and-true spike removal methods? Watching the tech pull out a crude hand drill and pass it to the doctor caused my faith in modern technology to instantly evaporate. My eyes widened in horror. The drill was nothing more than a crank drill that handymen store in their garage.

"Is it going to hurt?" I again asked, now stuttering.

"Only while the spikes are coming out," the tech muttered. When the first surges of pain shot up my leg as Dr. Babb began cranking, I hollered, "Don't you have something faster that uses electricity or something?" My leg was being yanked from one direction to another.

"I'm sorry. This is how it's done," Dr. Babb answered. "I'll be done in a minute." (I'm reconstructing his response since it was difficult at the time hearing exactly what he was saying through the din of my screams.)

"Quit being such a baby," the tech said, unbelievably callous.

After the smoke cleared, the assistant and Dr. Babb wrapped me in bandages to absorb the drainage.

They gave us extra bandages and instructions about keeping the wounds clean and sent me home. Their instructions were hardly necessary since my mom was an expert in personal cleanliness. I still have scabs left from her vigorous shampooing methods when I was a little boy. Besides, she already was a veteran of wound care, thanks to me. My mom acquired these advanced skills early on in my recovery from orthopedic and gastro-intestinal surgeries.

She bathed me three times daily in a tub full of soapy Dreft detergent (made for baby clothing). After these baths, I looked like an old man—wrinkled and soft—but I healed marvelously.

Years earlier, doctors had remarked following the post-surgical healing after my ileostomy surgery, "Mrs. Smith! This is the finest rectum closure we have ever seen." (Doctors get their thrills differently from the rest of us.)

Just as it was with my abdominal surgeries, the wounds on my surgically fused knee healed perfectly.

Decades later, as a result of the encouragement and curiosity of others, I asked my orthopedic specialist, "Can my fused knee be replaced with an artificial one?"

"I think if we tried it, the extensive rehab time it would require to rebuild the atrophied muscles would make success doubtful. We'd then have to fuse the knee again," he said.

My parents and I were blessed with doctors who never had the "move it along," ten-minutes-per-patient kind of mentality. My physicians embodied the Hippocratic Oath, even when it was not convenient or simple. I am, and will always be, grateful for their professionalism and care. We depended on their vision for my future when ours was blurred.

"So we fix our eyes not on what is seen, but on what is unseen. For what is seen is temporary, but what is unseen is eternal." 2 Corinthians 4:18

"When it is dark enough, you can see the stars."
–Ralph Waldo Emerson

CHAPTER 19

A SHADOWY GLIMPSE OF THE FUTURE OR "HALO EVERYBODY, HALO"

⌒

The first time I noticed something wrong with my vision was after one of my older brother Dave's Little League games the summer between fourth and fifth grade. Just a week earlier, my Uncle Sheridan (Aunt Alyce's husband) had been charmed by my request to have 500 of my own business cards printed to my exact specifications:

Agent 007 Private Investigator
Jeffrey Smith
Mendota Heights, MN
Offices: New York, London, Bombay, Hong Kong, St. Paul

The inspiration behind these business cards was receiving my greatest Christmas present ever–a James Bond attaché case! The specially-equipped briefcase had everything a ten-year-old spy required, starting with a plastic 9 mm hand gun with attachable scope and barrel for sniper assignments, and plastic bullets that could be loaded into a magazine, and then snapped into the handgrip. That's not all! The case included a codebook, a pen that could squirt poison gas (or tap water for the sake of convenience), and a passport with several forms of ID. But wait! There's more! There was a combination lock that, when opened by an enemy agent or little brother, would set off a preloaded cap. When closed, the case could shoot out plastic bullets and allow a rubber stiletto knife to be drawn out.

As soon as my secret agent business cards arrived, I looked for an opportunity to distribute them. This nerdy but reasonably priced international spy was available for hire. I saw Little League as a potential market for my services.

Mr. Prettyman, the coach of the team, had assigned me the duties of batboy. I realized this was, for the most part, an honorary position since eleven year olds would just as soon carry their own gear. He had kindly offered this to me to help me feel part of the team. While we were at bat, I covertly slipped an Agent 007 business card into each player's fielding glove. When it was our turn to take the field, I tried not to smile when I heard kids saying:

"Hey, where did this card come from?"

"Hey! I got one too..."

"Agent 007, Jeffrey Smith? Who is that?"

"Dave, isn't that your last name?"

I looked over at my brother, who had scrunched up his face and hunched his shoulders in embarrassment; I took his look to clearly say, *Gee what a moron my kid brother is*. But I heard him say, "Well, yeah, but Smith is a common name." Chalk another one up for the pesky kid brother!

I loved to bug Dave, whenever the opportunity arose. I certainly had no vendetta toward my older brother, but I sought his attention, even at the cost of annoying him. For instance, before I would allow him to read my new supply of comics—Superman, Batman, and Archie, I would make him do humiliating things. Right before bedtime, I'd mess up my sheets and blankets by scrunching them to the bottom of the bed in a tangled mass, then I'd lie down in a fetal position quivering with excitement as I would politely ask, "Dave, can you tuck me in?"

I wouldn't tell him where I hid my new sack of comics until the sheets and blanket were snugly tucked under each side of the mattress and neatly folded under my chin. I can still hear his grumbling and seething.

Anyway, following Dave's Little League game that summer night, we squeezed into my mom's 1965 Mustang convertible and headed for home. We were nearly home when my mom cried out, "Oh, my gosh! We left Dana at the ball field!"

"Just keep going, Mom," Dave joked.

"It's already too crowded," I added with a laugh.

Dana, being the only girl in the family, and a middle child to boot, needed to stand up for her rights on a regular basis. (Dana, my mom, and my Aunt Alyce for a period of time, were all patients of the same doctor who once commented to my mom, "You three women are the most determined people I ever met.") Maybe that's why I had the feeling at times that we boys were outnumbered by Dana, one to four.

Finally, when we were a reunited family and driving home again, I said, "Everything I see in my left eye has a halo around it."

"You're seeing things," Dave said.

"Yeah, I'm seeing a halo."

"Do you see angels under the halo?" Dave teased.

"Shut up," I groaned.

"Don't make me stop the car," said my mom, borrowing my father's line. Of course, it was less effective coming from her. "We'll get your glasses checked, Jeff."

Over the coming weeks, I kept complaining about my ever-increasing fuzzy vision. My Aunt Alyce, continuing to be a valuable medical advisor, referred us to one of the top ophthalmologists in the Twin Cities. Following her recommendation, we made an appointment with Dr. Charles Roach, whose quiet nature led me to believe he had attended the same school as Dr. Thompson: the school of mime. After a long examination filled with countless versions of "Hmmmmmms," Dr. Roach sat back in his chair, pressed the intercom button, and said in a voice that always reminded me of Jimmy Stewart, "Would you have Mrs. Smith come back to the exam room?" When she arrived, he said, "Jeffrey has iritis and is developing a cataract."

"Iritis?" asked my mom.

"Iritis can be a secondary condition not uncommon to those with rheumatoid arthritis. I examined his other eye and see no evidence of it there. However, I recommend you take him to the Mayo Clinic where I interned and see my teaching professor. I can set up an appointment immediately; when can you go?"

Like Rome, all our roads seemed to be leading to the Mayo Clinic. Hold the Mayo, please!

Dr. Roach never mentioned the B-word, which is what my mother feared most, because the chances of iritis eventually leading to total blindness were miniscule at best, according to his considered opinion.

"Doctor, we'll work our schedule around your recommendations," Mom said.

We left, picked up some prednisone eye drops to be taken three-times a day, and went home.

A few days later, my dad, mom, and I headed to Rochester where we met with Roach's mentor. Following an extensive exam, he announced, "Dr. Roach's diagnosis is correct. Jeffrey has iritis."

"Is there a chance it will spread to the other eye?" my mom asked, fearing the worst.

Placing his hand on my shoulder, the doctor responded, "I wouldn't worry about it. There is no case study that has made the connection between one eye being affected by the other. It would have to be an independent occurrence. The chances of that happening twice to the same person would be extremely rare, maybe 100,000 to 1. Moreover, the odds of iritis leading to total blindness are even less likely." (So how come I haven't won the lottery?) "Continue the eye drops as prescribed," he concluded.

"That's a huge relief, doctor," my mom said; my dad nodded. We headed home with renewed spirits.

The following Saturday night, I watched the movie *The Miracle Worker*, the story of Helen Keller. I imagined how terrible it would be to go blind, one of the worst things my mind could imagine. The next morning, my arthritis was bothering me enough that I stayed home from church. As I half-listened to one of those Sunday morning, public service AM-radio programs, the host was interviewing a man who was blind. They happened to be discussing the previous night's broadcast of *The Miracle Worker*. The host asked a series of questions about what it was like to be blind. For the most part, the contents of the interview skimmed the surface of my attention until I looked out my bedroom window and then it clicked: everything I could see from the upper-story vista was suddenly and unnervingly juxtaposed against everything said in the interview. *I can't see those letters on the street sign up the hill anymore. If I were blind, I couldn't see as far away as I can now. In fact, I wouldn't be able to see anything! How come the guy on the radio doesn't seem very upset about being blind?* I pondered.

My musings about what it would be like to be blind were forgotten amidst the sleepiness of the following Monday morning and the start of a new school year. I was too embarrassed to explain to my fifth-grade teacher that I would need to take eye drops every two to three hours. My dad drove me to school the next day and explained the situation to my teacher. Mr. Anderson gave me permission to leave the classroom anytime I needed.

It felt like the nurse's office was my second classroom. Ducking in and out of class became very noticeable to my classmates and embarrassing to me.

Taking eye drops throughout the day wasn't the only reason I often needed to leave the room. I didn't realize it at the time, but my intestines had formed scar tissue from the ileostomy surgery two-and-a-half years earlier. The scar tissue was slowly strangling the movement of my stool. As stool collected within me, an odor became obvious to me and to others. When I, or other kids, noticed the smell, I would excuse myself to the nurse's office to investigate. I assumed the bag was faulty and I had some kind of leak.

This caused me to become slightly paranoid; I started to imagine that every ambient unpleasant odor was coming from me. At one point, I remember leaning my head up against the bathroom wall wondering, *God, why is this happening? I've had enough! Please stop it!*

It would only become clear to me years later that I was being refined by fire to deal with what was to come.

"He is the Rock, His works are perfect, and all His ways are just." Deuteronomy 32: 4

"The art of living lies less in eliminating our troubles than in growing with them." – Bernard M. Baruch

CHAPTER 20

SICK AND SICKER OR "BATHROOM OR BUST"

I wasn't so much blaming God as calling on Him to simply stop this inexplicable odor. I even tried ramping up the showers, and don't think this wasn't an effort for a typical eleven-year-old. My parents noticed and asked, "Is there a special girl in your life at school?" I thought, *Oh, brother!* but was too embarrassed to confide in them.

Several days before Thanksgiving, I came down with flu-like symptoms. The nausea became worse, and I barely touched the array of delicious foods Mom had prepared for the holiday.

My dad had been awarded a trip to Puerto Rico and the Virgin Islands for achieving record insurance sales. My parents considered canceling their trip since they were due to leave just after Thanksgiving, but finally conceded to have me stay with my grandma for one-on-one care. They hired a retired woman to stay at the house with my siblings.

After several more days of nausea at my grandma's house, even turning down her delicacies (homemade scotch shortbread, chocolate chip and million dollar cookies, and hot cocoa), I was feeling so lousy I couldn't get off the lounge chair in her den. Knowing I was in bad shape, she called my Aunt Alyce late that evening.

"What's wrong, Irene?" asked Alyce. "It's Jeff."

"How's he feeling?"

"Horrible," said my grandmother.

"How much stool is Jeff producing in his bag?"

"Nothing since yesterday evening," responded my grandma. "Call Dr. Gallagan's answering service and explain the situation. We're coming right over."

When they arrived at Grandma's house, she reported to my aunt what the doctor had said. "Dr. Gallagan told me we need to call Dr. Lynn in Rochester."

"Bring Jeffrey down here now," Dr. Lynn, my ileostomy surgeon, urged my aunt and uncle. "Now" was around 1 a.m.

In the middle of that December night, we drove down to the Mayo Clinic. I was in so much pain that Uncle Sheridan carried me in. The emergency room at St. Mary's Hospital had been notified by my pediatrician and was prepared for my arrival.

A catheter was inserted into my stoma and the attendants determined that waste material wasn't getting through. They manipulated the drainage tube within my intestines to open the blockage. They continued probing until they broke through. What happened next reminds me of a mix between the movie *Krakatoa: East of Java* and the theme song from the Beverly Hillbillies: *"Then one day he was shootin' for some food and up through the ground came a' bubblin' crude."* Almost a gallon of waste spewed out of me. They were amazed that so much could come out of such a little person (I weighed 60 lbs).

Manipulating the drainage tube relieved one kink, but the other larger kink had to be released surgically.

With the immediate threat passed, doctors had Aunt Alyce call my parents' hotel in St. Thomas, Virgin Islands. "We'll catch the first flight out of here, Alyce," my mom said straightaway.

"No! Please, Martha, the doctors know what needs to be done. You and Lloyd need this vacation. Dr. Lynn only needs your permission to operate."

"Of course," my mom responded, "give the doctors permission to do whatever is necessary."

After more debate, Alyce convinced my parents that the doctors had things under control, to finish their vacation and assured them she'd keep them updated on my condition. My parents stayed, but any relaxation and enjoyment from the vacation was out the window.

After allaying the threat of peritonitis, doctors spent a couple of days removing any remaining toxins. With my parents in Puerto Rico but wanting to come home, my grandmother stood in for them and lodged at the Kahler Hotel near the hospital.

My parents were at ease regarding the care being provided for my other four siblings, at least. A retired woman had stayed with us kids in the past, and we saw her as a kind of grandmother. Unbeknownst to my parents, since last hiring her, she had slipped into a degree of senility.

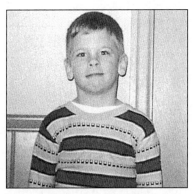

My well-fed four-year-old brother whom I affectionately nicknamed Boobie Benson. Family lore has his diet consisting of 75% protein and 25% grass, that he and the dog shared because my mom wanted him to stay outside to provide her with a respite.

High school-aged baby brother Mikey, a.k.a. Boobie Benson, taking after our dad. (1980) Maybe there IS something to a grass-rich diet, after all.

Amongst our freezer full of offerings, my mom kept expensive, prime-cut steaks for her and my dad. Don't get me wrong, we kids were better-fed than most kids in both quality and quantity, but we were envious that Mom and Dad had prime steak while we were fed the family cut—flavorful, but on the tough side.

Unaware of this practice, the babysitter thought it would be nice on her first night to serve the "good" steak for everyone. The next day, my brother Dave asked her, "What's for dinner tonight?"

"How about steak?" she suggested, forgetting she had served it just the night before. When the sitter suggested steak on the third night, Dave responded, "Again?"

"But Dave, last night we had spaghetti," she retorted.

Not understanding what was going on, but seeing an opportunity, Dave said, "OK." He issued a gag order to the brothers and to Dana. Steak dinners continued every night throughout my parents' vacation.

Eventually when our folks returned from Puerto Rico for a quick repacking before joining me at St. Mary's Hospital, my mom opened the freezer and gasped, "What happened to all my nice steaks?!"

The morning of my surgery, my parents totally surprised me by walking into the room with big smiles as they said, "Good morning, Jeffrey." To me, they looked like a million bucks. It was true: they were tan, well rested, and dressed to the nines, but the real reason they looked so good to me was that they were now there with me at the hospital.

A nurse came in later and asked, "Are your parents famous?"

"Why do you ask?"

"Your mom is so beautiful and your dad so handsome, I thought they were movie stars or something."

What Mom and Dad meant to me was more than Hollywood could ever imagine.

"…but we also rejoice in our sufferings, because we know that suffering produces perseverance, perseverance, character; and character, hope. And hope does not disappoint us, because God has poured out His love into our hearts by the Holy Spirit, whom He has given us." Romans 5:3-5

CHAPTER 21

CHRISTMAS BELLS, HOSPITAL SMELLS

D r. Lynn operated, cut away, and removed the damaged intestines, then positioned and re-sutured the new stoma through my stomach. Christmas was upon us, and here I was for a second time stuck in the hospital.

Once my mom was registered at the Kahler Hotel, she thanked my grandmother and settled in for this new twist in my health. Dad brought my grandma back to stay with my siblings to enable him to continue running his business.

Mom decorated my hospital room for Christmas as best she could but was running out of gas, especially with the prospect of shopping for five kids and several relatives yet ahead of her. When she finished decorating, the centerpiece was a one-foot-tall Santa Claus, accompanying reindeer, and proportionately-sized sled loaded with colorful packages. In fact, it looked so nice she gave it to my dad to take home and put on the middle of the dining room table. Well, so much for goodwill toward men and little sick kids in the hospital!

With little time left before the big day, my mom furiously began her Christmas shopping for me and everyone back home. She soon realized she couldn't be with me and shop at the same time.

In those days, department stores offered more customer services than today. She went to Dayton's, the long-established department store owned by the parents of Mark Dayton, Minnesota's current governor. She gave the names and ages of my siblings and relatives to a personal shopper, whose eyes bugged out upon seeing the magnitude of the task ahead of her.

Years later, Mom told me that my siblings had said to her, "Mom, this was the worst Christmas we ever had!" I'd like to say this was because their dearest brother Jeffrey was away in the hospital. But as it is with most kids, their assessment was based on pure materialistic motives. I gotta admit, I couldn't argue with their thinking. Besides, nobody knows the toy needs of her kids better than a mom.

Between my stay in the hospital and recovery time at home, a couple of months had transpired. From a physical point of view, I was ready to return to school but all the embarrassment with my ileostomy caused me to be gun-shy about facing some of those classmates again. The services of Mrs. Shackle were needed once more.

I didn't return to fifth grade until the last week of school; even if for only one week, I wanted a chance to reconnect with some friends, and I thought it would better equip me socially for the start of sixth grade. Great as the presents of Christmas may be, none provide the sustenance that comes from friendships.

"There are different kinds of gifts, but the same Spirit distributes them." 1 Corinthians 12:4, TNIV

"Laughter is the closest thing to the grace of God." – Karl Barth

CHAPTER 22

THE JUNIOR ENTREPRENEUR OR "BIG DADDY SMITH, I AIN'T."

I n fifth grade while at the hospital, I received a Christmas present that I thought might be the kick-start to send me on my way to a future of financial and social success. It was a Hasbro hand-cranked movie projector. It even had sound. Since the sound was dependent on the crank being turned uniformly, which was difficult to do, voice fluctuations on the soundtrack were to be expected. But what a toy! I spent hours watching the same cartoon.

This projector got me excited about the idea of making money by operating a movie theatre right out of my basement.

You've heard about those people who have made lots of money in their lives and still remember the first dollar they made? I remember my first dollar. Of course, it's much easier to remember the first dollar I earned compared to Donald Trump because I've had far fewer to remember.

I discovered ads for old movies and cartoons in the Johnson-Smith novelty catalogue. I began ordering silent 8mm "shorts." These were three-to-five-minute versions of famous motion pictures, such as Frankenstein, Abbott and Costello, the Keystone Kops, and cartoons like Popeye and Bugs Bunny.

Hey, maybe I can make money showing these movies to the neigh-borhood kids, a little voice inside me said.

I had inherited my dad's entrepreneurial spirit (he was a commercial property owner and award-winning insurance salesman). *This idea has to turn out better than my first try at earning money,*

I thought, recalling the disappointment that had come with having been a salesman for the National Youth Sales Club. The previous summer, I had spotted their ad in the back of a children's magazine that included myriad testimonies. "I made $50 last week," read one of the testimonials.

This company depended on the gullibility of kids and the reliability of relatives and adults feeling obligated to purchase stationery. I presented my stationery portfolio at the next family party and scored a big hit. I earned fourteen dollars, most of it paying for my start-up costs.

My enthusiasm for quick riches was dashed the following weekend after going door-to-door at a large townhouse development. I knocked on every door and gave my sales pitch, which has been permanently etched in my memory: "Good afternoon, my name is Jeffrey Smith. I am a representative of the National Youth Sales Club. We sell personalized and decorative stationery. Would you care to look at my samples?"

Despite this irresistible and snappy sales pitch (at least on paper, since it actually took me several minutes to say it thanks to my stutter), no one purchased a thing. My career in stationery sales ended then and there.

But this time, I thought for sure I had a money-making winner by presenting these popular old movies to kids in the neighborhood. Twenty-five cents for a movie, forty cents for a double feature. Overhead costs? Not a problem! Soda could be found in our refrigerator and bags of popcorn and chips were stocked in our cupboard by my unwitting supplier. I could even offer candy around Halloween and Valentine's Day thanks to my overly enthusiastic Mom, who thought running short of food was the ultimate crime. Since my movie inventory was limited by my modest weekly allowance, the show biz carnival huckster in me welled up, and I padded my library by pinching my parents' collection of home and vacation movies.

Even my best friends showed little enthusiasm for paying to watch my movie features. They were only interested if I offered them free soda and popcorn, candy if we had it. Becoming a movie mogul wasn't going to be as easy as I had figured. I learned yet another hard financial lesson—always offer products that the customer wants.

The onset of my money-making ventures paled in comparison to my little sister Dana, whose career as an entrepreneur began at age three. Once while Dana was supposedly napping, my mom received a call from a neighbor lady:

"Martha, I thought you'd like to know I have a little salesgirl at my door calling herself 'Mrs. Brown' selling old magazines for two cents," said the neighbor.

"What! Do you mean Dana?!" My mom's circuitry was overloading. While she had been ironing in the other room, Dana had gotten up, dressed herself in her Sunday best, climbed out the window, filled a Red Flyer wagon with old magazines from the garage and went out on her first sales call. Evidently, she had too many places to go and too many things to accomplish to be wasting her time with naps.

When she got home, a couple taps on the bottom persuaded Dana to hold off on any further business enterprises until naptime was over thenceforth.

"Dishonest money dwindles away, but whoever gathers money little by little makes it grow." Proverbs 13:11

Chapter 23

Who Says I Don't Love School?

Teachers have had a profound impact on how I have dealt with my disabilities. A bright star in grade school was my sixth-grade teacher, Mr. Rayburn; he made me feel part of the class. He looked like your typical junior high teacher, but he acted very differently. Rather than subjecting me to derision by other students, he was sensitive enough to give me dignity by making phy-ed optional. "Jeff, you can choose to spend phy-ed time in the library, the classroom, or the gym," Mr. Rayburn would say. I sometimes participated in gym when there was a group game or activity that wouldn't subject me to injury, such as "Pin Guard."

Once when the other students were in phy-ed, Rayburn asked me to read a short story on tape. "If you make a mistake, here's how you can rewind the machine and record over, Jeff." With a lot of editing on my part, I recorded it. Stuttering was still heard on the playback, but it was an acceptable amount to me.

My lack of confidence in speaking discouraged me from raising my hand in school. Making a recording could be my way of participating and making up for my classroom silence. Several mornings later, as students were congregating in the hall before the bell, several kids were greeting me and saying things like, "Jeff! You're on the school speaker reading something. You aren't even stuttering!" I had forgotten about my recording session from the previous week, so I thought they were all kidding. I suddenly stopped and listened. Although my focus was on the remaining speech disfluencies on the recording, the positive reaction from fellow students delighted me.

One of Rayburn's greatest triumphs in encouragement was giving me a leadership opportunity in the school play. He made me head director because he realized how stressful it would have been for me to have a speaking part in the play. He didn't leave me alone to fail; he also gave me assistant directors to carry some of the communication load.

Since I had been given final say in the production decisions, I noticed that even the students who teased me the most about my stuttering or physical limitations were beginning to show me respect. By making just a couple of simple decisions, Mr. Rayburn transformed my outlook of sixth grade from being yet another year- long struggle to endure to a school year that I thoroughly enjoyed and where I felt equal with my peers, including in the area of getting in trouble.

Having recently discovered the marvel of free catalogues offering novelty items and magic tricks, I routinely purchased and showed off these little wonders at school. Other kids wanted to know where they could get them. I gained a level of prestige as their supplier.

"You got smoke bombs?!" one of the kids marveled, slack- jawed.

"Sure do!" I responded, feeling like a big shot. I had bought them because they sounded like something James Bond would use, but I really didn't know what to do with them.

"I'll bring some matches and we can light them off here at school," suggested a classmate named Mark.

"Well, o.k." I said with some uncertainty.

"Then we'll put it into Mr. Rayburn's closet, close the door and watch the look on his face when he opens the doors!" added Craig, my best friend at the time. (Craig reappears 33 years later to orchestrate one of the most significant events in my life.)

During recess, we went over our plan. It was agreed that we would be last in line to go to lunch, but instead, turn back into the classroom to perform our shenanigans, then join the others in the lunchroom. As we lit the fuse, we all agreed it was the perfect plan. At least we thought so until a girl (why is it always a girl?) overheard the details of our plot and ran off to tell Mr. Rayburn. We closed the closet doors and headed off to the lunchroom.

The rest of the afternoon passed uneventfully and we thought we were off the hook. Then Mr. Rayburn said to us, "You three follow me down to the principal's office."

I had heard about the stern discipline of our principal. He met us in the hallway. Rayburn relayed to him what we perpetrated and, to make our stunt sound worse, what may have resulted: "They could have burned down the entire school!"

Well, maybe he's right, but does he have to be so dramatic about it? I thought.

The principal grabbed Mark by the shirt, lifted him bodily and pinned him up against the wall. "Not you again!" he shouted. "I am sick of seeing you down here!" He punctuated every one of his words by shoving my classmate against the wall. "You go wait in the office," he spat, looking at me. He gave Craig a warning and dismissed him; Craig gladly ditched his partners in crime.

"D-do-o y-you kn-know what the pr-pr-principal's going to do with me?" I asked the secretary. She shrugged and 20 minutes later flatly announced, "You can go to your bus now, Jeffrey." Next time, James Bond would have to handle a mission like this solo.

"Wisdom will save you from the ways of wicked men, from men whose words are perverse." Proverbs 2:12

"The mediocre teacher tells. The good teacher explains. The superior teacher demonstrates. The great teacher inspires."
— William Arthur Ward

CHAPTER 24

ORIGIN OF AMAZING JEFFO
OR "WATCH ME!"

I developed an interest in magic beginning in fifth grade after watching the movie *The Great Houdini*, starring Tony Curtis. I was moved by the power of magic. I don't mean some dark, mysterious force; rather, the powerful reaction that followed each trick that he performed.

The next day, I went to our school librarian and asked, "Do you have any books about magic?" The librarian, whom I had always thought of as a mysterious figure himself, silently led me to a corner of the library I had never before noticed. I was amazed to find at least a half dozen books that taught magic tricks. *I can't let anyone see me check out these books,* I thought, trying to keep this treasure trove of secrets to myself.

From that point on I had my mom and dad buy me all magic- related items for my birthday and Christmas: magic sets, books about magicians, methods for performing magic—you name it. I had a real thirst for learning, especially about Houdini.

My fascination became the incentive to read my first adult- length book: a biography about (who else?) Houdini. After that, I read two additional biographies about this magician, whose real name was Erich Weiss and whom most experts consider the greatest of them all. I became heady as I read about the respect and adulation that Houdini commanded. I craved that same kind of love.

I became an eleven-year-old expert on the subject. My parents would often have me come downstairs and do a Houdini Q&A session to entertain guests.

Something that revved up my burgeoning magic fever was seeing ads in the back pages of my brother Dave's *Boy's Life* magazines. The ads offered "Free Magic Catalogues." I ordered several catalogues: Johnson-Smith, Flosso-Hornmann, and Abbott Magic Co. to mention a few. My first order was for a levitating magic wand. Being an adrenaline junkie, I still remember the pure rush of every day getting off the bus and making a beeline to the mailbox, hoping this was the day my order would arrive. My mom allowed me the pleasure of being the first to get the mail, as she had too many other duties to tend to. Even if my package hadn't arrived on a given day, my excitement continued as I'd speculate, *I bet it will be tomorrow for sure!*

After what seemed forever (actually about three to four weeks), I opened the mailbox door. *Could this be my magic wand?* I thought upon seeing a tubular cardboard package. I read the return address: Flosso-Hornmann. It had finally come!

Besides its special mechanical quality that enabled it to "float," the clever marketers pointed out its "added value" because it could be used for general wand waving purposes as well!

My brother Mike—the one who signed his name on my Harmon Killebrew autographed baseball—broke my levitating magic wand after about a week. But I'm past all this now. However, at that time, duplicitous revenge was my only option, since I couldn't catch Mikey to give him the licking he so richly deserved.

"Do you want to make a trade?" I asked Mikey, smiling.

"Trade what?" he responded curiously.

"I'll give you four big nickels for your four baby dimes." I proposed.

"OK," he said, relying on his four-year-old logic which assigned greater value to things that were physically larger.

"Actually, you should really give me five dimes instead of four, Mikey," I pressed.

"Why?" he argued.

I patiently explained, "Because four big nickels have more metal in them than five little dimes, understand?"

I tried this same ruse the next time he had collected some coins. "Forget it!" a wiser Michael retorted.

The overall thirty cents I made neither gave me the satisfaction I expected nor restored my busted wand. If Mikey hadn't generally been such a funny, endearing little kid, I probably would have tried selling him to a Bedouin tribe. Fortunately for him, we didn't live near a desert.

For the next couple of years, until I lost most of my sight, I'd save my allowance, birthday, and Christmas money and continued to order tricks from magic catalogues as soon as I could afford them.

Once the tricks arrived, performing the tricks became secondary to the captivation I had with its gadgetry. More importantly, I didn't perform these tricks because of my fear of showing them in public. Learning the trick gave me satisfaction in and of itself, just as setting up little plastic army men was more fun than acting out warfare with them. I was even nervous about performing for members of my own family. This, however, was mostly due to the rude behavior of a certain brother grabbing the trick out of my hands and saying, "Ah-ha! That's how it works!" (No names mentioned, but Mike still does it today.)

Notwithstanding these nuisances and my trepidation, doing tricks for my family empowered me and was my first taste of that positive rush that comes from performing.

At that time, everything associated with magic served as unintentional therapy, providing me with self-confidence and, for the first time, a sense of purpose.

"The Lord will fulfill his purpose for me; your steadfast love, O Lord, endures forever." Psalm 138:8, ESV

Mikey cozying up to me in the wake of yet another hurricane of destruction aimed at my favorite stuff. My Harmon Killebrew autographed baseball, transistor radio, and first trick, a mail-order magic wand were never the same sheer minutes after a Mikey encounter.

My Johnny Express truck minutes before destruction at the hands of you-know-who.

CHAPTER 25

LIGHTS! MICROPHONE! ACTION!

For my thirteenth Christmas, I received a cassette tape recorder; it was during this time that I began losing my vision. I was drawn to old-time radio shows that were being rebroadcast on a weekly basis on a local AM radio station. I began recording and accumulating a cassette library of these broadcasts. I was fascinated by how these radio shows used sound effects and actors to paint vivid images within the theatre of the mind. I thought: *I'm going to try it myself.* I had the production equipment (a tape recorder) and plenty of actors: two younger brothers and a sister. My older brother Dave thought we were all nerds and stayed away from our activities.

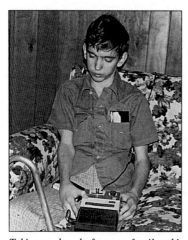

Taking a break from a family skit recording session. The majority of my eyesight was gone as a result of a massive vascular hemorrhage caused by iritis earlier that year (1971). My rheumatoid arthritis was also beginning to create bone malformation throughout my body.

My first creative juices began flowing as I figured out how I could make sound effects using common household objects and created a script that could be taped by my younger siblings. They were clay in my hands. I felt a sense of power as I had them repeat ridiculous lines that they would never had repeated if they actually knew what they were saying.

I developed parody versions of old radio shows into new creations such as

"The Blue Hornet," "Pa Perkins," and "Pretend Theatre." These productions became a big hit at the adult parties my parents hosted. The freely dispensed cocktails, I'm sure, made my productions funnier and more entertaining.

One of the shows starred my youngest brother Mikey, whom I at some point nicknamed "Boobie Benson" because he was such an oversized lovable klutz (he weighed forty pounds at age one). He was the funniest actor in my troupe because of his idiosyncrasies and mispronunciations, such as his substitution of *F for Tr* at the beginning of words, or pronouncing *L's* like *S's*. Once my mom turned crimson while shopping in the toy section of a local department store when Mikey announced at the top of his lungs his desire for a shiny red truck, "Mama, I want that f—-!"

Taking full advantage of Mikey's talents, I developed a script starring my brother as the little boy coming home with a bad report card and me in the role of his mother, with my squeaky prepubescent voice.

"I see you have your report card." "Yes, Mom."

"How did you do? Did you get all A's?"

"I hear on the weather we might get some chinook winds." (Announcer [me]: "Due to FCC regulations prohibiting violence on radio, the following segment of our show has been deleted.") "Well, did you show your grades to your father?"

"Yes, Mom." "What did he say?"

"Should I leave out the swear words?" "Yes! Of course."

"He didn't say a thing."

All the old radio shows to which I listened cultivated my imagination and, I believe, helped steer me toward a future where it would serve as an indispensable aid to my profession. I got a thrilling sense of accomplishment making these programs, just as I get a sense of fulfillment today developing a trick from its inception to its performance on stage.

"A happy heart makes the face cheerful..." Proverbs 15:13

CHAPTER 26

WARNING: BABY BROTHER
AHEAD OR "OH, THAT MIKEY!"

In the summer following sixth grade, as the sight in my right eye continued to deteriorate, God provided me a respite of laughter through the antics of my not-so-little brother Mikey. He was an oasis of humor in a desert of challenges. Through his escapades, I learned to laugh at life despite my circumstances.

Once when my mom was trapped under a hairdryer at the beauty salon, he locked in on an obese lady under a nearby dryer. Pointing at her with his chubby finger, Mike einquired, "Hey, lady! How come you so fat?"

My mom was a strict disciplinarian who emphasized to her children the importance of manners and respect for elders. At that moment, she felt like pulling the heating cap over her face and turning it to full blast. You can imagine her relief when the accosted woman started laughing and responded right back to Mikey, "Well, how come you're so fat?" poking her finger into his substantial belly.

A look of indignity covered Mikey's face. "I no fat!" he protested.

Mike wasn't trying to be mean; he just considered his comments simply as conversation starters. He actually had a favorable bias toward chubbiness. This bias was expressed through one of his quirky behaviors we'd encourage. Mikey would painstakingly feel our earlobes and then give an edict whether they had "good chub" or "bad chub." We'd play it up by acting all nervous and fearful as he determined his verdict. Fat, corpulence, blubber, and things related were an early and ongoing fascination of Mikey's childhood.

I often stayed at the kitchen table after a meal for long periods of time. Because of the anticipated discomfort and strain that came with lifting myself off the chair, it would sometimes take me as much as an hour to psych myself up before standing.

One night sitting at the table following dinner, Mikey asked me, "What are you listening to, Jeff?"

"A talk radio show." The radio format had just been introduced to the Twin Cities that year (1970) on WLOL, an AM station. The conversation on this talk show revolved around the geo-political justifications of American involvement in Vietnam. This subject held absolutely no interest to me, but I had no choice but to listen because I was stuck in my chair, too achy to get up and leave.

"Who are those people talking?" Mikey asked.

"They're people who call in to the show."

"Can I call in?"

"No! The program is for adults." "I'm going to call on our phone!"

"If you try, I'm going to hang it up," I warned. We had a phone in the kitchen, and I figured its relative proximity and my heightened level of annoyance would give me the impetus to get up off my chair and disconnect the call.

Mikey grabbed some paper and a pencil and waited to hear the call-in number as I continued making threats. As the announcer began saying the number, I tried in vain to yell over the announcer's voice. Once Mikey wrote down the number, he announced, "I'm just going to use the phone in the basement, and you're too stiff to catch me."

"I'm dialing!" Mike yelled up the staircase. "Hang it up, you idiot!" I yelled back. "It's ringing!" he continued taunting.

He's not really doing this, I rationalized. *He's just trying to get my goat.* "Some guy told me to wait for my turn," I heard Mikey bellowing up the stairway. My protests were falling on the ears of a seven-year-old on a misguided mission to grab for his 15 minutes of fame, and no one was going to stop him.

"You're on WLOL," said the host.

"How fat is the fattest man in the world?" asked Michael in his best adult-like manner.

"Pardon me?" asked the confused announcer.

Now annoyed, Mikey slowly repeated, "How fat is the fattest man in the world?"

"That's irrelevant," responded the host.

"Huh?" was the last thing I heard before the announcer disconnected Mikey and moved on to the next caller.

Thankfully the radio station used a seven-second delay in case of inappropriate comments by callers. But not before I experienced an overwhelming embarrassment as I clearly heard my own voice on the radio, shouting in the background, "Hang up that phone, you idiot!!"

Professional wrestling was a favorite of the Smith boys, especially Mikey who didn't realize it was scripted. Through a muddled understanding of the Sampson story, Mikey interpreted the male pattern baldness of the American Wrestling Association champ, the legendary Vern Gagne, as the key to his strength. Since every kid wants to be like their idol, he cut off all the hair on top of his head. That summer my mom constantly reminded Mike, "I'll tell you when you can take that ball cap off!"

"Even a child is known by his actions, by whether his conduct is pure and right." Proverbs 20:11

CHAPTER 27

THE VICTORIAN AGE REVISITED OR "THE GIRLS"

⁓

Long hospital stays provided me with lots of attention and opportunities to be pampered. This was sometimes expressed in the form of receiving gifts, including money.

In February of 1970, when I was 13 years old, Dr. Thompson recommended another surgery when X-rays revealed the cause of an ache in my left hip: the joint was starting to dislocate. The plan was to screw a metal plate into my femur and affix it within my hip socket. So much for the rest of that school year. In fact, the various disruptions from medical treatments between kindergarten and seventh grade resulted in missing roughly half my years of school. (Thank goodness this magic thing worked out. I keep my formal educational gaps hidden, right with my rabbits.)

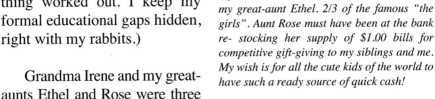

My dad's mom, Nonnie Irene, and her sister, my great-aunt Ethel. 2/3 of the famous "the girls". Aunt Rose must have been at the bank re- stocking her supply of $1.00 bills for competitive gift-giving to my siblings and me. My wish is for all the cute kids of the world to have such a ready source of quick cash!

Grandma Irene and my great-aunts Ethel and Rose were three elegant sisters whom our family affectionately referred to as "the girls." They were the last of a dying breed from the Victorian Era. "The girls" were raised with an emphasis on education, style, and manners. Their attire portrayed quiet elegance. They believed it was more important to have a few quality pieces rather than quantity, such as first edition books, period antique furniture, and fine china. Their apartments were made up of doilies, silver services that held crystal decanters of sherry (used nightly), and authentic Persian rugs on polished dark wood flooring. Old-world decorum mandated sophistication and civility; a polite facade always covered over personal differences, regardless of their severity.

"The girls" visited me while I convalesced from hip surgery. After the ladies sat down, pulling their chairs up tight around my bed, they asked me how I was doing. Without a word, my grandmother slipped a one-dollar bill in my hand. "Oh, thank you, grandma," I said, hearing my mom's voice echoing in my head: "Jeffrey, what do you say to your grandmother?"

This got the ball rolling. I hadn't realized how competitive these elderly sisters were. My Aunt Rose immediately upped the ante by slipping two dollar bills in my other hand, quietly, but obvious enough for her sisters to notice. I said, "Oh, Aunt Rose, thank you. That's very kind of you."

It was now Aunt Ethel's turn. I barely had time to empty my hands of the cash when Aunt Ethel slipped me a five-dollar bill in clear view of her sisters.

"Excuse me, I need to go freshen up," announced my grandmother as she quickly moved into the bathroom. I suspected she excused herself to check her available cash supply to pace herself in the event of a drawn-out money gifting battle with her sisters.

My grandmother returned just in time to see Aunt Rose sitting back down in her seat after also contributing five dollars to the kitty.

"What are you doing, Rose dear?" asked my grandmother suspiciously. Aunt Rose simply smiled.

"Rose gave Jeffrey another dollar while you were away," chimed Ethel.

"It was actually five dollars, Ethel," explained Rose.

My Grandma then slipped me a ten dollar bill as she said, "Here's a little something to buy yourself a treat with, but don't mention it to Ethel and Rose," whispering loud enough for everyone to easily hear. Gee, why would I bother?

Suddenly everything became a green blur. I felt like a phony TV evangelist on the take, following an impassioned "earn your way to Salvation" sermon. By the end of their two-hour visit, I had raked in over 35 bucks and change.

"...for God loves a cheerful giver." 2 Corinthians 9:7

"I made my money the old fashioned way. I was very nice to a wealthy relative right before he died." — Malcolm Forbes

CHAPTER 28

NEW MODE OF TRANSPORTATION OR "FOUR ON THE FLOOR"

After leaving seventh grade in February of 1970 to have my left hip surgically repaired, my recovery time was slow, not only from the effects of surgery but also because my RA was taking a turn for the worse. I continued using crutches throughout the summer. Mega doses of aspirin were no longer giving me the relief they had the previous eight years. Range of motion and exercise, a bulwark of former years in providing me with relief from arthritis pain, was also having little effect.

After the completion of an indoor pool that summer, my dad hired a swim teacher to offer me another form of exercise to help my arthritis, but I had to first overcome my water phobia. The swim teacher was more than qualified to accomplish both tasks, having participated in Olympic trials. "Don't worry, Mr. Smith. Jeff and I are going to do just fine," my coach reassured.

Notwithstanding the efforts of my swim coach, my dad was hoping he could write off the cost of the pool by declaring it as therapeutic relief for my rheumatoid arthritis—which can be a wonderful incentive to learn, and learn fast. Dad had hired the coach hoping to teach me how to swim before a visit by a tax auditor where he'd be forced to hoist me up and throw me into the pool while saying, "Of course Jeffrey can swim! Swim—d—n you, swim!"

After about 10 swimming lessons, I politely fired my coach.

"Mom, call Dr. Gallagan and ask him if he can do something about my arthritis," I pleaded as my stiffness and pain increased. Despite my age, Dr. Gallagan wished to continue being my physician because he was so knowledgeable about my medical history. "We're going to try something new, Jeff," Dr. Gallagan explained. "Besides, I don't like what 16 aspirin a day are doing to your stomach lining. We're going to try using prednisone on you. It's been mostly used on older people. We're not real clear on its long-term effects, especially in someone your age."

He sent us home with a prescription for 20 milligrams a day for several days. I soon discovered one of prednisone's side effects – elevated metabolism. Normally, I slept in late. But this Saturday morning my eyes shot open at 5 a.m. I was too restless to continue lying around. I got up, made myself breakfast, and turned on cartoons.

"What are you doing up this early?" asked my mom after starting the coffee later that morning.

"I'm not tired!" I explained brightly.

Another side effect of prednisone is that it gives the user a "moon" face. Eight years later, still on prednisone and attending Southwest State University in Marshall, MN, an assignment in health class had us develop an inventory of our physical health. The calculations were based on body weight. "No way you're only 88 pounds!" the health teacher exclaimed looking at my puffy "moon" face. The rest of my scrawny body was covered by the winter coat I'd typically wear in class.

If I had tried out for the Olympics that summer of 1970, I surely would have been banned for using a performance-enhancing substance. The prednisone made me now feel, relative to how I had felt, like an Olympic athlete. I was very active that summer, going everywhere, crutches and all, feeling like a new man. The crutches were no longer an inconvenience. My new limberness enabled me to use them in acrobatic ways. They increased the length of my stride to the pace of jogging.

Throughout the summer, my doctor whittled down the initial mega dosages of prednisone. My speed, euphoria, and increased energy gradually diminished as I was reintroduced to my old friends, Mr. Stiff and Mr. Ache, who brought with them their associate, Mr. Blue.

"When anxiety was great within me, your consolation brought me joy." Psalm 94:19, TNIV

CHAPTER 29

THE NIGHT CRAWLER OR "WHO TURNED OFF THE LIGHTS?"

As the prednisone dosages were reduced, my eyesight began diminishing at an accelerated rate. I had used glasses to correct ordinary nearsightedness since the third grade. But now, the strange halo effect that I had been seeing for the past two years was becoming a pervasive cloudiness. I stopped wearing my glasses because the effects of iritis were greater than the benefits from correction. "Jeff, you're not wearing your glasses. Your eyesight must be improving," commented the mother of a friend with unintended irony. I undiplomatically responded, "Actually, Mrs. Stiles, I've gone blind in my left eye, and glasses aren't able to help my right eye." I went off to play and couldn't understand why she seemed so suddenly crestfallen.

As fall approached, I was eagerly looking forward to duck hunting with my dad and older brother, Dave. The previous year, my dad had arranged a hunting trip for us, along with my dad's best friend and his three boys. I never was much for sitting in a cold duck blind at sunrise, but I was very excited about the activities surrounding the hunt. I had been on previous duck hunting trips and enjoyed everything about them—except for the duck hunting part. My dad's friend owned a large cabin which had a loft with about a dozen beds. This supplied us with ample ammo for pillow fights. The adults stayed in bedrooms on the lower level. The cabin had a large cabinet filled with board games and a color TV. We'd make paper airplanes, throwing them from the loft to see which one flew the best. They even had a slot machine. The rule was as long as you used your own nickel, you could keep any winnings. I also really enjoyed being a part of the four a.m. breakfast assembly line. It was a circus atmosphere. There were four men and ten boys ranging from seven to twelve years old. My dad, who never cooked anything at home, was the pancake flipper. Other men fried eggs, bacon, and sausages. Dave was in charge of buttering the toast. Older boys poured milk and juice. I laid out napkins and plastic ware. I was looking forward to our upcoming trip with great excitement.

The day before we were to leave on our duck hunting adventure, I experienced a hemorrhage in my right eye. (A hemorrhage results from one or more capillaries bursting in the eye.) I don't remember it being particularly painful as it would be with future episodes, but it left many particles floating around in my "good" eye. *This shouldn't keep me from going hunting since I'm not allowed to shoot anyway,* I reasoned.

My parents called Dr. Roach who explained, "As long as Jeffrey's comfortable, there's not much that can be done about the floaters. We'll see if they move to a part of the eye that's outside his vision field, which should enable him to have some clarity again."

"Jeff, I think it would be for the best if you don't go on the hunting trip," my mom said regretfully.

"My eye hardly hurts and I can still see, kind of," I pleaded. "I'm sorry," she said, "but the doctor wants you to rest to prevent more hemorrhaging. I tell you what—tonight you can go out for dinner with me and your sister and the Sutmar kids."

"What! A bunch of girls? Forget it, I'm staying home!" When all was said and done, I ended up going to dinner and was miserable. To top it off, my steak could have doubled as a patch kit for Goodyear tires.

My eye became more painful as the weekend progressed. I remember flailing my support cane back and forth trying to find my dad's comfy lounge chair, looking for sympathy and for the pain to subside.

In spite of the many physical challenges I've had to deal with, this was, I believe, the only time in my life I remember feeling sorry for myself. I attribute this general absence of self-pity to the support of my parents and siblings who have never treated me as a person with disabilities. Physical and other setbacks have also been softened by the caring doctors and educators who provided the assistance I needed. Withstanding all of the above, I know there are people in situations similar to mine, who have had great difficulty adjusting. Maybe I'd feel likewise if it not for the grace of God. Only His intervention in my life can make sense out of the inexplicable.

At this time, my mom's hope of a bright future for our family was also being cast into darkness. Besides *my* smorgasbord of physical challenges, my mom had myriad family crises herself. One was dealing with my dad. He used work and an over-dependence on alcohol to escape the accumulating stress from continual bad news about my illnesses and other family issues. We didn't have that positive model of leadership a dad should provide. We may have had money, but we weren't rich where it mattered. My dad's increasing drinking was a huge influence in his decision to move out and live away from our family at the St. Paul Athletic Club. The light at the end of the tunnel representing hope for our family was only a glimmer.

During this period, I drew closer to my mom, not only to befriend her through her difficult time but simply because my dad was around less. Through all my mom's many challenges, some couldn't understand how she was emotionally able to hold up under the strain. I believe her resilience came out of prayer. "It's easier asking God for strength when you're desperate," she's mentioned to me more than once.

The sincerity of her prayers proved effective as she maintained her equilibrium while keeping the sadness from overwhelming her.

"God is light and in Him there is no darkness at all." 1 John 1:5

How I went blind? I had my eye on a seat in the bus, and someone sat on it, which was no problem because I had double vision in the other eye.

CHAPTER 30

THE LINDSAY ALL-STARS OR "I'M ONE OF THESE GUYS?"

The delay in getting me off crutches was one of the considerations that led my doctors, parents, and school officials to recommend temporarily removing me from the public school system for a year to have time to heal and become more mobile. The greatest rationale for removing me from the public school system, however, was the prospect of totally losing my eyesight. Doctors and school officials felt it would be easier on me to learn blind adaptive skills in a setting where teachers were used to working with children with disabilities.

It was decided that my eighth grade year would begin at Lindsay, a school for the handicapped, the standard term at the time for people with disabilities. Lindsay School was built around the turn of the 20th century, and within a few years after I left, its campus was closed. I'd like to think I did my little part in its demolition, and just with the use of a hollow, plastic baseball bat at that! (More about the baseball bat, shortly.)

Lindsay's student body consisted of 75 to 100 children with a variety of disabilities. I was in a class of seventh and eighth graders combined. What an education! I had been pulling D's and C's in the public seventh grade. But with the very small class size at Lindsay (about a dozen students), and the increased one-on-one attention, I began earning A's. The class was led by Mrs. Mildred Berkstrum, a sixtyish grandmother type with a hip attitude that betrayed her years.

She had a different approach to teaching from what I had experienced in my former school district. Occasionally, she'd have us listen to the words of a current, popular song, then ask all of us, "What did the words mean to you?" One of the songs that sparked a long discussion was *Eleanor Rigby* by the Beatles. The song describes a lonely woman that society has rejected. I realize today that this was Mrs. Berkstrum's attempt to help her students deal with their sense of disenfranchisement and isolation from historical societal attitudes toward the disabled.

Even in 1970, the ignorant viewpoint by some of the parents of my Lindsay classmates created emotional scarring, because those parents saw their disabled children as mistakes or objects of humiliation. One of my classmates had been isolated in an attic; another had been given up as a ward of the state though his parents were financially well-off. I became quick friends with a wheelchair-bound student named Bill Guerin. He had advanced muscular dystrophy. His keen wit and sarcastic nature tickled my funny bone. One of our favorite games was to get Mrs. Berkstrum laughing uncontrollably. Right after she'd reassume a serious posture and tell us to get back to work, we'd throw out a one liner that would cause her to lose it all over again.

Another positive aspect of the Lindsay School was its speech pathology program. Speech therapy was very ineffective in grammar school, but Ms. Connors, Lindsay's speech pathologist, enabled me to enjoy, for the first time, speech therapy sessions. She smelled good, had a warm voice, and praised and encouraged me. She developed exercises for me to improve my fluency. She had me act out real-life situations by having me call Target stores and ask for the availability of products. If I performed well, she would reward me with gentle touches on the shoulder or arm and say, "Good job, Jeff." The incentive was incredibly strong. I wanted to speak like Cicero for this woman. She was everything an eighth grade boy could want. Although her physical presence gave me motivation, it was her encouraging spirit which allowed me to progress in my quest against stuttering.

The educational focus of Lindsay promoted the concept of "being all that you can be," which was the greatest lesson I learned there. Lindsay offered adaptive sports teams, theater opportunities, and even a glee club. In an effort to promote school spirit, the principal of the school thought it would be a wonderful idea to have everyone learn a school song sung to the tune of a popular college fight song: "We welcome you to Lindsay School, we're mighty glad you're here! We'll fill the air reverberating with our mighty cheer. We'll sing you in! We'll sing you out! Listen to our mighty shout! Hail, hail, the gang's all here. Welcome to Lindsay school."

I've always seen myself as a normal person trapped inside a malfunctioning body. To my surprise and delight, the rest of these kids felt the same way about themselves. This made for what I felt were real-world opportunities to laugh in the face of disabilities. We all felt comfortable about poking fun at each other's physical shortcomings. More importantly, we were learning how to laugh at ourselves. This worked as a self-empowering therapy that reinforced a positive self-image.

Now back to that hollow plastic baseball bat. While attending Lindsay, I tried things in the area of physical competition that I'd avoided before because of feeling inferior to able-bodied kids. Adaptive floor hockey, basketball, and especially baseball were my favorites. Sure, it might take ten throws of the tetherball before I'd connect with my hollow plastic bat. But when I did, the adrenaline rush and the residual good feelings that came from the smack of the bat to the ball built my self-confidence. My batting prowess became legend. If I hadn't been so worried about being caught, I would have requested a little bronze plate be affixed next to the school window that I smashed with a wiffle ball from one of my herculean swings (just doing my part for urban renewal). Although, truth be told, a good sneeze alone would have disintegrated that ancient window.

Lindsay offered us all the usual activities you'd find at a public school, including going to hospitals at Christmas and singing. We sounded pretty lousy but brought down the house; staff and patients alike were crying. I mistakenly thought, *"Man! We may not be professionals, but we aren't that bad!"* I now realize their tears were based on sympathy, seeing a bunch of severely "handicapped" kids doing something for others deeply touched them.

My parents' perspectives were also broadened by hearing, on a regular basis, my stories about all these kids and their different disabilities. I think it helped them understand in a practical way that there were parents like them who were up against monumental challenges. It's no surprise, therefore, how readily my parents agreed to have a big pool party at the end of the school year. My dad stayed home that weekday from his busy schedule.

My Aunt Alyce joined us. She helped take kids with quadriplegia into the pool, splashed and played with them. Stevie, a quadriplegic from cerebral palsy, had an alphabet board fixed to the arm of his wheelchair to make it possible to communicate. After pool time with my aunt, he slowly touched different letters on his board for her to see. As Alyce announced the letters that Stevie was pointing to, she suddenly realized Stevie had spelled out, "I love you." Just as my mom was on the verge of tears seeing this, she noticed one of the aides placing a thirteen- year-old boy without legs on the end of the diving board. She saw him use his arms to push himself off the board. My mom and dad were ready to leap into rescue mode. Their tension was relieved as they saw him swim effortlessly by use of his arms. They hadn't realized he regularly used the pool at Lindsay.

As Mrs. Berkstrum quietly shared some of the children's stories, she drew my mom's attention to a pretty seventh grade girl who used "Canadian walking sticks." She said, "This lovely girl is a ward of the state, in spite of her having wealthy parents." My mom shook her head.

Encouragingly my mom asked the girl, "What do you want to do when you grow up?"

"I'm going to be a singer and a movie star," she quickly responded. My mom had to turn and face the wall to hide her tears. "Would you like me to sing a song for you, Mrs. Smith?" she asked. Just when my mom had composed herself, Lucy began playing *Leaving on a Jet Plane* on her ukulele and started to sing. Her voice was as pure as an angel's. This caused my mom, who wasn't subject to outward emotions, to let tears flow unashamedly.

Fun was the overriding emotion that day, however. Dad grilled burgers, and Mom brought out all the fixings. Everyone ate like pigs. "Martha, I want you to know what this means to these kids. Some of them never get out; never have much to look forward to," Mrs. Berkstrum quietly shared with my mom.

"I must admit, at first I was overwhelmed seeing the situations of these children," my mom said to Mrs. Berkstrum. "You see, I look at Jeffrey every day and see him as my child and don't focus on his disabilities. In just the few hours I've spent with these kids, I'm seeing them as *just kids,* too."

By the end of that transition year at Lindsay, I had learned Braille, typing, abacus for arithmetic, and independent travel skills, all making me feel more like a student than someone disabled, and was ready to be mainstreamed back into the public school system for ninth grade.

"...the blind receive their sight and the lame walk, lepers are cleansed and the deaf hear, and the dead are raised up, and the poor have the good news preached to them." Matthew 11:4-5, ESV

I hope this book sells better than my first book. It was a book that explained a method to teach yourself how to read.

CHAPTER 31

THE FORECAST TONIGHT CALLS FOR DARKNESS, FOLLOWED BY MORE DARKNESS IN THE MORNING.

On January 1, 1971, my parents hosted a dinner party. Although I'd always enjoyed being the center of attraction at these parties, I would have preferred, on this particular day, being just one of the crowd. That morning, the eye with most of my remaining vision hemorrhaged, causing pain unlike anything I'd experienced before. The stabbing, pounding pain was excruciating. My mom called and left a message for Dr. Roach, my ophthalmologist. He called back after what seemed hours. His order was for me to lie very still, and he would order some medication. Following this advice, my eye still felt as if someone had poked a finger into it and just left it there. I remained on the couch in the basement where the attack had begun. I tried listening to the college football games playing on the TV, hoping it might distract me from the intensity of my pain. The pain had become so bad that I asked my brother to get my mom.

"How does your eye feel?" she asked, squatting alongside the couch.

"Don't talk so loud. Quit bumping the couch," I whispered. "What would you like me to do for you, Jeff?" she asked, understanding that it was the pain that was causing me to be difficult to deal with. "How can I help?" she asked.

One of their dinner guests was a doctor, although not an ophthalmologist. "Have the doctor come downstairs, Mom," I pleaded.

"But he's not an eye doctor, honey."

"Just have him come down and look at it!" I demanded out of desperation.

"I just put another call in for Dr. Roach, but I'll see if Dr. O'Brian will come down and look at it."

Their doctor friend came downstairs, lifted my eyelid, looked, but had no ability to help in this situation. When Dr. Roach called back, he prescribed something called Diamox. He warned us to take it only when absolutely necessary because of its potentially severe side effects. I didn't care what the side effects were; I just wanted relief.

I'm just guessing, however, that one of the side effects must have been abdominal gas. I say this because after taking it and getting noticeable pain relief, I had the longest burp in my entire life. I had to cut it off at about seven or eight seconds, fearing I might lose my innards in the process. (Will Ferrell's *Elf* has nothing on me!)

By the time the episode had ended, my vision was reduced to light, shadow, and limited color perception. From the myopic perspective of a 13-year-old, my most immediate concerns revolved around how I was going to continue reading my precious super- hero comic books: Action Comics, Adventures of Superman, The Legion of Superheroes, etc.

"You, O Lord, keep my lamp burning; my God turns my darkness into light." Psalm 18:28

My superhero alter-ego is "Blind as a Bat Man."

CHAPTER 32

EVERY MAN FOR HIMSELF, AND GIRL TOO OR "A MASOCHIST AND LOVING IT!"

To me, the fact that my brothers could tease me proved they thought of me as a typical brother, subject to the same treatment as any other brother. They didn't focus on my illnesses and treatments that, at times, were my dominating feature.

My oldest brother, Dave, was the loner of the family. He loved to read. I can't remember when there wasn't a big stack of books on his side of the dresser. In his quest for quiet, he would search out remote corners of our large home where he could settle down with a book. One of his favorite spots was the couch in our basement. This presented me with the perfect opportunity to coordinate a gangland-style attack on him with my younger siblings. I'd assign them *West Side Story*-type names, such as "Honda Baby" for Mikey, "Honda Shark" for Steve, "Honda Girl" for Dana, and I was "Honda Chief." Why Honda? Honda just seemed to be a cool name to me in light of the proliferation of that brand of motorcycle.

No one wanted to be the first to jump on Dave. Despite their naive ages, three to six years old, they were well aware of the consequences that came with being on the frontline of the battle field and the wrath that would follow for disturbing their biggest of brothers. I only garnered their support by employing the most powerful appeal to kid-dom: the Doctrine of Fairness. They all took their turns getting a licking.

First, all three would get on top of him making it safe for me to sit on Dave's legs. Just when it appeared we had successfully subdued him he would eventually reach his breaking point and yell, "OK! That's it!" Then the carnage began. Once I saw a sibling getting tossed off, I'd bail, leaving whoever remained as the sacrificial lamb. Dave's patience wore thin as we'd repeatedly perform this routine on him.

Despite my physically frail condition, my brother found creative ways of getting back at me. He'd wrap me up in elastic bandages and leave me in the basement with the lights off. (Thank goodness I'm blind and not afraid of the dark!) Other times, he'd subdue and tickle me until I screamed like a girl. I often resorted to the "Mr. Spock mind-control" technique to make him finally stop. I would focus as best I could and repeat aloud in my best Leonard Nimoy, "Your tickling is useless. It is childish and illogical." Sometimes I could maintain my composure through this facade—and, sometimes *not!* But, I admit, I always loved the attention.

Steve and Mike didn't even have to be in Dave's presence to irritate him. They found Dave's twin bed to be the most suitable place for wrestling. They used it so often, in fact, they'd play right through the cracking and crunching sounds as its screws loosened and the supporting slats began wobbling. I'd be in my bed listening to them pretend to be their favorite professional wrestlers and mimicking what they had heard on TV as they brazenly warned their opponents of the dire fate that awaited them. But at the first sound of Dave coming through the front door, they'd simultaneously say, "Dave's coming! Quick! Make the bed!" They'd straighten out the sheets, blanket, and bedspread then run into their room, turn the TV on, and act naturally. They could do all this in about 10 seconds. Then Dave would walk into our room saying, "Man, am I tired... can't wait to hit the sack!" He'd climb into bed, turn off the light, give a big sigh, and then...CRASH! The head end of the mattress and box spring would be on the floor. There would be a moment of silence in the dark as Dave lay inverted, and then I'd hear a string of mumbled swear words. Sometimes he'd be too tired to even bother leveling out the mattress and would just sleep at a 25-degree slant. It was actually funnier for me to *hear* it rather than *see* it, and I'd try to choke down my laughter.

Dave would reserve his fury until the next day. At just the right time, he'd exact his revenge by (what he called playfully) tossing them down the stairs; most of the time, they'd just bounce up and run right back for more action. Once in a while, someone would get a little too rambunctious and Mom would come to investigate and discover the epicenter of the crash. "It's all fun and games until someone gets hurt," she would warn.

Honestly, my mom seemed more concerned about the ceiling crashing down over our kitchen table than someone really getting hurt. My brothers were the sturdiest kids in the neighborhood. My mom attributed this to her steady diet of protein, protein, and more protein. Which is why I didn't think the occasional moderate whack of a crutch or cane from me (only when it was justified, of course) would really hurt them with all that extra muscle on their frames. One such occasion happened when Mikey noticed a large, white area remaining on my Harmon Killebrew autographed baseball, my prized possession. In his best seven-year-old printing, he signed his name, crooked letters and all, "Mike S." He even printed the letter S backwards, adding insult to injury. (Did I mention yet that my greatest birthday present—a Johnny Express truck—met its untimely demise the day after receiving it? Also thanks to Mikey!) Maybe saying this in print will finally allow me to put it to rest.

My family home, where I spent most of my time in my second floor bedroom (upper left corner). Tree on the left obscures the 50 ft. indoor pool room, where I fired my swim coach. Good thing our house was large, otherwise my brothers' horseplay would have blown its sides out.

My seven-year-old sister Dana loved to express her nurturing and maternal instincts–sometimes in rather dramatic ways. When she was about seven, she was determined to discover a way to make our brother Mikey appreciate her maternal urge to comfort him. Normally, he didn't go in for the huggy stuff, so she tried a new approach. "I've got bad news, Mikey," she said in a somber tone.

"What!?" he asked, alarmed.

"I'm not supposed to tell you, but you're going to die soon."

"I'm going to die!?" And as Mikey started to cry, Dana immediately comforted him. I overheard it from the next room, shaking my head but amused just the same. I was just as guilty by association and apathy for letting it happen. (Sorry, Boobie…)

"There, there, Mikey. It's okay. I was just kidding," Dana soothed.

"Really?" he asked as he looked up at her through watery eyes.

"Yes, really," Dana reassured him.

After Mikey calmed down, she said, "You know when I was telling you that I was kidding about you dying? Well, I was kidding about that. You really are going to die." And on and on it went. Little Mikey was gullible enough to keep falling for it.

For those amateur psychologists who think that this childhood incident irreparably scarred my brother, think again. Mike is a jovial, 49-year-old husband and father of three, and probably the most well-adjusted of the entire Smith clan.

In the same vein, if you think my sister grew up to be a sociopath, think again. Dana has grown to be a woman whose steely determination has enabled her to triumph over diabetes, rheumatoid arthritis, colitis, cancer, two extremely difficult childbirths, multiple corrective orthopedic surgeries, and a broken back. In sheer numbers, my sister may have overcome more physical challenges than I have. Mine are just more obvious.

"Children are a heritage from the LORD, offspring a reward from him." Psalm 127:3, TNIV

I win every "Whoever blinks first loses" contest.

My disabilities may have protected me from the physical assault of three rowdy brothers, but when it came to verbal assault, game on! They loved to verbally torment me, not because they were cruel, but because they couldn't *physically* beat me up as they did one another (a time-honored tradition of brothers everywhere!). They referred to my fused knee and the lift in my shoe as being my *Frankie foot.* "Hey! Get your Frankie foot out of the way!" Sometimes they would lay me on my back and say, "We want to see you flail around like a turtle who can't turn over." My brother Steve referred to me as "Stammering Stu" because of my stuttering. He'd give me a hard time, telling me how my dad (who already had a nervous, intense personality) would be screwing up his face and squirming uncomfortably in his seat while I went on and on, trying to pronounce something.

My brother Mike was inspired after listening to the old *War of the World's* radio broadcast that described how Martians were releasing a poisonous gas that was wiping out our military. He took my tape recorder and adapted his own version so he could have a little "fun" with me. Playing the part of the reporter, he described how a green, slimy gas was oozing out from under the bathroom door that I happened to be occupying at the time. He held his hand over his mouth to mimic speaking while wearing a gas mask. Gasping, he reported on his mock radio broadcast, "I don't know how much longer I can go on, ladies and gentleman, before the toxic fumes overcome me!" He acted out the sounds of the soldiers in their death throes and finally gave a Sarah Bernhardt treatment to his own demise.

The sibling teasing which I received I sometimes saw as mistreatment, but now look back on it fondly and realize it was all part of growing up.

"For everything there is a season, and a time for every matter under heaven: ...a time to weep, and a time to laugh; a time to mourn, and a time to dance..." Ecclesiastes 3: 1, 4, ESV

I admit I don't practice the principle of "let the buyer beware." I buy everything sight unseen!

CHAPTER 33

"GOING, GOING...
ALMOST GONE!"

At this time, I discovered a new passion for Major League Baseball. Although this new interest of mine coincided with my rapidly fading vision, radio broadcasts of baseball games enabled me to use my mind's eye to follow the game and make it as—or more— enjoyable than before. The methodical pace of baseball lends itself to being described. Other than day games that coincided with school time, I listened to all but a handful of games throughout the decade of the 1970s—over 1,600 total! Thank God for baseball. Being limited in what I could do, I don't know how I would have occupied the many long hours without it.

Statistics are part and parcel of baseball, more so than any other sport. I was fascinated by how a little box score in the sports section of the newspaper could relay every recordable aspect of a game.

As blindness became more apparent throughout the summer of 1970, I was only able to read the newspaper scores by the illumination of the natural light of outdoors. "Why aren't you using that magnifying glass I paid $7 for," my mom asked with irritation as she watched me trying to read with a three quarter inch toy magnifier I had retrieved as a prize from a cereal box.

"Because it isn't strong enough!" As ridiculous as it may sound, this cheap hunk of plastic from the box of my favorite cereal—Quisp— actually magnified better. Its only disadvantage was that I needed to hold it one inch away from the newspaper print.

"You look ridiculous with your faced plastered to the paper," my mom added. She assumed I was using this silly toy as an alternative to her nice magnifying glass just to be contrary.

As my sight diminished, no longer seeing my face literally buried in the paper, my sister Dana one day asked, "Why aren't you using that little magnifying glass anymore, Jeff?" I ruefully told her it was no longer strong enough. "I'll read you the scores if you scratch my back," she proposed, and I agreed.

After describing where to find the box scores, she was able to relay to me the vital information, though she never could remember what the abbreviations all stood for. "Let's see," she said as she found the box scores. "Well, Harmon got one H. That's good, right?"

"Not really," I muttered.

"But he got five AB's and four SO's! That's pretty good...right?"

"AB's mean 'at bats'," I explained, "and SO's are 'strike outs.' He had a bad game. Just read the numbers. I'll let you know."

Around this time, my two younger brothers and I had a chance to attend a sportsmen's banquet where many of my baseball heroes would be. I sent Steve and Mike up to the main table to ask for autographs from my favorites (I was too tongue-tied to attempt talking with them myself). Following the banquet, Steve was walking me out of the hotel while my dad was getting the car. I came to the top of a long flight of steps without realizing it. Leading with my right foot, I began falling forward, unable to correct myself due to the fact my fused left leg was still on the higher step. Somehow Steve hung on to my arm as I kept falling one step at a time, swinging to and fro. Neither of us was able to get a firm grip on anything to stop my lurching progress. It looked like a bumbling, careening, marionette performance. Spasmodically, down the flight I went, my dad waiting in the car white-knuckling it, watching every teetering step I made. (Where's *Funniest Home Videos* when you need it?)

"...though he may stumble, he will not fall, for the Lord upholds him with his hand." Psalms 37:24

"I don't have to look up my family tree, because I know I am the sap."- Fred Allen

CHAPTER 34

TO SIR, WITH LOVE OR
I'LL DRINK TO THAT!

I met Tom Dosch in eighth grade. He was a curious blend of the scholarly and earthy. He could instantly switch from discussing political theory to telling off-color jokes. Originally a high school history and English teacher, Dosch's interests shifted and he acquired a license to teach visually impaired kids. Two years later, he earned a Master's in blind rehabilitation, with an emphasis on orientation and mobility. Initially during my eighth grade year, he served as a jack-of-all-trades, introducing me to Braille, keyboarding, abacus, and basics in mobility. Betsy Mertz, fresh out of school, became my vision teacher later that year. I didn't see Tom again until my junior year when he was specializing exclusively in orientation and mobility. At that point, we began twice weekly training sessions with a white cane. Now using the white cane in my right hand and the support cane in my left hand, it occurred to me that I must have looked like a cane salesman carrying my samples.

I called him "Tom" instead of "Mr. Dosch" because our relationship was more friendship-based than teacher-student. He had a vast array of pipes from all over the world which he smoked regularly during our mobility sessions, since they occurred after school. Inevitably our contact would start off with any new jokes we had heard. These jokes tended to be crude, which gave me a sense of masculine identity, normalcy, belonging, and connection. No matter how my disabilities separated me from my peers and regular social functions, Tom's salty humor reminded me that deep down I was just one of the guys. I remember with fondness how we directed personal shots at one another regarding political points of view. I considered Dosch a radical liberal and myself a reactionary conservative. Truth be told, I had no political affiliation. I just enjoyed getting into lively discussions.

My mobility training was giving me a sense of independence that I had not yet experienced in my life. Mobility lessons enabled me to leave the dreaded wheelchair and begin maneuvering independently from class to class. I was trained to use auditory and directional cues to accomplish tasks both small and large. It wasn't long until Tom's assignments had me independently traveling on public transportation, shopping at a large department store, purchasing an item, and returning home with the proof. Later, this kept me from becoming overwhelmed by the enormity of negotiating the University of Minnesota with its east and west campuses and its 60,000 students.

Dosch always treated me as an adult, even though I was pretty immature and still had plenty to learn about life. He often took the opportunity to develop my sense of significance and dignity by posing questions about my worldview in the areas of politics, religion, and personal philosophy. This gave me my first chance to think outside of my own little world and about how I might fit into the real world. Trust and friendship developed, which resulted in expansive conversations after work hours including, once I became an adult, symbols of adulthood: drinks and pipes. Dosch served in large part as a positive male role model in my formative teen years.

As mentioned earlier, my stuttering had been a great barrier to developing relationships and expressing myself. For as long as I could remember, my style of speaking has included big words and long, involved sentences with lots of clauses. This tendency, in combination with stuttering, is a conversation killer. My inclination to use complex sentences served as a compensatory method of getting around difficult-to-pronounce words and, in part, to build my self-image through big words. Tom was a rare being who was patient enough to sit and listen to me work through complex, philosophical ideas. Since

I believe in strictly a worldly, not spiritual way, in Descartes' idea of "I think; therefore, I am," Dosch helped me develop an identity by allowing me to talk through my ideas. His unconventional approach regarded the student as a person, which was effectively different from the traditional student-teacher relationship at that time.

A regular conversational theme of ours revolved around my blatant attempts to take advantage of Tom and then try to spin it as a good deal. He didn't exactly encourage this kind of behavior but he appreciated my attempt at cleverness.

I once bought a couple of 6 foot inflatable vinyl rafts with plastic oars. One of the rafts ended up with a hole in it because I had left it inside our sauna for two days after accidentally leaving the temperature gauge on high. Since I didn't have any use for a raft that couldn't hold its air, I offered it to Tom, an inveterate fisherman. "I'll sell you the good one for $10 or the one that has a hole in it for $4," I proposed.

"What good is a raft with a hole in it?" he said in mock anger. "I'll throw in a patch kit for a buck," I said, seeing another opportunity to profit.

"All right, you chiseler, I'll take the one with the patch kit," he grumbled with a detectable chuckle.

The next time I saw him, I asked, "Did you take your good deal out for a spin yet?"

"Good deal my–! I was in the middle of the lake when the patch blew off the raft," he retorted.

Sarcastically I responded, "It's your own fault for letting me take advantage of you!"

"Remind me next time not to buy your junk," he said.

Maybe I'd have felt more sympathy about Tom getting the short end of the stick if the memory of him walking me into a pillar during a high school orientation and mobility session hadn't left such an impression on me—in more ways than one.

Not only was Tom blind to my blindness, but he raised his children in the same way.

"I'm taking the family to see the Minnesota Twins—want to come along?"

Baseball and free are two of my favorite things.

To make sure I kept up on all the current statistics, I'd typically bring along with me a transistor radio and ear buds to the ballpark, in the same fashion sighted folks enjoy carrying along a pair of binoculars. Tom's 9-year-old daughter, Rochelle, sat next to me and kept up with the game using her set of binocs.

She turned to me and proposed, in all innocence, "How 'bout I use your radio for a while and you can use my binoculars?"

"Okay…but I don't think it's a fair trade," I said with bemusement. Everyone howled as poor little Rochelle turned crimson.

Thirty-five years later, Tom and I still get together regularly, but now the Manhattans and Scotch have been replaced by tea and water.

"I have not stopped giving thanks for you, remembering you in my prayers." Ephesians 1:16

"Laughter is the valve on the pressure cooker of life. Either you laugh and suffer, or you got your beans or brains on the ceiling."
– Wavy Gravy

CHAPTER 35

VISION TEACHER OR FEELING BRAILLE IN MY SLEEP

I worked with orientation and mobility specialists, such as Tom Dosch, on a less frequent basis as I developed independent travel skills, however, I worked with vision teachers such as Betsy Mertz daily throughout high school. "Vision teacher" is the title of someone who orally administers tests, teaches Braille, keyboarding, abacus, and other adaptive tools that enable people who are blind to function in school settings. Mrs. Mertz became my vision teacher late in eighth grade. Her style was authoritative, which came across to me as bossy, and we'd often butt heads. This was much to the surprise of my fellow students who considered her "a total fox," which was seventies' lingo for a knock out. She wore the miniskirts of the day that displayed her attractive legs. My buddies drooled over her and were befuddled by my less-than-favorable view of her.

Mrs. Mertz demanded excellence and, like my mom, didn't let me use my disability to my advantage. Her dedication to this was demonstrated when she decided to have me spend the summer between eighth and ninth grade working on reading Braille so I would be equipped when I'd be mainstreamed back into the public school system. That summer we practiced reading Braille for three- hour sessions two to three days per week; my fingers were set to the grindstone. I couldn't escape. My immature and myopic thinking was *she's drilling me unmercifully!* I couldn't believe that Betsy Mertz wanted me to practice Braille during my leisure time on top of our scheduled sessions.

"I'm getting bloodshot fingers, Mrs. Mertz!" I complained. Mertz had long, blonde wavy hair—reminiscent of Farrah Fawcett, or so my high school buddies informed me. Her hair would tickle my neck and face while she leaned over the Braille exercises. She had a sweet, high-pitched voice that I've always associated with attractiveness.

My half-hearted attempts to complete the exercises would often be interrupted by her exclamation, "No scrubbing!" ("Scrubbing" is an incorrect technique for reading Braille where the fingertips move up and down instead of correctly moving left-to-right.) "I'm not scrubbing." "I'm just itching my finger tips!" I'd lie. "Keep your elbows in. Read with your lead fingers, trail withyour left hand. Find the next line with your left hand," were some of the commands I still remember today.

The fastest I ever read Braille was between 60 and 100 words per minute. Mrs. Mertz could read between two and three hundred words per minute, but of course, she peeked. Mertz was passionate about my learning, knew I could do better, and slammed the desk countless times to make a point in her pursuit of excellence. It worked—my speed increased dramatically over the summer. Besides giving me the adaptive tools I needed to help me succeed in school, she gave me the discipline and transferable learning skills to do things that I didn't want to do, an inevitability in everyone's life. Thank you, Mrs. Mertz, for putting up with my subversive nature.

When I still had my vision in fifth grade, going blind was my worst nightmare. But not long after going blind, my perspective totally changed. My fear of blindness had been mostly rooted in not knowing all the resources and support that would be available to me. Later on, I discovered among blind friends and acquaintances a similar point of view: the reality of having gone blind is more manageable than the fear of the unknown.

Though I share this truth to reassure others going through a transition, the greatest impact seems to come from what I unintentionally share when people see me live my life amidst constant change.

"Each one should use whatever gift he has received to serve others, faithfully administering God's grace in its various forms." 1 Peter 4:10

Did you hear about the Braille greeting card proofreader who worked his fingers to the bone last holiday season?

CHAPTER 36

MORE LOW SCHOOL
THAN HIGH SCHOOL

Tenth grade posed many challenges. One of the challenges was building relationships with my peers. Stuttering and the sheer size of the high school were my main obstacles. My lack of confidence in speaking discouraged me from raising my hand in class. One of the few times I did feel comfortable enough to go vertical occurred in ninth grade. Mr. M., my economics teacher, always encouraged participation and cultivated open communication.

One of Mr. M.'s students named Kevin must have needed to absorb oxygen through his vocal cords because he never stopped talking. Once, as I started saying something, Kevin interrupted and began running off at the mouth. In a shattering bellow, Mr. M. yelled, "Johnson, SHUT... UP!" Kevin literally jumped out of his desk...everyone was hushed. Once composed, Mr. M. calmly said, "Now, what were you saying, Jeff?" Feeling a strange sense of honor, I proudly finished my comment.

The very first day of class when the lunch bell rang, everyone rushed out of the room, leaving only me and another student named Don Dinger (who would play integrally in my personal and professional development). "Don, would you mind escorting this gentleman to the lunch room?" requested Mr. M.

Without Don, the photo on the front cover of the book would have never become a reality. Under his tutelage, I tooled around the high school parking lot after hours while Don, who had only recently received his driver's license, sat in the passenger seat. I took audio cues from Don to brake or turn left or right based largely on the pitch and urgency of his voice. I would have never advanced beyond being a student blind driver to a fully accredited blind driver without Don's assistance. I wonder if our sessions had anything to do with his premature graying?

At this juncture of my adaptive training, I had yet to work with Tom Dosch to learn orientation and mobility with a white cane instead of the wheelchair. State and school officials felt that student volunteers should take me in a wheelchair from class to class because of my RA. Being blind and wheelchair-bound increased my sense of isolation, and my self-image suffered. I couldn't partake in the normal hallway conversation during class passing time since I had an escort wheeling me through the halls five minutes before the bell rang. I felt powerless and frustrated, which only increased my stuttering, further limiting peer interaction. Because of this, I often used inappropriate behavior to get attention and make a statement that would communicate my sense of independence to other students.

The nurse's office had assigned me a wheelchair. It was rusty, old, and oversized, which made me look like a little twerp. It was a far cry from what I viewed to be sleek, aerodynamic wheelchairs from my early childhood days at Saint Joseph's. I wanted to make it obvious to my high school classmates that I was just using this wheelchair rather than really needing it. I decided to show my disdain for it by slowly and surreptitiously taking it apart. I wanted to enjoy the reaction of my escorts as they witnessed the gradual deterioration of the wheelchair and say, "The wheelchair isn't moving right, Jeff." My thinking was if I broke the wheelchair, they'd allow me to walk from class to class. Even with a sighted guide, walking was my preference over being wheeled.

The first step in my plan to destroy this rolling albatross was unscrewing the front of the metal sides of the chair; this caused a rolling claptrap sound going down the hall which turned the heads of every student in the "open style" designed school as we wheeled by. The next step was waiting for an opportunity to see what would happen when, inevitably, one of my escorts decided for fun to begin running, part and parcel of having a wheelchair joy ride.

"Jeff! Let's put this puppy in gear!" one of my escorts announced.

"OK," I responded, laughing for reasons of which he had no clue. His abundance of exuberance disappeared immediately after I thrust out the loose metal plating of the wheelchair until it dug into the spokes of the wheels. My now alarmed escort, unaware of my master plan, said, "Man, your wheelchair just blew up! You lost half your spokes!"

"You're kidding!" I feigned seriousness, trying not to laugh out loud. Some of the remaining spokes had wound their way around the axle, giving the chair a sound similar to the clicking sound of a playing card being placed in the spokes of a kid's bicycle.

I did my handiwork slowly and methodically while in class—unscrewing and removing bolts on the sly without detection. From this point on, nature took its course. The large side wheels began loosening, and my weight caused the bottoms of the wheels to bow out and come back in, which gave me a fun sort of up and down ride. But something was missing: the coup de grace. It finally came to me. I removed all but a single bolt on each metal hand rim of the wheels. Gravity caused the rims to roll ahead and then be pulled back with each wheel rotation, giving a locomotive type of motion, not to mention the sound of the metal rims dragging across the tile. Finally it reached its Waterloo. Rolling down the hall one day, one of the wheels just rolled off the chair. Fortunately, my quick-reacting escort managed to hold up the right side of the chair and half wheel, half carry me into the nurse's office. I claimed complete ignorance to the nurse.

"We were rolling along, minding our own business, Mrs. Sengi, when the chair just fell apart. I don't know what happened! I never thought it was that well-built to begin with."

"Just fell apart?" she said laughing, knowing my history of pranks. Despite my master plan to be wheelchair-free, I was assigned a brand new wheelchair. It looked nice, but it was still a wheelchair.

Hijnks such as these bonded us and helped me to be seen for my personality, rather than my condition.

"Therefore encourage one another and build one another up, just as you are doing." 1 Thessalonians 5:11

What value! A recent e-mail to me from Lasik states in their subject line, "Lasik New Year's offer – Regain Your Vision in 2012."

CHAPTER 37

OLD METHODS MAKE A NEW MAN

As a Christian, I don't believe in superstition, coincidences, or jinxing, but their irony certainly makes life more interesting.

In the spring of 1973, I remember thinking en route to a routine annual checkup with Dr. Thompson, my orthopedic specialist, that it had been, like, three years since I had my last operation. Seeing me walk to the exam table, the doctor said, "Jeff, I don't remember you having this limp. I'd like you to try straightening your right leg." I couldn't, nor could I straighten my right hip. This constriction in my knee and hip had come about as a result of my decision two years earlier to replace my orthopedic shoes that had a two-inch lift with stylish regular shoes. But style always comes with a cost.

"You have some scoliosis in your back," Dr. Thompson assessed after examining me. "Has your back been hurting?"

"Well, maybe a little."

"Don't you have a lift for that shoe?" he asked.

"I used to have one," I responded, avoiding any self-incriminating details.

The doctor replied, "The ligaments in your hip and knee have constricted from walking without a lift in the shoe of your shorter leg. I'd like to release the ligaments so you can walk more comfortably."

In June of 1973, I was admitted into Midway Hospital in Saint Paul. Except for a two-week period between surgeries that released knee and hip ligaments, I would spend the entire summer of 1973 in the hospital.

Thompson had researched and discovered a ligament-releasing technique from 1923 that he decided was the most suitable for my condition. Ironically, we used old information to move forward in my recovery. I was admitted to Midway Hospital in St. Paul the afternoon prior to surgery. As x-rays and other preparation were taking place, I noticed the young and outgoing staff. Even the few staff over age 30 assumed the hip, relaxed nature of their juniors. It was easy joking and hanging around with them as many spent their break time in my room.

Despite all the pain, sweat, and tears that would be part of my recovery, meeting Kathy Johnson, a nurse's aide at the time, made up for it all. Kathy and I instantly hit it off. Since the average age on an orthopedic floor in that era was somewhere between 70 and dead, Kathy couldn't have been more tickled about working with a patient closer to her age. She was eighteen and I was sixteen. I brought the average age of the floor down to sixty-five.

From day one, we began teasing one another. I pretended to have a photographic memory, which she fully believed and still believes to this day. I had just completed listening on tape to the book *How to Develop a Super-Powered Memory* by Harry Lorayne. It taught me some relatively easy methods for memorizing a grid of one hundred squares, each containing a random four-digit number. I used these techniques to convince her of my ruse.

"Go ahead, say any four-digit number on this grid, and I will tell you the corresponding letter and number," I boasted to Kathy.

"First I'm going to tell you the letter and number, and you tell me the digit," she said. The method in the book worked either way. I smiled and told her the four-digit number.

"No way!" Kathy yelled.

This not only jump-started our friendship, but also opened the door to meeting the rest of the staff on the floor. Kathy dragged just about everyone of them into my room.

"Go ahead, try to stump him," she'd challenge.

I can reassure the reader that this feat had nothing to do with intelligence or possessing a photographic memory. I have just always liked entertaining people.

Dr. Thompson's surgical technique proved more than suitable—it was perfect. Despite having long incisions on both sides of the kneecap, I woke up pain-free, clear-headed, and had a full lunch a half hour after being returned to my room. This successful surgery, however, set up false expectations for the upcoming ligament release in my hip.

The Summer of Love

Following the successful ligament release in my knee, I came home for two weeks to continue physical therapy and healing. Then, as planned, I was readmitted to Midway Hospital for surgery to release my constricted hip ligaments. This procedure would enable me to once again stand erect.

The surgeons had to cut more muscle than they had first anticipated. (Remember, I'm a product of protein, just ask my mom). Awakening from surgery, I was in intense pain, a level of which I had never felt before. I repeatedly threw up as a result, and as the pain further diminished my appetite, it created a cycle of continued nausea. Strangely, what finally broke this cycle was the vending machine soup purchased for me by none other than Kathy Johnson. No wonder she and I became such great friends, with her saving my life and all. My relationship with Kathy expanded beyond hospital walls and has extended over many decades.

My recovery this time was long and arduous. Due to the large amount of muscle that had been cut, even with months of therapy, I could never again draw up my knee beyond a 90-degree bend.

Although the surgeries and recovery were painful and the separation from my family and friends hurt, to this day I still maintain that the summer of 1973 was the most hilarious time of my life because I became a part of the staff's social interactions. My self-confidence soared. Nurse assistants, techs and orderlies were college-aged, and I was in high school. We entertained each other in a variety of ways. Staff morale improved—and so did mine.

Orthopedic wards in general are places of positivity. Once the surgery is done, it's all about the recovery. People are working toward a goal of improving mobility. In between therapy sessions, there is a lot of downtime. This makes for a perfect environment where staff and patients are able to socialize, which I did every chance I got.

Fresh Rubber Chicken for Sale

During my long hospital stay that summer, I ordered a number of novelties from a magic shop; among them were a rubber chicken, fake vomit, and a pair of inflatable women's legs (more about those later). Once the novelties and practical jokes arrived at the hospital, I began a course of strategic implementation. I had someone hang the chicken from the exercise bar above my bed with a sign attached that read, "Chicken for Sale $1." This was crossed out, and below that was written, "$.50," also crossed out, and under that it read, "$.25," and finally, "What will it cost me to have this chicken taken away?"

I thought for sure my doctor would comment in some way about the rubber chicken dangling from my overhead exercise bar. *Not a word.* He didn't know what to make of this patient of his, an incongruent mix of multiple disabilities and perverse humor. In spite of the fun visual atmosphere that always pervaded my hospital room, my doctor checked my progress daily and then would leave without comment.

Eventually, my outrageousness caused Dr. Thompson to warm up to my mother and me. Over time, he actually became loquacious, something unthinkable several years earlier.

My humor helped the staff see me for who I was, rather than just a patient with a disability. They warmed up to me and before you knew it, we were busy trying to outdo one another with jokes and stunts. For example, once, just to find out if the kitchen would do it, I had someone check off every item on the order form for the next day's breakfast. And sure enough, the next morning a food tray arrived stacked two-feet high with my breakfast requests. The word got out about my breakfast bounty, and soon my room was full of orderlies, aides, and medical assistants chowing down and having a good time.

Adding to my hospital room's reputation as "party central" was my mom's regular contribution of a family favorite, Scotch shortbread. Once tasting this irresistible confection, staff were hooked and would return later asking, "Um, Jeff, would you have any more of that, what do you call it?"

"Scotch shortbread?" I'd reply, feigning innocence but aware of its power to not only provide me with ample company but it's use as a negotiating chip as well. "Hey, would you mind running across to Burger King to pick me up a Whopper on your break?"

In another instance, I told my mom in a phone conversation, "Mom, I need cotton balls for a craft project. I need a bunch of bags of them."

Mom, concerned about the effect the long-term hospital stays were having on my morale, thought this was a great idea and said, "Glad to hear you're using your time productively." The next day, she visited me with an armful of cotton ball bags and asked, "What exactly are you going to do with these, Jeff?"

"It's really kind of hard to describe, sort of a craft project, Mom."

That satisfied her, perhaps because she figured it would be a surprise and that interfering would limit the creative process of developing a masterpiece. The reality was, I was amusing myself and looking for additional avenues for getting attention, a forerunner to the motives of the stage hog known as the Amazing Jeffo.

I had recently discovered that when a water-soaked cotton ball is thrown, it has the same properties as a massive spit ball on steroids. I thought, *Maybe I can chuck enough of these wet wads up on the ceiling to create something like an upside-down minefield.* As the cotton balls dried, they would drop on the heads of the unsuspecting, or so I thought. Physics was never my strong suit. As the cotton balls dried, they cemented themselves to any surface they hit, including the windows. The cotton ball-covered windows attracted much attention from passers-by. For instance, an orderly, who thought his eyes were playing tricks on him, came into my room to investigate. The still-wet cotton balls plastered on my windows gave them a strange appearance. He entered my room and in a confused voice said, "Excuse me, but it looks like your window is melting."

"No, no, it's just a bunch of wet cotton balls stuck to the window," I said, stuttering and embarrassed.

"How did they get there?" he continued, still confused.

"Well, I threw them there." Still extrapolating from my flawed, scientific hypothesis, I continued, "I'm trying to make a solar eclipse effect in my room. When the cotton balls dry and fall off, the beams of light will kind of make for a homemade Pink Floyd light show."

In the same bewildered tone he said, "Oh," and walked out.

After exhausting my ammunition supply—three large bags of 300 cotton balls each—I asked my mom to bring more, but she had recently visited me and had discovered, much to her embarrassment, that my creative juices were being used for evil, not for good, and she firmly refused.

The cotton balls were scattered equally on the window, walls, ceiling, and TV screen. The nurses were annoyed because they couldn't watch their soaps. (I've never understood soap operas. They're not funny enough to be taken as comedy and too farcical to be taken as legitimate drama). Later Kathy Johnson told me that when the custodial staff removed the cotton balls from the ceiling panels, it left clean white spots on the otherwise dirty ceiling. Consequently, the entire ceiling had to be repainted. (Last time I help clean the ceiling!)

The greatest practical joke that summer was played on me by the staff and was inspired by Kathy. One day I was up having physical therapy and one of the orderlies said, "There's a girl waiting for you in your room, and she's pretty hot."

"Whatever," I said, not believing him figuring he was trying to get back at me for my Tabasco candy prank.

"I'm not kidding!"

Then a bit later one of the therapists came up to me and said, "We're going to speed up your session today because I heard there's a cute girl waiting for you downstairs."

"What?!" I exclaimed.

By the time my therapy session was done, two or three more staff had teased me about this mystery girl waiting for me downstairs in my room. I kept telling them, "Get out! I don't believe it," but thought to myself, *Maybe it's a girl from high school or something?*

Well, by the time they wheeled me back to my room, I was in a total tizzy, mostly not believing it at all, but kind of, sort of, wanting to. As we went in, the two orderlies acted surprised and whispered to me, "There she is, lying in your bed. Do you want us to help you slide next to her?" I wanted to yell out "heck, yeah!" but was also worried about getting in trouble.

Well, the staff had really yanked my chain. As I, oh so carefully, checked out who my visiting bed partner was, I discovered she was made up of a combination of pillows and ribbons sculpted together to make the curves in all the right places. A pair of inflatable legs (ordered from the magic novelty shop) had been fitted with a pair of four-inch heels and fishnet stockings donated by a nurse. A large corner of one of the pillows at the top was fashioned into a head by use of a colorful ribbon necklace. Another ribbon was around the very corner of the pillowcase to resemble a ponytail. This Bride of Frankenstein was wrapped with a lovely blue skirt, which in reality was a moisture absorbing pad used for patients who are incontinent. The staff had really outdone themselves in the practical joke department. I dubbed my fluffy girlfriend "Makeshift Maggie."

To preserve this moment as long as possible, they carefully placed her on my windowsill. It wasn't long afterward that my introverted doctor came by for his daily rounds. He stopped short when he saw "Makeshift Maggie" lying there and said, "Is this your girlfriend?" Comedy had broken the ice. From that time on, he really opened up to us about his family and personal interests.

Every amusing image of that summer at Midway hospital dwells in my memory as in a room visibly bright with light, ironic since I was nearly bereft of all my vision. By comparison, the dire images that are lodged in my mind of those early days at St. Mary's hospital are of a darkened room, in spite of having perfect vision at that time. The presence or absence of bright light in my memories is all about the surrounding events, not the actual luminosity of the room.

All the new relationships I developed that summer were so uplifting to me that my parents and I thought it only right to invite these "angels of mercy" to our home for a giant pool party and barbecue. My mom spent days preparing her homemade delicacies: potato salad, coleslaw, baked beans, all topped off with our family favorite—grilled baby back pork loin ribs, prepared in the manner made famous in my mom's birthplace—Kansas City.

That summer helped me realize that laughter was life's greatest medicine, and the camaraderie with the medical staff provided my daily dose.

"For God will give His angels charge over you to guard you in all your ways." Psalm 91:11, HNV

"Laughter is a tranquilizer with no side effects." – Arnold Glasow

I'll tell you what's frustrating: when I get so mad I want to stomp my foot. I can't do it with my right foot because I've got a bad knee. I tried doing it with my stiff left leg and fell over.

CHAPTER 38

HIGH SCHOOL: TRIUMPHANT RETURN

As the school year began in 1974, I had a renewed sense of self-confidence. My hip and knee surgeries allowed me to stand and walk erect for the first time in six years. I returned to high school determined to "fit in." I joined the pole vault team. With my fused knee, how could I lose? Just kidding!

Throughout high school, reading, writing and arithmetic were not the only areas in which I needed to develop. I still had a lot of maturing to do.

I worked the system as much as circumstances allowed. Our health teacher doubled as a football coach. He decided that 90% of our grade would be based on a health-related presentation that we would give to the class. I'm only guessing, but his motivation might have been based on the need to devote more of his time and thoughts designing plays for the upcoming football game.

The prospect of humiliating myself in front of everyone because of my stutter was averted when the teacher agreed that I could record my presentation (no matter how many tries it might take to get it just right) with accompanying slides. This also gave me an opportunity to do my research and recording in the comfort of my "private office." (The school was overbuilt in anticipation of population swells. This allowed school officials to assign me one of the unused offices, where I could meet with my vision teacher during daily study hour.)

I took a large sheet of construction paper from art class, had it cut to size, and taped it to the windows to exclude passersby from seeing

158

into my sanctuary. I didn't do this because I had anything to hide. Rather, it allowed for buddies who were on teacher- assigned errands to pop in and shoot the breeze for a few minutes. The room even had a sink. I called it my wet bar—my "cocktails" were in the form of powdered fruit drink mixes. The bulletin board was used to receive darts I brought from home. We put up pictures of people who were held in low esteem to serve as our targets. (25 points for an ear, 50 for an eye, 100 for the tip of the nose, at least until the Algebra teacher in the adjoining room got tired of hearing the "thump-thump-thump" of our darts and took them away.)

Every couple of weeks the health teacher wanted me to check in with him regarding the progress of my health presentation. "I'm working hard on it, Mr. Ben. I'm glad you gave us the entire quarter to finish; it's quite a big project!"

Needless to say, only a small portion of the allotted time was devoted to working on my project, which was on the subject of hypnosis. Coincidentally, I had actually at the time been going to a hypnotist in an attempt to control stuttering. Previously, I had my parents sign me up for transcendental meditation. I had not yet proclaimed Jesus as my Lord and Savior, so I found no conflicts with this practice of Eastern mysticism. The hypnosis actually helped my situational stress and improved my verbal fluency.

Some of the kids were grumbling that I was never in class, but I just smiled. By the end of the class, I received an A. The quality of my work must have met the criteria to achieve such a grade, but I could have as easily been awarded an A in the subject of sloughing off.

"A little sleep, a little slumber, a little folding of the hands to rest."
Proverbs 24:33

High School Privileges or "I'll Take Three Dozen, Please"

Growing up, I often received unmerited privileges because of my disabilities, except in the Smith household. Naturally, like any kid, I began to take advantage of these opportunities.

Once a substitute teacher held an open book in front of my (blind) eyes and asked, "Is this about the place in the book where your teacher left off?" I looked down for effect, moved my head a little, and said, "That looks about right."

I still wonder how that substitute felt when she later realized she'd been had by someone who didn't even stay for the class. My wheelchair escort and I had an important game of darts waiting for us in my "office" upstairs.

Another example occurred in my ninth grade economics class. The teacher needed to attend to some matters that required him to leave the room for several minutes. "You're all young adults," he said before leaving. "With age comes responsibility," he continued, "And I'm going to trust that while I'm gone, all of you will read your lesson with no talking. I'm counting on you." About thirty seconds after he left, desks were slid together and several poker games broke out. Playing cards were dealt and money exchanged.

We should have been responsible, or at least responsible enough to post a lookout to give us a warning of his return. In our excitement, we were creating quite a ruckus, which suddenly changed to the loudest silence you ever heard when the teacher suddenly reappeared in the doorway. We froze in mid-deal. I couldn't even play the "blind" card after he spotted my deck of Braille cards.

The punishment was that everyone had to write 1,000 times, "I will not play poker in Economics Class." As I suspected, I got off with a lightweight punishment. I was supposed to, on tape, record 1,000 times, "I will not play poker in Economics Class." I figured Mr. Mooney wouldn't sit there and listen to this for more than a minute or so. So that's how long I recorded.

Getting privileges because of my disabilities was a nice perk.

However, I now understand that any form of special treatment, motivated by pity toward someone with a disability, in the long term, is damaging to the development of that individual. I'm not looking for favoritism; I am looking for equality.

"Whoever works his land will have plenty of bread, but he who follows worthless pursuits lacks sense." Proverbs 12:11, ESV

"All life demands struggle. Those who have everything given to them become lazy, selfish, and insensitive to the real values of life." – Pope Paul VI

How many blind people does it take to change a light bulb? Does it really matter?

CHAPTER 39

HOT SUMMER JOB

Between my junior and senior years of high school, I was enrolled in a job skills training program sponsored by State Services for The Blind. The program was designed for students with disabilities to prepare them for future employment. Held on the campuses of the University of Minnesota, it would be the first opportunity I had to stretch my wings of independence. The six-week summer program consisted of vocational aptitude and work experience.

Our group of visually impaired teenagers lived in an older dorm, one without air conditioning. 1974 was one of the hottest summers ever in Minnesota. The low temperature that first night was ninety degrees with no breeze.

I did not want to be there at any temperature; my counselors had strongly urged me to attend. Likewise, my parents coerced me and argued that it was for my own good—as well as for theirs. "Jeffrey, you need to have a taste of independence," my mom insisted.

"I think your mother is right. Besides, what's so bad about making a little dough in the process, Jimmy Slicks? At any rate, it's a free program," added my thrifty dad.

Making money, huh? Well, the man DOES have a point, I thought. After all, the apple doesn't fall far from the tree…the money tree.

Victor Hugo said that our destiny is determined at the crossroads in our lives—this was a crossroad for me. My first foray into independent living.

The first two weeks of the program were devoted to aptitude testing, including hand dexterity assessment for piece work. I knew early on that this kind of thing wasn't for me. To determine the level of my manual dexterity, they wanted me to fill in hundreds of teeny tiny threaded holes on a large metal plate with hundreds of teeny tiny screws, and then unscrew them all. Not exactly meaningful work. To relieve the tedium and my frustration, I screwed in just enough teeny tiny screws into a certain pattern of teeny tiny threaded holes to spell out a not-so-teeny-tiny epithet. I don't recommend this approach.

The last four weeks of the program matched student interest and aptitude to a real-world work experience. Every student was paid $85 a week. This gave us a chance to learn about budgeting as we were also responsible for paying our dormitory housing, $170 a month.

I was assigned to work in a cigar shop within the Minneapolis Courthouse. Pete McCann, owner of the stand, said I didn't have to pack a lunch but instead could help myself to what was available in his stand. He didn't realize that despite my 85-pound frame I could really pack it in, especially when it came to junk food, typically unavailable at home. Realizing his profit margin was going down the tube fast, Mr. McCann said, "A microwavable hamburger, package of Slim Jims, Twinkie, bag of chips, bag of peanuts, and a grape soda... isn't that a bit much, Jeff?"

Once I saw the error of my kid-in-a-candy-store ways, I toned it down, and Pete and I had a great relationship. He was a veteran of WWII and lost his eyesight during the Normandy invasion. I've always had a fascination with hearing the endless stories surrounding this watershed world event. Pete was a great storyteller, even more so as he fielded question after question about his war experiences. He'd get so wrapped up in his stories, he'd constantly forget to keep up with his cigar stand duties.

In addition to Pete's companionship, being thrown among a group of other blind high school students gave me a chance to see these kids for what they really were: people who just so happen to be blind, just like me. Even though my physical differences never did me any favors relating to my self-image, I have always seen myself as a normal person trapped in an uncooperative body. And again, this is how I saw most of the other kids in the summer program, with the exception of one. His name was John.

My parents and I sat with John and his folks at the orientation luncheon. John's parents had gotten wind of this innovative program and had flown all the way from Pennsylvania to be a part of it. After we were introduced, I noticed how awkward and withdrawn John acted and the uncertainty of his parents toward everything around them.

"I've been observing your family and your son. Is this Jeff's first time here like it is with my son, John?"

"Yes. It is," my mom responded. The mothers exchanged information about their sons.

"How is it that your son seems so unaffected by his blindness and other problems?" asked John's mom. "He doesn't seem to need much assistance."

"Jeff has had some training by Minnesota's State Services. Does Pennsylvania have a program like this?"

As the conversation went on, John's mother and father admitted they were overwhelmed by their son's situation and didn't know where to turn.

"How long has Jeff been blind?"

"About three years," my mom responded.

"We feel so sorry this happened to our son," she confided to my mother. "John has never been away from us before."

"Has John been blind from birth?"

"Yes. So his father and I decided to have him attend a school for the blind."

Personally, I have nothing against schools for the blind, but I feel it's equally important to expose children who are blind to people and experiences outside that safe environment. After all, the goal is to be fully integrated into society.

It was immediately clear to me and to my parents that John had inadequate social skills, which I knew couldn't be attributed to having gone to a school for the blind. In listening to John's mother tell her story, my mother conjectured that John's parents had from early on, out of purely good motives, coddled—maybe even pitied—him.

"Jeff, try to be friends with John. He looks like he could use one," my mom said to me before leaving. "It would be nice for you to get to know John, joke around a little."

Once all the parents gave us their good-byes, we were ready to begin learning independent living skills for the next six weeks.

I wanted to get to know him but, honestly, I was at a loss trying to understand John's odd behavior. He repeatedly interjected phrases such as "fuzzy teddy" and "catfish," neither of which were within the context of any conversation. Moreover, when he pronounced these two favorite expressions, he'd extend the "Z" and "Sh" sounds to several seconds in length. He classified everyone as either a "good" catfish or a "bad" catfish, but only John knew the difference between the two.

When our group would ride the city bus together, we'd be embarrassed by the things he'd blurt to other passengers. For example, he'd ask complete strangers, "Are you a catfish or a fuzzy teddy?" and would ask passenger after passenger if they would go fishing with him. We took our turns saying, "Knock it off, John," then would smile apologetically in the direction of the person he was addressing.

It's not uncommon for a child who is blind to engage in self-stimulation behaviors, sometimes also referred to as "blindisms", which are unnecessary movements, i.e., when you see Stevie Wonder twitching, rhythmically tapping, rocking, or the like. This is especially manifested in those born blind. Unless corrected, this behavior can become habitual and will cause a child to stand out from his or her peers.

This has even happened to me, someone not even born blind. One day in high school my vision teacher, Betsy Mertz, abruptly said, "Stop that!"

"Stop what?" I asked in surprise.

"That rocking you're doing on a chair that's not meant to be rocked." I wasn't even aware of what I was doing.

Because it was an unbearably hot summer in Minneapolis, our group spent a lot of time on the roof at tables and in chairs. Every night after the rest of us went inside, through our open windows we heard John, still on the roof, loudly singing away, while rocking violently on a metal chair as a form of self-stimulation. Inevitably the chair's momentum would flip it backward and it would come crashing down, followed by a loud string of curse words, then some mumbling, then once again rocking, gently at first, then violently, followed by another crash, and so on.

Sadly, his behavior was mocked by the group. I tried to get to know him. He was intelligent and knew, for example, everything that there was to know about houseflies, including every scientific classification and eidetic detail of body part names and functions.

A couple of weeks into the program, I happened to be waiting in the lounge for my ride when I overheard one of the coordinators say to John, "We are very sorry to say this, John, but we're going to have to excuse you from the program."

"You mean I can't stay here?" asked John, heartbroken.

"I'm sorry John, but you've caused too many disruptions for the other students. It's just not working out."

Several years later, our cleaning lady, Mrs. Libhart, was recounting an experience she had while riding the city bus. "For several weeks now, I've been riding on the same bus with this very strange man. He's blind," she said. As I heard her telling more and more about this fellow passenger's bizarre behavior, I could hardly believe what I was hearing. Her description perfectly fit John. I asked her, "By chance is this guy's name John?"

"Yes! It IS John! How did you know?"

"It's a long story…"

John had a sharp academic mind, but his social intelligence was unfortunately quite impaired. This created a condition far more disabling than the mere loss of vision.

"Blessed are those who find wisdom, those who gain understanding."
Proverbs 3:13, TNIV

"Patience, n. A minor form of despair, disguised as a virtue." – Ambrose Bierce, The Devil's Dictionary, 1911

CHAPTER 40

A DEAD END LEADS TO MORE SURGERY

I began my senior year of high school with optimism that my string of surgeries was a thing of the past, but my hope was tempered by a growing concern regarding the changing dimensions of my ileostomy stoma. Along with its increasing size, another more embarrassing sign something was wrong was its giving classmates the raspberry indiscriminately. In reality, my stoma was losing its elasticity. I guess Cyclops was doing his impression of his favorite Pharaoh, "Tootin' Common."

One morning while getting ready for school, I couldn't get a fresh appliance around my stoma. For the umpteenth time, we called Aunt Alyce for her assessment. She came over and said, "Oh, my gosh, your stoma looks terrible—you need to go to the hospital." I was shocked. My thoughts of that day's history midterm were obliterated. She made a quick call, and we headed off to the emergency room.

Surgery was immediately scheduled—although not before being the case-study for several surgeons in residence. They gathered around my bed and took notes as they studied my grossly swollen stoma. They had never seen a gangrenous stoma. ("Gangrenous stoma" sounds like the name of a punk rock band, doesn't it?) Afterward my surgeon told me, "We pulled out about a foot worth of infected intestines, Jeff. This leaves you with a nice pink end, but you only have a few feet of intestines left," he added. So few guts inside me might explain why I have never dealt with a beer belly. (Is that cheating?)

After a week in the hospital, I was ready to get home. It was Christmas Eve day. "Jeff, I don't like the idea of your coming home this soon. You should stay in the hospital a few more days," Mom said. I told her that I just couldn't spend a third Christmas in the hospital.

"You better stay off your feet, mister, and keep things low key," my mom threatened.

Exasperated, I told her, "Mom! Quit bugging me."

That evening she prepared one of my favorite meals: rib eye steaks, twice baked potatoes, asparagus, and Caesar salad, topped off with homemade apple pie. After dinner I returned to the bedroom. My dad carried in the TV. "Don't stay up all night. You need your rest," my mom said as she passed my room en route to bed.

"I was kind of thinking it would be nice to watch the Pope say midnight Mass."

"Well, I guess that's OK," my mom said, softening. I watched the Pope give his final blessing and say "Merry Christmas" in 42 languages.

I woke up later, checked my Braille watch, and saw that it was 2:30 in the morning. Never knowing how much Cyclops decides to expel, I instinctively check it throughout the night. On this occasion as I reached down, I was alarmed to discover the bag was bursting full. *Crap*, I thought. *It's leaked out.*

"Dave? Are you asleep?" "What?"

"Can you get me a washcloth? My bag leaked." "Can't you get it yourself?"

"No. It's leaking." Grumbling, Dave flipped on the light and headed to the bathroom. I tossed off the sheets and sat up. My head began spinning and ringing so loudly I thought it was a siren outside. Even though I was blind, I saw black spots rapidly growing before my eyes. Quickly, I laid back down. Dave returned with the washcloth.

"Jeff, you're all bloody." "I am?"

"I better wake up Mom and Dad," he said, his demeanor changing from annoyance to alarm. "Something's wrong with Jeff," I heard him say from down the hall.

As my dad entered the room, I heard him mumble something. I couldn't tell what, but I knew it wasn't good. I was hoping Dave was wrong and turned to my dad for a second opinion.

"Is it diarrhea?" I asked hopefully.

"No," he said. "It's bright red blood." My mom appeared at the doorway.

"Martha, you better call the doctor." She called and left a message with his answering service. I couldn't make out her words but clearly heard the urgency in her voice.

"Cover Jeffrey up, Lloyd," my mom said when she returned. Hearing this, I thought, *Who cares? I feel like I'm dying and she's concerned that I'm naked.*

Ten minutes later, the doctor called. Up to this point, my dad was having me hold a washcloth over the blood leaking from my stitches. "Lloyd, the doctor said to put an ice cube against the stitches."

Even though my dad knew little about medicine, and in fact intentionally stayed clear of it, he said, "Ice cube? That's not going to stop the blood. Call him back." Not wanting to be a nuisance, my mom was hesitant about calling him back.

"Mom, call him," I said weakly.

After talking to the doctor again, she said, "He thinks the stitches have broken loose and wants us to meet him at the ER."

"Can you walk if we help you, Jeff?" my dad asked. I sat up, but the sirens in my ears once again wailed.

"No, I can't." My dad got the car started and had my mom get blankets while it warmed. When he pulled down the sheet to lift me, my mom gasped, "Oh, my Lord, Lloyd, the sheets are soaked with blood!"

"I've got the car going, Martha, we're leaving! What else can I do?"

He carried me to the car and placed me in the back seat with my stiff leg between the front buckets, Mom seated next to me. "I can't sit up, I gotta lean on you." I whispered.

"You go right ahead, Jeff," my mom responded.

"I'm so cold." She removed her coat and laid it over the blankets already wrapped around me.

After checking into the emergency room, we waited for the doctor. As luck would have it, my doctor was on vacation and it would take time for his associate to arrive. As I lay there, it was clear to me what I needed.

"Can you start an IV to give me fluids until the doctor arrives?" I pleaded. Based on what my parents had seen and on my low hemoglobin count, I had already lost one to two quarts of blood. Laying on the gurney, I began uncontrollably shaking and once again started hearing those sirens in my head. This time, though, it wasn't from the strain of trying to sit up.

"We have to wait for your doctor," the ER doctor reminded me. When my doctor arrived, he did a blood count and announced, "We're going to have to admit Jeff, and begin blood transfusions."

That's what I already told them, duh! I thought, angrily.

"His hemoglobin is extremely low and we're not sure why the sutures broke open," said the doctor.

Once re-sutured, with blood and saline lines inserted, I was moved to intensive care.

This was my third Christmas Day in the hospital.

Once I was stabilized, Mom went home with my dad, showered, and continued her preparation for the Christmas morning brunch she was hosting for the extended family. Since it was close to six a.m., she decided she may as well just stay up. She was emotionally spent and physically exhausted as the first of 25 relatives arrived at our home.

I later was told my Aunt Rose, known to march to a different drummer, said to my mom during brunch, "My dear Martha, I don't know what it is, but there's a glow about you. Your eyes are sparkling like diamonds!"

Her spinster sister, Ethel, characterized by having a realistic attitude toward life, interrupted, "Rose, for heaven sakes! Those aren't diamonds in her eyes. Poor Martha has been up all night. She's exhausted!"

"Well, they still look like diamonds."

My dad and brother Steve, being the most reserved of our family, excused themselves from the festivities to come down to the hospital and watch the Vikings game with me.

I was in the hospital for three or four days. My first day at home, my mom brought lunch to my bedroom. "My bag is filling up with something," I said with trepidation. "Is it brown or…?" Mom started crying.

"What is the matter with those doctors?" she hissed.

We caught it early enough for my mom to drive me in to be re-stitched. I returned once more to be re-sutured later that week. We were at least grateful that it never again occurred while I was asleep. Doctors finally determined that six years of high dose prednisone had compromised my tissue's ability to heal. Not only that, it was also elevating my blood sugar level and decreasing my bone density.

"We have to wean you off prednisone," my rheumatologist said in no uncertain terms. He immediately cut my dosage in half.

As my senior year in high school wound down, I noticed my hands beginning to swell, and my fingers curling inward and sideways. While sitting in class I'd rub my now swelling, painful wrists for relief and force my hands flat, stretching out my fingers on the desktop. But by the end of my senior year, my hands and fingers had become permanently malformed.

With the latest turn of events, I began wondering if my chances for stable health were destined to career into a dead end of perpetual problems.

"Turn your ear to me, come quickly to my rescue; be my rock of refuge, a strong fortress to save me." Psalm 31:2

My family in 1976. Note how young I appear as a full grown adult; I got into drive- in movies free until I was 24 years old. Front: Dad and Mom. Rear, left to right: Dave (22), Steve (16), Dana (18), Me(20) and Mikey (14).

CHAPTER 41

COLLEGE: GOING ABOUT IT THE HARD WAY

I was looking forward to joining many of my high school friends at Inver Hills Junior College. As the summer progressed, and the start of college drew near, my stoma was doing its best to reverse what it had done months earlier. The stoma was now receding back into my abdomen. Just a week prior to starting IHJC, another ileostomy stoma revision was required, but this time not on an emergency basis. A stoma, like a belly button, can be an "innie" or an "outie." Mine had become an innie and needed to be repositioned one inch out to ensure proper fit. I was concerned that this surgery would delay the start of college and put me behind the eight ball right off the bat. Much to my surprise, my hospital stay was uncharacteristically short. I was in and out of the hospital in one week and started college on time.

In the meantime, my mom was doing whatever she could to hold things together at home. From a physical standpoint, she somehow got through it all. Popeye had his spinach, Underdog had his energy pill, and Martha Smith had her coffee! Yes, I'm being facetious. But another part of me wonders... the sheer amount of caffeine she ingested, complemented by three packs a day of inhaled nicotine until she quit smoking twenty-five years ago—most probably contributed in some way to her ability to blast through the challenges, not even giving herself a chance to dwell on them.

During a class called "Drug Use and Abuse" at Inver Hills, my teacher, a pharmacist, was describing the effects of caffeine. "Caffeine is addictive," he explained. "Large amounts of it can cause nervousness, insomnia, heart arrhythmia…even hallucinations."

"Mr. Brundage," I said, raising my hand. "How many cups of coffee would it take to become hallucinatory?"

"Oh, I imagine someone would have to drink at least twenty cups a day for that to begin to happen."

I went home and casually asked my mom, "How many cups of coffee would you say you drink every day?"

"I've never counted. H-m-m, maybe thirty?"

"Well, what's your daily minimum?"

"That is the minimum. Sometimes I have more."

Figuring there must be some mistake with Mr. Brundage's information, I was eager to tell him what my mom had said.

"She said she drinks about thirty cups a day."

"Thirty cups! No way! How little are the cups?" he asked.

"She uses mugs and cups," I responded.

"Still, Jeff, if that were true, she'd be bouncing off the walls ready for the loony bin."

Later that school year, Mr. Brundage, who had become a personal friend, was a guest at our home. He found my mom to be anything but bouncing off the walls and ready for the loony bin. If coffee was the magic elixir that helped to keep an immaculate house, serve home-made meals daily, chauffeur, shop, and be a shoulder for five kids, then, hooray for coffee!

But coffee was hardly the panacea my mom was looking for when it came to my dad's issues with drinking. Incidents at home were coming to a head. In a desperate attempt to keep the family together, my mom hired the toughest divorce lawyer in the Twin Cities and served my dad with papers. My dad was shocked back into his senses, suddenly realizing he could be financially ruined and, more importantly, lose his children. He realized how much we loved and needed him. He quit drinking. My dad has been sober for 33 years, and recently he and my mom celebrated their 57th wedding anniversary. He could not be a more supportive dad over the last 33 years.

I never intentionally shrink from a challenge. I have discovered time and again that I grow the most when I am outside my comfort zone. Besides, not participating in something that I know to be enriching would always make me wonder "what if?" But neither do I look for the absolutely most challenging way to go from point A to point B. That's why I appreciated starting post-secondary education at Inver Hills Junior College. Its campus consisted of six buildings surrounding a plaza, which I could easily navigate in light of my arthritis.

Although the setting was new, I was experiencing the same old standard of low expectation of high school and elsewhere.

Some faculty members could not acknowledge that I was ready for a greater challenge. For example, a well meaning but misguided economics professor would not let me fail a test. He always gave multiple-choice tests, which he would orally administer to me.

"All right, Jeff, here are your choices. A, or *BEEE*, or C, or D."
"Uh, C?" I responded.

"Let me read those choices to you again. A, or *BEEE*, or C, or D."
"Um, D?"

The instructor took a deep breath and said, "It's a little noisy in here. If you just focus a little more I think you'll be on the right track. Is it A, or BEEEEE, or—well, we already know it's not C or D."

I didn't study for the test, so just fail me like you should, I thought.

By the time the economics final came around, I was so defeated that I was succumbing to the effects of self-fulfilling prophecy. I just didn't care. The instructor gave permission for a buddy of mine to orally administer the test. "Jeff, is it, A, B, C, or D?"

"Tom, just fill in all the letter B's." "What!?"

"Well, at least I'll get 25% right," I sighed. I somehow passed the class with a C, if that's any surprise.

When the course finally ended, a fellow classmate and I decided to drown our shame with jazz music at a local club. As we began getting into the music, my buddy noticed our economics teacher sitting at a nearby table. My buddy, equally ashamed of his grade, shifted his chair to avoid eye contact.

Maybe it's just coincidence, but it seemed wherever I turned that night, there was our teacher. Later when we went to use the restroom, our economics instructor was following right behind. We kept our heads down. Thank goodness for the dim lighting of a jazz club. At the end of the evening, as we headed out to the car there he was again! It was like the Twilight Zone. I was getting sweaty. I never again wanted to feel the guilt that resulted from having taken the easy way out.

My abysmal failure in economics should have come as no surprise given my real life experiences with micro-economics. While at IHJC, my desire to earn money was heightened by seeing friends whose part-time jobs offered them the independence and the self-confidence I craved. During my ongoing effort to find a job and experience its benefits, I was introduced to a multi-level marketing company that featured a vast array of powders, pills, and potions—all designed to cure what ails you. I was deluged with cassette tapes extolling the wondrous effects of these health products. Some of their propaganda mentioned that taking B-Complex in large doses would instantly eliminate the effects of intoxication.

My friend Joe was very much a party boy. He often enjoyed tying one on. Besides this lifestyle being a path to nowhere, Joe's behavior risked feeling the wrath of his dad who was a strict disciplinarian and former drill sergeant. Unlike the vast majority of my friends who were tired of me going on and on about the wonders of vitamins and minerals, Joe was intrigued.

"You mean, Jeff, I can get drunk and take a bunch of this—what do you call it?"

"B-Complex."

"And I'll sober up?"

"Yup—guaranteed," I said, desperate to make a sale.

The next time I saw Joe, I assumed he'd had an opportunity to try the B-complex hangover cure.

"So Joe, did you try the B-Complex?" "I sure did," he said dryly. "Did it work?"

"It cleared my head right up."

"Great—do you want to buy some more?"

"I don't think so."

"How come, it sobered you up, didn't it?"

"It sure did. I ground it up like you said and mixed it with water and drank it down in the driveway before I went into the house. I only had a couple of beers, so I thought for sure your vitamins would take care of it."

"And...?"

"I got into bed, and a minute later I puked all over the place! I heard my dad yelling, 'What the hell is going on?' He came running into my bedroom. 'You're drunk again!'

'No I'm not, Dad—I swear—I think I got some bad vitamins.' 'Right, Joe, bad vitamins—just how stupid do you think I am?'"

Right then and there my vitamin sales career ended, but I had laid down another stepping stone on the road of hard knocks to eventually becoming a successfully self-employed magician

Looking ahead to a four-year degree, I began considering my major while completing general requirements at Inver Hills Junior College. I had always enjoyed writing as a creative exercise and thought advertising copywriting might be a good field to use this skill set. Besides, creative writing seemed fun, at least based on how it was portrayed in the TV show *Bewitched*.

A counselor at IHJC recommended Southwest State University in Marshall, Minnesota. "Do they have a degree in advertising copywriting?" I asked.

"Not per se, but they have what's called an inter-disciplinary program that enables a student to customize his own major."

"Sounds good to me." (What did I know?)

"Besides, Jeff, it has a wonderfully designed campus where everything is indoors except for the residence halls," she added.

It turned out that this was the most useful aspect of her recommendation and not their "inter-disciplinary" program. SSU offered a degree in marketing but nothing specific in advertising copywriting.

After spring quarter of 1978, I returned to the Twin Cities where my State Services for the Blind counselor recommended I improve my independent living skills and enroll in a blind skills refresher course. I met a girl named Stacy who also was totally blind, and we became an item for the next two years. (You know what they say about how low lighting makes everyone look more attractive...)

While attending the eight-week course, I lived in a building for seniors that had a floor dedicated to students who were part of the training program. I was assigned a mobility teacher to improve my travel skills. This teacher had been previously introduced to me in high school by Tom Dosch.

Like Tom Dosch, my new mobility instructor had unconventional teaching approaches, but unlike Tom, no wisdom behind her methodology. She had liberal ideas about mixing business with pleasure. That part I didn't mind. During one of our sessions, I said, "Hey! How about we stop and take a little break?" Standing in front of a drinking establishment, I suggested, "Let's pop in for a quick brewski." Just 21, it was only the legality of my age and not the level of wisdom that caused me to come up with an idea that should have been squashed by the older—and supposedly wiser—mobility teacher. It was a very hot day, and I hadn't had anything to eat yet. My empty stomach, combined with the fact that I weighed less than 100 pounds, made the beer really disorient me, but I wasn't about to admit it.

My assignment was to practice crossing a busy city street at the intersection by listening for parallel traffic on my left and to walk alongside it until reaching the curb on the other side. The light turned green, and I started off on a straight line until a semi-truck on my right began revving his engine in order to get off to a fast start when the light turned green. With each rev of his engine, I began unconsciously veering more and more to my left until I unknowingly missed the entire corner of the curb on the far side. In my altered state, I was thinking, *Wow! This has to be the widest street I've ever crossed!* I was thinking these things as I merrily walked up the middle of the street up to the next intersection. Finally I stopped because nothing I was hearing was making sense to me. At that point, my mobility teacher announced her presence and explained what I had done wrong. Her explanation contained no mention of the real cause of my mishap—the beer!

In the fall, I returned to Southwest State and continued my studies. Because SSU didn't offer an advertising copywriting curriculum, I became discouraged and changed my major three times over the next year. I was confused and apathetic about attending classes and, not surprisingly, developed an ulcer.

One day an area State Services for the Blind counselor scheduled a meeting. "Jeff, I'm sorry, but everything you have demonstrated here at Southwest State leads me to no other conclusion than to have to discontinue our support of your plan— if, for that matter, a plan even exists." (*"I was so dedicated, they actually had to kick me out,"* or so I spun it to my friends after returning home.)

But my time at Southwest State certainly wasn't a waste. My enrollment at SSU resulted in additional transferable credits and the opportunity to meet Mark Roesler, a student who would be an indispensable encourager and play a key role in my future.

Saving all 88 lbs of me or, "Where Trouble Goes, Angels Follow"

Throughout my life, God has sent guardian angels and encouragers to lift me up when I needed it most. A guardian angel moment once happened en route home from Southwest State. Temperatures were hovering around 20 below zero, nothing unusual for the dead of winter here in Minnesota. I was shaken awake by an abrupt jerk.

"What's happening?" I asked no one in particular.

"A bunch of wheels came off the bus," someone behind me yelled. Somehow, our driver kept the fishtailing bus from ending up in the ditch.

Shaken after the harrowing experience, everyone was talking at once. "Man! The highway's smokin'!"

"That groove's got to be a mile long!" "Look! The axle broke off."

The rattled driver encouraged calm and asked if anyone had been hurt.

After being reassured everyone was okay, he said, "I've been driving for 35 years and nothing like this has ever happened before! We might be here for a while, but we can run the engine for heat. I'm going to try to flag someone down."

A camaraderie commenced among the passengers as we decompressed. Camaraderie gave way to fatigue as we waited five hours until a new bus arrived. Our emergency parking job left us on the edge of a three-foot ditch. This was compounded by the angle of the bus, which tilted away from the ditch. This made the last step truly a doozy, about five feet! One at a time, people were lowered off the bus into raised, waiting arms.

My encouragers have been from all walks of life and have helped me through all different times of my life. Mark Roesler, whom I met at Southwest State, has been an extraordinary friend and encourager. He had signed up to be an attendant for students with disabilities and was asked at the start of the 1978 school year to serve as my sighted guide until I could acclimate to campus life.

I now regret the grief I gave this poor man.

Some students considered Mark the nicest guy on campus. This mild-mannered gentleman later told me of the impression I made on him, "Jeff, I was *that* close to punching out your lights." What would drive such a kind soul to the brink of violence? I was never on time when he came to my room to escort me to breakfast, which made him late for his first class, which he coincidentally ended up failing. I'd turn the thermostat in his room to 90 degrees after he'd fall asleep. He'd wake up thinking he had a case of malaria. I'd draw a funny face on his mirror with Magic Marker then urge him to look at himself in the mirror because I was concerned he didn't seem healthy.

After piling up long distance minutes into hours talking to my girlfriend, I ended up not being able to pay my bill and the phone company cut off my privileges. No problem. I simply began using Mark's phone until the phone company discontinued his unpaid long-distance services. "I'm not going to enable your irresponsible behavior by paying my bill just so you can start abusing my phone again," Mark complained.

Other times I'd coerce Mark to get up after midnight, throw a coat over his pajama shorts, and peddle to Taco John's to satisfy my regular cravings for one taco and two burritos. For his trouble, I'd buy him a taco. He quit making midnight runs for me when he found out I had bought two tacos and a burrito for someone else making the same fast food run. "What?! I do way more for you than Ron, and all I get is one stinking taco?" he argued.

Some people get bent out of shape so easily; touchy, touchy, touchy. "Nothing personal, Mark. Ron's price is just higher," I reasoned.

But Mark must have seen in me the man I'd eventually become: someone who's working on improving and becoming the man God desires. I put Mark into uncomfortable situations in our relationship even when I wasn't trying to give him a hard time. Once he was leading a Bible study in his dorm room. The group was discussing how the Bible says, "If someone wants your cloak, give them your coat as well." The group was discussing the Christian principle of giving money to someone and having the attitude of not expecting it repaid. Unknowingly, at that very moment, I knocked on Mark's door and said:

"Mark, excuse me for interrupting, but could I have ten bucks?" Mark, of course, didn't want to appear to the group as a hypocrite. "All I've got is a twenty. Keep it," he said sighing.

"Wow! Thanks a lot, Marky!" (I must confess that I've left out a few incidents when I *wasn't* so nice to him.)

The reason I consider Mark so special is that he saved my life on three occasions. The most important of these salvations was in the spiritual sense. One night Mark asked, "Jeff, do you know for sure where you're going when you die?" It had been my understanding that we could never be totally sure of our salvation. Only God would truly know. Mark showed me from scripture that we can be assured of our eternal destiny:

1 John 5:13, "I write these things to you who believe in the name of the Son of God so that you may know that you have eternal life."

Romans 10:9, "If you confess with your mouth Jesus as Lord and believe in your heart that God raised Him from the dead, you will be saved."

Acts 4:12, "And there is salvation in no one else, for there is no other name under heaven given among men by which we must be saved.", ESV

Moments after having prayed what some have called "the sinner's prayer," where I trusted that Jesus' act of dying on the cross had forgiven and removed the penalty of my sins and any sin to come, I sat quietly in my dorm room really not feeling any different—nor did I even know if I was supposed to.

In fact, the next day when Mark brought me to the little country church he had been attending, whose number of pews totaled three (and always reminded me of being a part of a playhouse experience) I raised my hand when the pastor asked the congregation whether there was anyone who wanted Jesus' forgiveness. After the service I was escorted to a room where an elder asked me if I knew that the humility and sincerity of my raised hand had allowed God's gift of forgiveness to enter me and had guaranteed me eternal life. Not feeling I could presume such a thing, I responded, "No. I didn't realize that."

"Well it's true. It's clear as night from day in the Bible," he said confidently. "And not from anything you did, but everything having to do with what Jesus did," he added.

Those in the church who had already received the gift of salvation shook my hand or hugged me following the service. Mark and I walked out of the church and I felt a brightness inside, difficult to describe. As God had appointed the weather for that morning—sunny with a fresh light breeze—I wondered if He had designed such a day for me or for another reason only known to Him.

A part of me didn't know whether my feeling of brightness was the action of the Holy Spirit or an adrenaline rush. But in the following days all I wanted to do was spend hours listening to the Bible on records in my dorm room because of the comfort it brought me, even to the concern of dorm-mates. "We don't see you hanging out anymore, Jeff. You're in your room all the time. What's wrong?"

Only God's grace can save us through faith in Jesus Christ when we believe that Jesus suffered the penalty of death as a substitute for our sins. God is calling everyone to make a free decision to choose life everlasting and sometimes uses messengers to spread this Good News. I believe Mark to be a divine messenger sent to watch over me.

This was further illustrated one stormy, blizzard-filled afternoon in Marshall. This town is located in the middle of nowhere, unless you consider mile after mile of graded farmland to be somewhere. By eliminating natural windbreaks, a normal wind speed can be 15- 20 mph. This January day, by every definition, was a windy day. Wind velocity was 40-50 mph. Temperatures were well below zero with wind chill factors hovering close to 50 degrees below zero. As the snows swirled and began drifting, many of the students skipped class and stayed in their dorms.

Having learned how to navigate the campus, I decided to make my way to the central academic building. (It was probably to practice on the pinball machine in the student center. Yes, yes. I sure play a mean pinball.) It had been arranged at the start of the school year that I would live in the dorm closest to the academic building because of my arthritis. But the combination of slippery footing, a curvy, uneven sidewalk, and the fact that I was packing a full 88 pounds at the time enabled a big gust of wind to lift me off the ground and throw me into a fresh snowdrift. There I lay, realizing my potential peril as no one was around. There was no way I could stand up on my own given my surgically fused left knee and general overall arthritic stiffness. After about 10-15 minutes, I was pretty cold.

Suddenly someone was yelling at me, "What are you lying there for?" It was Mark Roesler, now laughing uncontrollably.

"Well, I'm not making snow angels!"

He climbed into the drift, lifted me up, and brushed off the snow. My pinball appointment was rescheduled.

In life, eventually, things have a tendency to balance out and justice is served.

One day I said to Mark, "I think you need psychoanalysis," and told him to lie down on my dorm bed. Naturally, Mark grumbled about this stupidity, but before he could tell me to take a hike, I rushed out my door intending to grab a pen and notepad from his room next door. Unfortunately, I hadn't realized someone had moved out and left a metal bed frame leaning up against the wall. Hearing me cry out, accompanied by the crashing sounds of the bed frame, Mark ran out into the hallway and discovered me moaning and semi- conscious. I was dangling upside down by a couple of my belt loops caught on a bedspring. The only part of me touching the floor was my now aching head. Mark helped me down and back into my room. A couple of girls who had wandered by asked if I was okay, and Mark explained what had happened. They came in, gently stroked my head, and said, "You poor thing." I decided their attention was worth a bump on the head! (Making lemonade out of lemons, huh?)

Mark's mission as a special divine messenger, unknowingly sent to protect me, continued following our time at Southwest State. Don Dinger (more about Don later), Mark, and I went on a camping trip the following summer. We pitched the tent. OK, *they* pitched the tent, while I advised and they ignored me.

"Here," Mark said, "You've got plenty of hot air. Blow up your own mattress."

It was late, so we climbed into our sleeping bags. Mark could not fall asleep. He found my pattern of snoring, followed by sudden silence, then choking and sputtering awake a full minute later to be rather disconcerting. He kept waking me up whispering, "Jeff! You're not breathing. Something's really weird with your snoring." Annoyed, I said, "Quit bugging me!" He couldn't stand it any longer, so he left the tent and went on a long walk in the dark to relax.

My brothers had been giving me a hard time about my strange style of snoring for a few years. I thought they were just teasing me, but I should have put two-and-two together. I was sleepy all the time.

Finally, Mark convinced me that I should mention this to a doctor. I was diagnosed with sleep apnea, a condition where the breathing tube closes during sleep and causes the body to eventually gasp for air. This condition not only ruins quality sleep by not allowing entrance to deep sleep but puts great strain on the heart in the process. Individuals in far better condition than me have died from undiagnosed apnea. Reggie White, the NFL defensive end, was someone who died as a result of untreated sleep apnea. Frankly, I'm surprised Mark didn't quit saving my life after the first time based on how I treated him in college. I'll chalk it up to Mark's patience while waiting for the Holy Spirit to change my heart and make me aware of my shortcomings.

Even though Mark thought enough of me to save my life three times, he gave me my just desserts, literally. On three separate occasions, following our time together at Southwest State, he spilled a strawberry milkshake on my lap. The first time was the result of pouring it out of the metal canister into my fountain glass but ignoring the basic tenet of breaking up the frozen lump *before* pouring it. The second cold shock occurred after Mark dutifully broke up that pesky, frozen ice cream lump but the metal canister slipped out of his hands because of the surrounding condensation. The wet lap triple play was completed on a subsequent occasion shortly after I said, "Here, let me do it this time, I don't want you to spill it."

"Don't be insulting; what do you think? I'm going to do it again?"

"I'd really feel safer doing it myself," I insisted.

Well, with the combination of Mark's pride being at stake and rushing things a bit—the stir spoon knocked over the glass filled with milk shake. Maybe there really is something to what psychologists describe as demonstrating passive-aggressive behavior.

In case you think the scales of justice were still imbalanced, restitution of my past sins continued as the mantle passed from father to son. After Mark and his wife Laura had their first child, his son Carl did his unwitting best to remind me not to mess with his daddy. Mark and Laura thought it would be a good idea for Carl, at the time a precocious lad of five, to guide me to their parked car because their arms were full of stuff. I thought this would be a nice learning opportunity for Carl. I held on to his shoulder instead of his arm because of his short stature and reminded him to be sure to tell me when I should step down off the curb. He approached the curb at an angle so I ended up at the curb first. Because I happened to step off the curb with my fused knee still atop the curb, I tipped forward like a tree being felled and pulled Carl down with me, landing on top of him in the street. After we were helped up with a few bruises and a torn shirt to show for it, I asked Carl later in the car,

"What did you learn from this lesson?"

He thought about it and after a while said, "The next time you fall when I'm walking with you…"

"Yes?"

"I'm going to be sure to get out of the way!"

"He reached down from on high and took hold of me; He drew me out of deep waters." Psalm 18:16

184

"It is not the destination where you end up but the mishaps and memories you create along the way!" – Penelopy Riley

"It is one of the blessings of old friends that you can afford to be stupid with them." – Ralph Waldo Emerson

CHAPTER 42

ARE THE WALLS OF ACADEMIA CLOSING IN OR IS IT JUST ME?

After I was kicked out of SSU in 1979, I wasn't ready to move back home after enjoying my taste of independence. A college friend, Mario Murga, from Lima, Peru couldn't afford to go home for the summer and needed a summer job anyway to pay for tuition. We shared an apartment in south Minneapolis that happened to be located next to a Dairy Queen. After three months of living it up with daily visits to the DQ, I was surprised to see I had gained 30 pounds, which put me at a more normal weight for my height—120 pounds. *Wait 'til Mom and Dad hear THIS*, I thought as I dialed the phone, remembering their myriad appeals over the years for me to gain weight. *No one's gonna call ME scrawny anymore!* I smiled to myself, waiting for my dad to answer.

"30 pounds?! You need to go on a diet!" said my surprisingly disapproving dad. At first I thought he was joking until he began to detail a weight-loss plan for me. Who'd a thunk someone who was chronically malnourished all those years would have to become a calorie counter in three short months?

In the fall, State Services for the Blind recommended a course in remedial English and more vocational aptitude testing that included piece work. I went along with their recommendation, since my vocational aspirations had reached an all-time low.

Returning to Inver Hills College one day to visit my favorite teachers, a counselor different from the one who had recommended Southwest State asked how things were going. She was surprised by what had happened at SSU, and was astounded by the proposed plan of action. Over lunch she said to me, "You are capable of so much more, Jeff. I know this, just from my familiarity with you." After discussing my goals, she said, "I think you should go to the University of Minnesota. They have advertising copywriting within their School of Journalism." She arranged a meeting with a counselor from the Office of Disabilities at the University of Minnesota.

"Will I be able to handle navigating this huge campus?" I asked the U of M counselor.

"We can work with the office of registration to make sure your classes are not too far apart from one another," she reassured me.

That very same day my mom was lamenting to a friend about my lack of vocational direction.

"Martha, I know someone who's a counselor at the University of Minnesota Office of Disabilities. Let me call her and see if she can set up an appointment to see Jeff."

These two events happening on the same day, I took as a sign.

I passed the written entrance test and enrolled in the School of Journalism, eventually becoming its first blind graduate.

Before starting at the University of Minnesota, I remembered back to seventh grade and how much territory I could cover using crutches. Now I was about to begin navigating around one of the largest college campuses in the world and wasn't looking forward to it. It was obvious I couldn't go back to crutches! That left me with my specially made leather orthotic shoes that were stiff and uncomfortable and prevented me from walking for long distances without pain. My doctors said I couldn't wear tennis shoes because they lacked support. This made no sense to me since I knew I wouldn't be running in them anyway. I was lamenting to my buddy Mark Roesler about all the walking that lay ahead of me at the U of M.

"Let me take you to Duggan's shoes and find you something comfortable," Mark suggested.

"Good luck," I responded, knowing the difficulty in fitting one foot that was a size three in adults and the other foot a size five.

"They're supposed to be able to fit anyone," he encouraged. The store employed an old fashioned, middle-aged shoe salesman who, with his measuring tools, sliding foot sizer and angled foot rests, suggested I try New Balance walking shoes. I discovered a whole new world after being fitted and purchasing a pair.

"It's like floating on air," I instantly remarked after trying the shoes out. It took a little getting used to balancing on this softer surface—funny, given their name. I went from being able to only walk two to three blocks before experiencing painful feet to now being able to walk one mile before my feet felt sore.

If I had known about these comfortable shoes years earlier, maybe I wouldn't have had to suffer the consequences of staying on crutches so long following my hip surgery in seventh grade. The crutches led to atrophy and imbalance in my legs, necessitating the permanent use of a cane. My improved mobility from the new tennis shoes greatly lifted my spirits.

Timing is important in a magician's performance. But in my case, it's even more important on the stage of life. There have been more magical moments in my *real* life than during any time on stage. One of the magical moments that ultimately led me to where I am today came as a result of attending the U of M. There I was exposed to a large variety of people, ideas and opportunities.

When I finally graduated from the U of M in 1985. I could brag about the fact I had a ten-year degree or tell the truth that it took me ten years to get through a four-year degree.

Some of the additional time it took me to graduate was due to a misguided plan of action, recommended by the junior college counselor. But the other delay was due to my fears about how I would complete specific requirements to graduate.

One of the requirements was to complete three term papers in Latin history studies. The other requirement was to complete one year in a foreign language. My lack of writing experience resulting from the missed years of school, and the difficulty I had using Braille to assist in composing papers due to arthritic fingers, was enough to keep me from completing my degree. The alternative to Braille was almost as ineffective: using a tape recorder on which to compose my papers. Writing is a process that requires constant rewriting and changes. Using a tape recorder to come up with a finished piece of writing is awkward at best. If I wanted to insert a later thought within the recording, I'd have to talk really fast and hope I wouldn't be erasing something I'd already recorded.

Again God used encouragers, this time Mark Roesler and Roxy Hale, to help me overcome obstacles: three "incomplete" grades on my transcript, which included a foreign language requirement, that delayed my graduation until 1985.

Notwithstanding my trepidation about completing three term papers, I couldn't see how I could complete my foreign language requirement. Spanish, which everyone told me was the easiest language to learn, would require speaking it in class. A cloud of negativity hovered over me as I visualized the difficulty and embarrassment I'd have stuttering in a whole new language.

"I've wanted to learn Spanish for a long time anyway. Why don't we take it and study together?" my friend Mark suggested. At the same time, his wife Laura, to whom writing came so naturally and who also knew Spanish, said:

"You can hire me as a writing coach to get those term papers done and use me as a Spanish coach, too."

"Great. OK. Here's what I want you to write about, Laura," I said excitedly.

"No. You're going to write it, Jeff. I'll be here if you need help," she clarified. The day before the Spanish class began, Mark called me.

"How's it going, Jeff?" He seemed a little nervous. "Fine. Why are you calling?"

"Well, I have wonderful news for one of us."

"Don't tell me...does it have something to do with us taking Spanish together?" I asked in alarm.

"I just got a call from UPS. They're going to pay me $12 an hour to throw boxes around! Isn't that great news!"

"You promised to hold my hand through this thing, Mark!"

"I'm sorry. I can't pass up this opportunity."

After calling the Spanish language office at the University, they set me up with a tutor at a very affordable price. Her name was Roxy Hale. She supplied me with all the help I needed, and in fact she, her husband, and I became good friends. In spite of consolidating a year of Spanish language into nine weeks of summer, I finished the class with straight As. I finally graduated at the end of the summer of 1985. The next day, I forgot everything except for no and si...maybe because I no see! (Sorry, I couldn't help myself.)

While plowing our way through Spanish, Roxy invited me to a Christian camp later in the summer. She encouraged me to realize and develop my natural talents of humor and creativity by suggesting I bring a few magic tricks along with me to the camp. I attribute so much of my success to encouraging people like Roxy who said I was more capable than I believed myself to be. This camp had a safe and loving atmosphere and used fun icebreakers such as having a talent show to create bonding among the campers. The name "Amazing Jeffo" was first invented there when nobody else had the nerve to volunteer for the talent show. In spite of stuttering and never having performed in public before, I was desperate for attention. That desperation led to the introduction by the camp director and my divinely inspired name of Amazing Jeffo!

At the show, the emcee invited campers to come up on stage and share their talents, but no one would volunteer. Roxy jokingly whispered in my ear, "Jeff, you've got to go for it! With your talent, the worst that could happen is you'd end up placing second!"

"Gee, thanks," I said. But my desperation for attention won out, and I did it. I performed five or six tricks and screwed up every one of them. In my panic, I tried to cover up with jokes, hoping no one would notice the mistakes. When the ordeal was done, several people came up to me and said, "What a great comedy routine you have, screwing up the tricks on purpose and then pretending to be all panicky! Great act, Jeff!"

Who's pretending, I thought, but out loud with a hitch of my pants and a confident sniff a la Barney Fife I said, "Awww....it's just a little something I've been workin' on lately."

"But He said to me, "My grace is sufficient for you, for my power is made perfect in weakness." 2 Corinthians 12:9

"If you only do what you know you can do, you never do very much."
– Tom Krause

NUDIST COLONY MEMBER ALERT: The naked dress code require-ment will be waived for members with ileostomies. Trust us, it's in everyone's best interest.

CHAPTER 43

MAYBE WE CAN LOSE HIM IN THE CROWD

⌒

I n 1984, my brother Dave was the second among my siblings to marry; our sister Dana had married three months earlier. Since I had memorized and recited a reading from the Bible at my sister's wedding, Dave asked, "Jeff, could you do a reading at our wedding?"

"Sure," I said hesitating, still dealing with severe stuttering. I had made it through my reading at Dana's wedding only because I had ample time to memorize and practice the long reading. With months of preparation under my belt, I felt reasonably happy about my performance at her wedding. But Dave's request of me was only weeks before his November wedding date. Without having had effective speech therapy up to that point, I tried to combine what little methods for fluid speech I had, but simply didn't have enough time to practice. My recitation sounded terrible. At least some of the attention was taken off me and instead focused on a professional opera singer who, right before the wedding day, had come down with an upper respiratory infection. What my uncle played on the organ as accompaniment came across sounding like a totally different song because the singer was so off-key. (Poor Dave. Well, at least he and Linda are still married.)

On Dave's wedding day, I had a wonderful opportunity to apply the "Mumzy Dearest" nickname I had given to Mom several years earlier following her describing to me a tell-all book called *Mommy Dearest*. Dave's reception was held at the majestic St. Paul Athletic Club. My brother Steve and I, both groomsmen, drove to the reception from the church. Steve, never much of a partier, left the reception before the rest of the family. As there were hundreds in attendance, Steve's early departure did not become obvious to the rest of us.

I was enjoying working the crowd table by table. As the evening drew on, tables began emptying.

"Can we bring you to another table, Jeff?" someone would ask me before leaving.

"Sure. Just bring me to another table and I'll hang out there."

That table would eventually empty, and someone before leaving would ask, "Are you riding with someone from your family, Jeff?"

"Oh yes; don't worry. I'll catch a ride with one of them," I responded confidently. Steve and Mike still lived at home and drove. *Plenty of rides for everyone,* I thought.

At some point, I realized no one was coming over to invite me to their table. In fact, once the band stopped playing, it was uncomfortably quiet. Not wanting to look like a helpless, abandoned blind guy, I stood up, nonchalantly put my hand in my pocket, and slowly made my way to where I guessed was the entrance to the ballroom. As I casually moved along, trying to disguise what really were cautious steps because I had no white cane with me, I periodically stopped to give the appearance that I had everything under control, sniffed, took a sip of my drink and continued on.

I finally made my way to the elevators. It took me a while to find the down button. The building had 16 floors. I stepped into the elevator and the elevator started down before I could feel if any of the buttons were marked with Braille. It eventually stopped, the doors opened, and there, strolling by, was the bridegroom Dave and his bride Linda making their way toward the exit. Linda saw me and said in surprise, "Jeff? What are you doing in there?"

"I don't know," I said honestly.

"Well, where's Mom and Dad?" Dave asked.

"I guess everyone went home. You're not doing anything. Can you guys give me a ride home?" I asked, knowing the answer.

Dave answered tersely, "No, Jeff. I've got stuff to do! Wait right there." Dave shortly returned with his friend Evan and his wife Shea.

"Sure, Dave. I can give Jeff a lift," Evan laughed as he headed to the elevator. "So everyone just took off without you, huh Jeff?" "I guess they figured this was their chance to lose me in the crowd. Just when you think you know your own family…" We laughed about it all the way home.

"Remember me, Mumzy Dearest, your son?" I said after my mom opened the front door with Evan alongside me. I reserve the "Mumzy Dearest" label particularly for when there are other people around.

"Evan, I'm so embarrassed. You probably think I'm a terrible mother!"

I milked the situation for all it was worth. In general, I've always enjoyed rattling people's cages, not only because it forces interaction, which recharges me as an extrovert, but also helps people more easily see me as a person first.

"And he has given us this command: Anyone who loves God must also love their brother." 1 John 4:21

Don't you just hate it when you can't find something because someone moved it…two inches to the left?

My brother, Dave Smith, 1985 Mr. Minnesota Middle Weight champion. (Not grass-fed like Mikey.)

194

CHAPTER 44

"TH-TH-THAT'S ALL FOLKS" OR IT REALLY IS HOW YOU SAY IT

O ne of the reasons my purpose and place in the world was slow to evolve was due to my negative self-image, rooted in my struggle with stuttering. The various physical disruptions to my life between kindergarten and seventh grade amounted to missing roughly half my years of school. My long-term absences made me feel more like an outsider and kept me from establishing friendships, which only added stress and contributed to my worsening speech. My inability to effectively express myself skewed my thinking about what I could offer others. Before ever becoming a professional presenter, opportunities were offered to me to help others by sharing with them what I had gone through. "How could I?" I argued, both to those asking and to myself. "I stutter!"

Stuttering was my albatross. It has been the thorn in my side, even more so than rheumatoid arthritis, ulcerative colitis, blindness, joint repair and replacements, family alcoholism, etc. I felt embarrassment and frustration as I labored to communicate my thoughts and release my frozen vocal cords.

What must they be thinking about me? My over-active imagination was in full throttle feeding me self-destructive possibilities: *What a babbling idiot...Why does he sound so nervous? Come on, I've got places to go and people to see; spit it out already!*

The content of what I had to say was lost amidst the way in which it was being said. "Uh...what was that, Jeff? I didn't catch that," they'd say.

Are you kidding? I thought. The resulting frustration made my second attempt even more overwhelming. The most damaging dagger to my spirit, however, was my own attitude of resignation and failure to attempt to communicate. I don't even want to think of the number of times I sat motionless at my school desk while the teacher waited for someone to answer a question. Even when I knew the answer, or had an idea to offer, there was no way I was about to expose myself to more humiliation.

Stuttering is more than a physical manifestation of stress. It affects all aspects of a person's being. Emotionally, it is frustrating not being able to say something when you want to say it. Intellectually, it can keep you from verbally sharing your thoughts and ideas. Spiritually, it leads you to think of yourself as less than God's beautiful creation; psychologically, it's a barrier to being a whole person. Stuttering was a major disability for me, particularly as a blind person. I believe having clear, verbal communication is more essential to someone who is blind, if for no other reason than that more description on their part is required. I base this statement on the axiom that a picture paints a thousand words (That is, if you know where the picture is.)

My college buddy, Mark Roesler, said to me, "I see stuttering as your biggest disability, but, ironically, it's the thing you can do the most about." What my good friend was saying was attitude is the most disabling thing in life. I could let it defeat me, or I could keep working to improve it.

One day around dinner time, while I was attending a stuttering support group at the U of M, my dad, who never said much but could be very funny when he wanted, asked my mom, "Where's Jeff, Martha?"

"He's at stuttering class," she responded.

"He doesn't need stuttering class—He stutters just fine!" quipped my dad.

On another occasion, Mr. Oslund, a friend of my dad's, arrived at our house before my dad got home. He joined my brother Steve and me at the kitchen table to wait. Mr. Oslund struck up idle conversation to pass the time. "How have things been going, Jeff?" My longwinded answer contained few actual words but many incoherent syllables. When Dad eventually arrived home and went on his way with Mr. Oslund, my ever "supportive" brother Steve said, "I'm kind of surprised that Mr. Oslund didn't have a nervous breakdown. I was watching him listen to you while you tried to answer his question. His whole body was twisting and tensing with every stuttering word you tried to say. It looked like he was trying to will it out of you. He white-knuckled it all the way through. Jeff, the more you'd stutter, the more it looked like someone was sticking a pin into a Mr. Oslund voodoo doll."

I don't really know how much of this was truth and how much was a brother giving another brother a hard time. However, I did notice when Dad finally got home, Mr. Oslund seemed awfully excited that my dad had arrived. "Lloyd, how are you? I mean, it's really good to see ya!"

I can still hear Steve snickering in the background.

In 1985, my Aunt Alyce, a nurse at United Hospital in St. Paul, had noticed the opening of a new department: speech pathology. She talked with a speech pathologist named Katie Dauer and explained the difficulty I was having because of stuttering.

"Jeff, you should make an appointment with this woman. I think she could help you." Always open to suggestions, I made an appointment and began what ended up being one-on-one sessions that lasted five years.

Katie was a great listener. She and I developed a hybrid version of a type of speech therapy originally developed by Dr. Martin Schwartz out of New York University. He called it the passive flow, soft and slow (PFSS) method. Basically it involved re-learning how to talk. The premise of the therapy was based on the fact that as long as air is flowing through vocal cords, stuttering cannot occur. Putting this idea into practice is possible by beginning a sentence slowly and softly. Moreover, air flowing out before any sound is made keeps the vocal cords from locking up.

Since I wasn't employed, Katie and I were able to meet three times weekly for several months. It took this many sessions to adopt this new style of speech. I was self-conscious of my new speaking style, especially when at times I needed to talk extremely slowly to avoid locking up my vocal cords. During these periods, my rate of speech made Alfred Hitchcock sound like an auctioneer.

As the months passed I became more comfortable and confident about my new speech. Our sessions became fewer and fewer as Katie continued to encourage me that I could do it on my own, much as a mother robin tries to separate her hatchling from the nest. Our official last session was five years from when they had first begun.

I liken my newfound fluency, in a way, to what I saw in my dad's sobriety. Notwithstanding the night and day difference in my speech, only with constant vigilance can I maintain what has been accomplished.

Katie is more than a competent clinician. She's a friend who regularly reminds me of how proud she is that I mastered my speech instead of letting it master me.

I have moved from self-doubt, defining my core identity as a stutterer, to embracing the encouragement from those who valued me for my true self.

Moses raised another objection to God: "Master, please, I don't talk well. I've never been good with words, neither before nor after you spoke to me. I stutter and stammer." God said, "And who do you think made the human mouth? And who makes some mute, some deaf, some sighted, some blind? Isn't it I, God? So, get going. I'll be right there with you—with your mouth! I'll be right there to teach you what to say." Exodus 4:10-12, MSG

"The most wasted of all days is one without laughter." –E.E.Cummings

Was I tongue-tied? Heck, as a kid I counted on the Scouts having a merit badge for tying your tongue into a square knot.

CHAPTER 45

DO YOU HAVE ANY OPENINGS FOR A BLIND MAGICIAN?

Late in 1985 more testing at State Services for the Blind confirmed my interest and aptitude in the area of advertising copywriting. SSB provided me with assistive technology training to enable me to access the information on a computer screen. Since Braille never was my forte, I had the option to learn how to navigate and read the screen by use of synthetic speech. My thinking process is not linear, so it took many months before understanding and feeling comfortable around a computer with a DOS operating system and assistive software commands. After initial one- on-one training, I was scheduled for long blocks of time (3 hours a day) for independent computer training using tutorials on cassette tapes. The tediousness of this activity, along with the droning voice of Mr. Synthetic Speech, caused me to doze at the keyboard. I'd be awakened by what I thought was a mechanical man mocking my stuttering, until I realized I had been leaning on one of the keyboard keys.

After completing my computer training, I was introduced to a SSB job placement counselor named Doug Tourville. "Jeff, I've gone through every job title currently held by the blind, and there's nothing that shows up about an advertising copywriter."

That just proves I'm not your typical blind, stuttering, arthritic job seeker, I thought.

"But if you're really willing to go for it, I'll support your efforts," he reassured me. Since we were breaking new ground, he recommended I first do informational interviewing to try getting my foot in the door before it ended up in my mouth. "You're going to need to show them something, like a portfolio of your work," he added.

So in the spring of 1986, I began going to friends and family to offer my copywriting services to their businesses, gratis. One business to whom I gave a pitch was a floor covering store owned by the older brother of my close friend, Don Dinger. I developed a radio commercial and print ad along with a slogan, "You're covered at CLT." Since it is true that "a prophet is not known in his own land," I should have been prepared for the indifference Don's brother expressed after reviewing my copywriting ideas. For that matter, neither was my dad all that excited when I approached him about writing ad copy for the Smith Brothers Fitness Center, a new family-owned-and-operated business.

Professional photograph used in an ad showcasing my advertising copywriting skills, circa 1986. The headline read, "Who better than someone blind to use their mind's eye to create effective radio copy?"

Through the informational interviewing process, I was able to develop a portfolio by taking the suggestions of interviewers and coming up with imaginary ad campaigns. I also confirmed through informational interviewing what I had been told by my college professor practitioners: that the Twin Cities hosts some of the most creative, award-winning advertising anywhere, and anyone wanting to work locally in the field is expected to first gain experience in a less competitive market. So I felt blessed when Twin Cities advertising agency Cohen, Okerlund and Smith proposed a six-month internship that turned into a one year position.

The internship started auspiciously. Doug Tourville called me the day prior to starting. "Jeff?" he began slowly, "I don't know what to say..." "What's wrong, Doug?"

"I just came back from the ad agency—they were robbed! One of the items stolen was your computer that was outfitted with assistive software for you. I don't know if we can get you another one." Fortunately, Cohen, Okerlund and Smith had a good insurance policy and another computer and software package was ordered, and I started one week later.

Upon completion of the internship, COS recommended I begin my copywriting career in a small town market. "Your greatest strengths, Jeff, are best suited to writing copy for a radio station."

I wasn't willing to move to a small town because they wouldn't have the resources available to someone with my disabilities, such as specialized transportation. So there I was with a degree in advertising copywriting and no place to professionally use it.

Maybe I'm better off not limiting myself to working only in advertising. Maybe I'll get a job easier if I broaden my job search. These thoughts kept my spirits from bottoming out. I connected with all sorts of vocational placement agencies, went to job fairs and seminars and checked out job postings everywhere on a daily basis. I even did some telemarketing from home. I kept thinking, *I got to get a job soon so I can relax. This job search stuff is killing me!* Any job openings I did come across I wasn't qualified for or really interested in. Nor were job openings matching up with my strengths in the area of creativity and communication, especially now with the great strides I had made following successful speech therapy for my stuttering.

Throughout this time, the organization then known as the St. Paul Society for the Blind had volunteers that regularly provided me with transportation. One day I was contacted by the organization about volunteering within their speaker bureau. The bureau was made up of people who were blind and spoke to school-age children about what it is like to be visually impaired. "Jeff, we've been helping you. Now it's time you should help us. We'd like you to talk to school-age children about what it is like to be blind," said the speaker bureau rep.

"I can't do that! I, I, I stutter!" I said.

"Well, okay, but if you want to have more rides from us... Besides, we know you have so much to offer the children."

I saw this as a case of clear-cut blackmail. But because I had a need for a lot of help growing up, this speaking opportunity clearly stood out to me as the point in my life when I had my first chance to give back and grow personally.

About the same time, Mark Roesler, echoing what many friends were saying to me, said, "Why don't you do magic shows for a real audience and maybe make a little money at the same time? After all, you're 32 years old!"

"Do you have to say that so loud?" I cringed. "The neighbors will hear!" I added, more than a little embarrassed about my age and lack of "gainful employment" experience.

Today, I thank God for these encouragers. Without them, I might have taken to heart my self-doubt and fear and never even tried to take the first step to becoming a magician. I often viewed my stuttering as something that stood out the most in the eyes of others. *How on earth could I be a magician? I'm just re-learning how to talk, and now I'm supposed to speak to kids about what it's like to be blind?* And the unimaginative words of some vocational counselors from a few years earlier kept echoing inside me, further hindering my confidence to begin stepping out on my own: "Jeff, we think you should pursue what many people like yourself do..." I translated this to mean assembly line-type work. (Assembly line work with crooked fingers like mine and the wear and tear on my joints? I'll never be able to pick my nose again!) Seriously, though, I know that if I had followed the conventional thinking of some, instead of risking pride by opting for new and often scary situations, such as talking to children about being blind, I'd always be haunted by another voice inside—the voice that said "What if?"

I knew that what the St. Paul Society for the Blind was asking me to do was a defining moment in my life. Somehow, I mustered up enough courage to face the kids, in part by preparing funny material at home. Every couple of weeks, I visited an elementary school and spoke to the students about what it's like being blind. This gave me my first chance to speak in front of anyone. To deflect focus away from my speech disfluency, I incorporated a little pocket-sized magic to illustrate speech points. With my magic on hand and armed with plenty of jokes, I brought adaptive tools from home, such as an abacus, a Braille compass, and a tablet of raised lined paper, all making me feel less vulnerable in front of the kids. Armed with these visual aids, I became more relaxed, and humor became an even greater part of my presentation.

Coinciding with the invitation to speak to children about being blind was a call from my old friend Kathy Johnson. "Jeff, do you know that there's a new magic store that just opened in downtown St. Paul? It's called Twin Cities Magic and Costume."

"You're kidding! In St. Paul? That's not very far from me. I sure could use some fresh tricks. I need something to hide behind when I'm in front of those kids."

Twin Cities Magic is owned and operated by Jim Berg and Fred Baish, veteran performers of the Shrine Circus. They were valuable resources during my formative years of learning magic and presentation.

"Well, how about I pick you up, and we'll check it out." Kathy suggested.

"Ben has been asking me to get him some magic tricks too." (Ben was her ten-year-old son.)

Around that time, a new transportation service called Metro Mobility and DARTS, designed for people with disabilities, began operating in my community. Not only did I begin ordering rides to Twin Cities Magic, but I was now able to get to Eagle Magic Store, established in 1899, making it the oldest store of its kind in the nation. Larry Kahlow, the owner, has provided me with many lessons and countless hours of engaging conversation on many topics, even magic.

One day back then, at Eagle Magic, on an impulse I bought a professional magic stand. I set it up in my room, which gave me a perfect vantage point to periodically perform for family members. It also provided for me a chance to begin imagining what it would be like to perform before the public.

Tori, my brother Steve's wife, had a boy in preschool. Since blood is thicker than water, her little Barrett already thought I was great. "Uncle Jeff, you're better than David Copperfield!" My brothers had already compared me to David Copperfield: "Compared to David Copperfield, Jeff, you stink!"

Tori charmed me into presenting my very first show for a less-than- discriminating audience: her son's kindergarten class. The kids often clapped even before the climax of the trick, which I didn't mind since I appreciated and needed every bit of their encouragement.

On a weekly basis, the St. Paul Society for the Blind provided a volunteer to stop by to read my mail and other things I enjoyed, such as superhero comic books. My parents, brother Mike, and I now were living in an apartment on the Mississippi River, having recently sold our family home.

"Jeff, I can tell that you enjoy showing off your tricks, don't you?" one of the volunteer readers commented one day.

"Yeah. It's fun."

"I have a son who's a math teacher for seventh and eighth graders at Highland Park Middle School in St. Paul," she continued. "I'm going to talk with him about you doing a show for his class."

"Oh, thanks for thinking of me, but I don't think I'd be interested," I said trying to hide my fear.

"If I could get $50 for you, would you be more interested?" My desire to earn money and have a sense of accomplishment was greater than my fear of presenting in front of middle-schoolers. "You got a deal!"

She knew her son Tim ran his class with an iron fist, which I too became aware of upon arriving. While setting up before students arrived, he provided for me a security net. "Jeff, I told the kids if any one of them smarts off or does anything even close to disrespecting you, they'll be immediately removed and have to stay after class for a solid week." *Wow! What a warm-up act,* I thought.

The seventh and eighth graders were certainly respectful during the show, or scared—it was hard to tell. They just kind of sat there. My show didn't have an intentional educational message tied in with the tricks. But after the kids left the room (yes, after, not during the show), Tim approached me and said, "I knew these guys weren't going to hassle you, but I didn't expect this reaction."

"What do you mean?" I asked.

"I've never seen them sit so still!" he continued.

"They didn't clap, so I figured they didn't like it," I said.

"They didn't clap because they're too cool for that," he laughed, "but I wish you could have seen how closely they were watching you."

My career path was perfectly on course — I just didn't know it yet.

"I will lead the blind by ways they have not known, along unfamiliar paths I will guide them; I will turn the darkness into light before them and make the rough places smooth." Isaiah 42:16

"The highest reward for a person's toil is not what they get for it, but what they become by it." –John Ruskin Cohen

I don't like sky diving because it scares the heck out of my Seeing Eye dog.

CHAPTER 46

INTERNSHIP OR I'LL PASS ON THE MAYO—JUST GIVE ME THE BREAD

~~~~~~~~

In 1991, State Services for the Blind arranged on my behalf an internship in the collections department of Mayo Clinic that had the potential of turning into permanent employment. Once again, this was continuing down the path of other efforts directing me to careers that were successful for many blind people, but weren't right for me. My strengths were so unsuited for collections; to start with, I kept falling asleep on the job. I thought at first, *Maybe I'm not getting enough sleep*. So I went to bed earlier. Not only did I continue to fall asleep at my desk, I even fell asleep during departmental meetings.

Our office situation was Spartan. Everyone sat at their cubicles facing one another with only a fabric wall separating them. One day I was having a conversation with a fellow employee. In the middle of our conversation, I once again fell asleep.

"Jeff!?"

I woke up and mumbled, "Yes?"

After I confessed I had fallen asleep, he said, "Most people who fall asleep in a conversation fall asleep while the other guy is talking. You just fell asleep when *you* were talking."

My supervisors and fellow employees were friendly and always willing to help me learn the process. I was overwrought trying to fit my round peg into this square hole that I believe the stress was shutting down my body. Eventually, after going to bed at 7 p.m. and still falling asleep at work, I realized *hmm…maybe collections just is not my thing.*

My nearly one-year internship at Mayo Clinic gave me more insight into my future than merely knowing I wasn't cut out for a desk job. While there, I contacted St. Mary's hospital and volunteered to perform a magic show for their pediatric ward on an upcoming Saturday. I remembered as a patient how lonely some weekends were. Weekends for parents were a time when they could reconnect with the rest of their family at home. I explained to the child life specialist, "I was here as a patient many years ago. I'd like a chance to show kids some fun at a place where at times they might be feeling scared. I know I had those kinds of feelings."

My next weekend back home, I assembled a gym bag of magic tricks, many of which had been recent purchases from Twin Cities Magic. I wore a sports jacket and tie to the show, which was part of the collections department's dress code anyway. Positive self- talk helped keep me calm during the show as I reminded myself that this audience was no threat to me but just a bunch of vulnerable kids, some of whom may have been filled with a sense of helplessness about their lives.

Afterward, the child life specialist thanked me while she helped pack up my stuff. Though I spent considerable time developing patter (magician's dialogue) for each trick, her words of appreciation were undoubtedly based purely on my effort, not the quality of my performance. This was only my fourth or fifth presentation ever. So I was thankful for the opportunity to get any precious additional experience.

My parents had decided that apartment living wasn't for them and were in the midst of building a retirement home. At the conclusion of my internship, my friend Kevin Scherer and his wife Kathy kindly helped pack me up and move me home. The day began with rain in Rochester, but as we headed north to the Twin Cities, it turned into sleet, then snow. By the time we arrived, the snow had accumulated to over a foot. Kevin's car had gotten stuck in the snow two or three times. My mom and dad invited Kevin and Kathy to stay overnight because of impassable roads. Mom had the apartment filled with tall stacks of heavy moving boxes waiting to be brought to their new house and was in no mood to lodge me any earlier than required. She said, "You can't stay here, Jeffrey! You're throwing a monkey wrench into everything by coming home early."

"Mom! Calm down! I'm trying to save some money! I don't have any other way to earn it!"

"Your father hasn't lifted a finger around here to help me pack." (I suspect, if he had offered, my take-charge mom would have said, "No, no, you're doing it wrong...I'll do it myself!")

"And now, I've got to deal with you?" (Ah-h...there's no place like home.) "All your stuff has already been packed! I'm calling your brother Steve. You can stay with him and Tori until we're settled into our new house."

I joined my parents at their new house on December 23rd (doggone it—I was going for a record: fourth Christmas away from home). Over the course of the next few weeks, my stuff had been unpacked at the new house and organized in places that worked for me. My mom, who feels most comfortable when in control, didn't mind where or how I had organized my stuff in her shiny new abode, since I pretty much had the lower level of the house to myself.

The last month of my internship, I commuted 100 miles each day with other Mayo employees who lived in the Twin Cities. During one of my commutes, guardian angels again flexed their muscles as we were heading home, going about 60 miles per hour. My driver noticed a familiar tire passing alongside us at 70 mph. As it faded into the horizon ahead, he put two and two together. He gradually slowed the vehicle, and we came to a stop. It was only then that the car leaned to the left because of its missing rear left tire. The lug nuts on his new tires had not been tightened. The tire shop should have been more correctly called "Tires Minus (lug nuts)." He flagged down a car and called his wife who came to our rescue.

Shortly after settling into my new digs, my Aunt Alyce called me one day: "Jeffrey, I was at a social gathering where I was talking to the superintendent of the Minneapolis school system about you. I told him about all you've been doing to find a job but hadn't yet been successful in your efforts."

"Oh yeah?" I said with interest, wondering where she was going with the conversation.

"Anyway, I told him how you've been talking to school children about what it's like being blind, and about your positive attitude toward life and your wonderful sense of humor."

"So what did he say?"

"Well, one thing led to another, and he wants to meet with you about possibly arranging some kind of residency going from school to school talking with the kids."

"Would it pay something?"

"The superintendent mentioned there are federal funds available to assist in funding the mandate for disability awareness training."

"Great!" I said, nervous but excited that this could be my big break.

A two or three week schedule was arranged on a trial basis, this time for me to talk to students from sixth to eighth grades, a more discriminating group than the lower grade school students I had been talking to.

The few hundred dollars weekly was my incentive to rise above my nerves and organize a presentation for the students. On my first day, I looked great, had my teaching props, and felt prepared but had a really bad cold. I began at the middle school talking to the sixth graders. My cold and my runny nose was distracting me. At some point in the presentation, I didn't have the time to turn around before I excused myself and held a tissue up to my nose and gave it a blow. In my haste or general nervousness, I'm not sure which, I missed the tissue altogether and blew it all over my tie. I figured at the time that the best response would be to try playing it cool and maybe no one would notice. Well, forget that! Right away I heard a bunch of kids shout in unison,

"Gro-o-oss!!!"

Considering it was one of the most embarrassing moments I remember, as well as it happening at my first presentation, I'm glad I didn't just hang it all up there and then. After my probationary period concluded, the superintendent decided not to have me continue addressing students in the district.

I continued buying tricks at the two local magic shops and tried to integrate them into my sporadic speaking engagements with school children on behalf of the St. Paul Society for the Blind. With no job, no prospects, and no advice, I decided, *Why not? I'm going to give performing magic a shot for one year and see what happens.*

Magic was an uncertain adventure, but as I reflected back on my experiences at the advertising agency and at Mayo Clinic, I realized that my strengths were too non-linear to be comfortable in the position of a "nine to five" type employee. The convenience and security that comes with being an employee might actually be limiting. Maybe for me, it's safer to be "driving blind," so to speak. Ironically, I began seeing a parallel between magic and life. The magical phrase, "Things aren't always as they first appear," seemed to be perfectly describing my real-world experiences at that time. Ironically, if I hadn't gone through all the disappointment of trying to find a traditional job, having door after door closed in my face, I wouldn't be resorting to self-employment as a magician, let alone a blind magician!

With my decision to head in a new direction, I tried to avoid treating it as merely a way to make quick money, but rather, see it as a career step. I thought I should dedicate as much time as possible to becoming a magician. I contacted the St. Paul Society for the Blind and announced my plans. "I'm sorry but I'm not going to be able to continue speaking to school children about being blind. I'm going to devote time to becoming a magician,"

"A magician?" questioned the bewildered speaker bureau coordinator. "There's no money in being a magician. You'll be wasting your time."

Expecting encouragement rather than scorn, I couldn't help thinking, *I'll show her!*

Fortunately, my methodical nature prepared me professionally for the many steps required to ultimately become a magician.

"And let us not be weary in well doing: for in due season we shall reap, if we faint not." Galatians 6:9, ASV

"A dream doesn't become reality through magic; it takes sweat, determination and hard work."–Colin Powell

I was fired just because of an eye condition. I couldn't see getting to work on time.

CHAPTER 47

BREAK A LEG OR RANDOM ACTS OF BLINDNESS

B ecause of my previous succession of failed and fruitless job placements, I went against the advice of vocational professionals and began thinking about what came naturally to me—creating and performing. In February of 1992, I began developing my interest in magic and sharing insights about blindness into a formal presentation initially intended for children. This was the only age level with which I felt confident enough to present.

I started my marketing efforts as simply as possible because that was the only way I knew how to go about it. I called a buddy and asked him if he could read to me from the phone book names of schools and their phone numbers. From the money I had recently earned by speaking to students in the Minneapolis school district, I purchased my own computer.

With sweaty palms, I made my first telemarketing call. "Hello, my name is Jeffrey Smith. I'm also called Amazing Jeffo." (This was sometimes met with a snicker.) "I am a blind magician who teaches disability awareness through the use of magic." (Sounds kind of stiff, doesn't it?) "Can I talk to somebody about doing a magic show at your school?"

The whole time I was thinking, *What's happened to all my speech training? I'm stuttering like I'm trapped on a cheap hotel bed with out of control "magic fingers."*

"Can you send us something in the mail?" the secretary suggested.

"Oh, sure!" I said, but thought, *I don't have anything to send!*

"What do you charge?" the secretary asked.

I fought the urge to respond, *Well, how much ya got?* But instead I responded, "$75 for one show and $125 for two shows."

As you might have guessed, I didn't close the deal. The secretary unwittingly taught me that I had a lot to learn about marketing.

The Holy Spirit must have been feeling particularly sympathetic on my behalf because suddenly, people began appearing in my life, each possessing different expertise in what was required for me to become a performer: how I should dress and market myself, what topics should be covered in my show, the groups with funding for this kind of thing, and so on. These encouragers enabled me to take my first giant step into becoming Amazing Jeffo. If I believed in coincidences, I may have chalked it up to that. Instead, it was becoming clearer to me that these events, at this time, were divinely coordinated.

One evidence of this sort of divine messenger, named Linda, had been in the audience at the Christian camp where I performed the previous summer. Linda had watched my comedy show which was originally intended as a serious magic show. The quality of my presentation decided that. In spite of all the laughter that came from my failed attempts to deflect attention from my mess ups, what she witnessed somehow inspired her with a bigger vision for my future. As I packed up my "highly entertaining" presentation, she approached me and said, "Jeff, I really liked the things you were saying."

"Like what? I was just trying to cover my butt."

"Yes, but in the things you were saying, I saw perseverance and tenaciousness. I saw how you drew from your experiences and shared it through a magic trick. You should develop a message about over-coming disabilities and put it into a magic show and perform it at my elementary school in St. Paul."

Since I didn't know how to contact her, I had pretty much forgotten this encounter. Then, following my Mayo Clinic internship, out of the blue, she gave me a call.

"Jeff, I talked with some other teachers, and they all seemed inter-ested to have you come to our school and do something like you did at the summer camp."

"Minus the mistakes, right?" I said with a chuckle.

"I'm not too worried about that," she said offhandedly.

A magic show to teach disability awareness... yikes! I thought. I stretched out on my bed with my tape recorder and started to mentally review my magic props. As I thought of each trick, I'd ask myself, *What is the effect of this trick and how can I relate it to disability awareness?* I was amazed how quickly the associations between the message and the magic flowed out of me. Tricks involving levitation elicited messages such as "rising above challenges"; those involving transformation inspired messages such as "changing negative thinking", and so on.

After the show I was paid $60 out of the petty cash drawer in the school office. Though it may not have been the most dignified way of being paid, I considered it on par with the level of my performance. Still, Linda recommended me to a teacher friend of hers at another school.

The promise of a few dollars gave me a reason to further develop and begin promoting the show, but I still had to apply the lessons I learned from my speech therapist to conquer stuttering. Anyone who has ever stuttered agrees that it is exacerbated by stress. I had good trick concepts and my prepared dialogue sounded great as I practiced at home, both bolstering my self-confidence. But never before having presented to an audience, my stress levels were off the charts. Consternation arose from all directions: making sure the driver got me to the site early enough to have the full one-hour prep time (necessary in the beginning of my career); hoping there was someone to assist me in getting ready; and praying I didn't mess up the tricks. At first it was difficult remembering my lines while correctly handling tricks, particularly with sweaty palms, and struggling with the timing of each trick.

On top of everything, my halting speech was distracting to the children. I thought following the show it would be a good idea to take questions from the kids, until the first query was, "How come when you talk, you do 'uh-uh-uh-uh-uh'?"

Caught off guard, I responded defensively, "How come you're so short?"

It took a good two years and about five hundred shows before I quit sweating and gained enough confidence to keep my stuttering under control and learned to respect my audience. Today, I can do a show with my eyes closed (no pun intended).

Thanks to the new transportation system for people with disabilities, I was able to frequently visit the local magic shops, and my knowledge increased. I made important contacts with other local magicians. One of these magicians was a precocious 14-year-old who happened to be helping out behind the counter at Twin Cities Magic. Michael showed me the most basic of tricks, but I thought they were plenty challenging.

"Jeff, would you like to come to a magic club meeting?" he asked.

"What's that about?" I said.

"It's a bunch of guys who get together here at the shop or at Eagle Magic every month to practice and learn new tricks."

"Does it cost anything?"

"No. It's free. They sometimes even get big-name magicians to come and teach."

Attending this magic club, I had the chance to listen and learn from other performers and have the visual elements described to me by fellow magicians.

In 1993, as my resume of magic shows gradually increased, I contacted a nearby church to see if they might have any volunteers who could assist me with marketing. Three volunteers from the church read phone numbers to me, directed me where to sign my introductory letter, and addressed envelopes. By the end of that year, youth programmers began referring me to adult programs and I quickly learned how inappropriate it was to present a kid show to adult audiences. For example, on the head of a distinguished businessman I once put a wizard's hat that magically changed into a plunger. I quipped, "My! You're looking a little flushed today!" The post-show evaluation card came back with the response "NO!!" next to the question, "Was the tone appropriate for the audience?", written in such large print it covered up the entire question card. Most of what I've learned throughout my career has come as a result of reacting to customer feedback and an ability to take criticism.

I booked 125 performances in 1993 without a website or even a brochure, but just by making a million phone calls. When I started, my skill level was somewhere between David Copperfield and Professor

Hinkle from *Frosty the Snowman*...with the scales tipped definitely toward the professor. I will admit, however, my fees were commensurate with my skill level: $75, or two shows for $125. I refined jokes and tricks that had fallen flat. I didn't need sight to see a good response and know whether or not my audience was tuned in. Some of my biggest laughs along the way came as a result of having to ad lib when something went wrong. For example, when a new joke would be met with total silence, I'd say, "My dog thought that joke was funny!"

One morning in early 1994 I was awakened by a phone call. "Hello?" I answered hoarsely.

"May I speak to Amazing Jeffo? This is Deb O'Connor from the Saint Paul *Pioneer Press*."

She was responding to my newly produced brochure I had mailed to the newspaper. "Yes, that's me," I said, trying to clear my throat.

"I want to write a human interest story about you for my column. Do you have a show this week that I can come to?"

"Yes, tomorrow at Gethsemane Lutheran School in Maplewood at 1:00."

"Great, I'll see ya there. Can we do the interview after the show?"

"You bet!" I said. I hung up the phone excited by the prospect of free publicity.

I arrived at the school and performed. Once the sanctuary was cleared of students, Deb and I sat in a pew and began the thirty- minute interview. The column appeared in the next morning's paper.

Returning from a show later that afternoon, I checked my answering machine. "I'm calling for Amazing Jeffo. I read a story about you in the newspaper today. I'd like to see if we can schedule a show..."

As I was removing my bowtie, the answering machine beeped again, "I am calling about the magician that was mentioned in the *Pioneer Press*. Can you please call me about a show..."

Great, two shows! I thought. My reverie was interrupted by another beep.

"My name is Sharon. I'm calling for Amazing Jeffo, the blind magician. I read a wonderful story about you in the Saint Paul paper. I'd love to talk to you about doing a show for our school." The beeps continued—14 more times. I thought my answering machine was broken and I was listening to old messages my machine hadn't deleted, but every one of them referenced the newspaper article. As a result of the publicity, I grew from an average of two shows per month to ten.

I networked with marketing professionals, some of whom I had known in high school, such as Theresa Wohlers who designed my first print promotional pieces. Two years later, with the assistance of free publicity, a snappy brochure, tons of telemarketing, and a willingness on my part to sometimes leave the house as early as 5 a.m. and not return until 10 p.m., I performed 360 shows between mid-1994 and 1995. In February of 1995, I presented 42 shows, including 17 in one week. The words of King David rang true that year: "You anoint my head with oil; my cup overflows" (Psalm 23:5).

It was no coincidence that I developed high blood pressure. A new design in the vehicles made to transport people with disabilities unwittingly helped slow my frenetic pace; I tore cartilage in my right knee attempting to climb its overly steep steps, ironic in a vehicle designed for people with mobility issues. I thought, *Until I can perfect the levitation trick, from now on I'll resort to using the lift to get into the bus.* I raised my fee; it lowered my blood pressure, and shows leveled out.

The thrill of earning money, having an outlet for my creativity, and making people laugh while teaching them about disabilities was a wonderful balm for my self-confidence. But teaching and entertaining through magic was, at least for me, uncharted territory, and there were a lot of bumps along the way.

Later that year, my great friend Don Dinger and I had two Cub Scout shows in two cities and not much time between them. This was in the month of February, when the Boy Scouts of America organization celebrates their founding. This time of year also happens to be the worst of the Minnesota winter. As Don was throwing my cases in the rear of his vehicle, he said, "Jeff, stay right there until I can help you into the car." He had already opened the passenger door. Between the piercing wind chill and our tight schedule, I thought I'd just help myself into the car. I didn't realize as I stepped off the curb that a ramp of sheer ice had collected in the gutter. I slipped and gashed my face against the metal luggage rack affixed atop Don's car. "You're bleeding all over the place!" Don said in alarm.

"It's so cold out, I can't even feel it," I responded. He grabbed some napkins from his glove compartment, and we headed back into the school that had hosted the scouting event.

Fortunately, one of the mothers of the cubs happened to be the nurse of the school. She opened up her office and cleaned me up, then taped the cuts closed with butterfly bandages and gauze.

"You're going to have to get stitches soon or you'll have a big scar, Jeff," she announced. Not wanting to disappoint the subsequent Cub Scout group, nor feel obligated to forfeit the check, I mustered myself and announced to Don, "The show must go on!" echoing the cry of many a past performer. Blood stains and all, we headed off to the next show. It actually gave me some great stand- up material. With crusty blood stains on my tuxedo and on the surface of the gauze, I worked it into the show by peppering the audience with lines like, "Talk about a tough audience!"

Following the second show, Don and I headed off to the closest hospital for stitches, not getting home until 3 a.m. from the emergency room.

"...struck down, but not destroyed." 2 Corinthians 4:8

For a while, Houdini used a lot of trap doors in his act, but he was just going through a stage.–Doug the Pun-isher

My rabbit only listens to hip-hop.

CHAPTER 48

RHEUMATOID ARTHRITIS AND SHOWBIZ: A SWELL STORY

With the sudden onset of income from magic shows, I exercised my independence and moved out from my parents' household into my own apartment in 1995.

Thrilling as it was at last to earn real money, the accompanying frenzy from all the show-related activity was exhausting me. Besides necessitating medication for high blood pressure, my frantic schedule was putting new demands on my rheumatoid arthritis. The anti-inflammatory medication I had been taking for years was now becoming ineffective.

Mollie, my sister-in-law and a registered dietitian, not only provided me with personal care but also with suggestions and advice about alternative therapies for arthritis. My newfound income and curiosity about different ways of treating arthritis spurred me to dabble in some of these methods. Over the years, surgery and medication had kept me going, but researching alternative treatments helped me discover the role that diet can play in managing arthritis.

After trying a number of food supplements, herbs, and homeopathic remedies, some of which were a total waste of money, I stumbled onto the fact that being selective about what I put into my mouth could reduce overall aches and pains. This awareness came about as a result of my dad, a rental property owner, talking with a city building inspector about his properties. During one of their meetings, the subject of arthritis arose, and my dad commented to the inspector how my arthritis had been bothering me more lately. The inspector shared about his once crippled father, a dairy farmer.

"Lloyd, because of his arthritis, my father thought he had no other choice than to retire early from farming," the inspector said. "In one year, he had gone from milking 18 cows a day to almost complete bed rest," he continued. "He passed his time by reading. A friend of his had given him a book about living with arthritis by Dr. Dale Alexander called *Arthritis and Common Sense*. He read it cover-to-cover and followed every suggestion it had about a special diet for those having arthritis. He was faithful to the diet and in one year he felt so good he was back milking 36 cows a day!"

My dad relayed this information to me, and I called around to see where I could get the book. I found out it had been out of print for years. I contacted the Library of Congress Recordings for the Blind, and they had it available in a cassette format.

I read in the book, and later in other studies, that certain foods aggravate arthritic symptoms, such as sugar, chocolate, wheat, red meat, tomatoes, potatoes, peppers, and others. Conversely, some foods seem to reduce inflammation, such as fish that has been baked, broiled, or grilled. Dr. Alexander's research confirmed what I had suspected over the years based on how I felt after eating foods that were either good or bad for my arthritis. I had never made a definite correlation between the food I had eaten and how I felt afterwards.

As I incorporated more "good" foods in my diet along with food supplements, my arthritic symptoms slowly went away. I suddenly realized the extent of my improved flexibility one day when I was able to touch the top of my feet while holding on to the kitchen counter with my other hand.

My symptoms had, in fact, become so minimal, I decided to discontinue some of the more expensive products that I had been using to augment my arthritis medicines. Over the course of several months, my arthritis not only returned but felt worse than before. My rheumatologist tried other medications, but nothing was working. Putting on the facade of smiles and laughter while performing on stage, I grimaced inside as I picked up my props and manipulated them in my hands. I called my doctor one day and begged, "Isn't there anything else we can try?"

"A new class of medication has just come out," reported my doctor.

"Oh yeah? How does it work?" I asked.

"Well, researchers have manipulated a protein molecule in the ovary of Chinese hamsters to create a host site to genetically regulate the tumor necrosis factor blocker to prevent your body from attacking itself."

"O-h-h, I see…" I fibbed. "Does it work?" I queried as my overloaded brain cleared.

"I categorize the results we are finding as revolutionary," my doctor boldly stated.

A flutter of giddy excitement arose in me, and I said, "Let's try it!"

"You'll be one of my first patients to try it. It's a weekly injectable; a nurse will come out to your house to give it to you," he explained.

On the morning of the third day following the first injection, I arose out of bed and immediately noticed how limber I felt.

This miracle medication, which I still use today, is called Enbrel. On days I have magic shows I use an anti-inflammatory in combination with the Enbrel to enable me to perform that extra little sleight-of-hand.

"'For I will restore health to you and heal you of your wounds,' says the Lord." Jeremiah 30:17, NKJV

"The Doctor called Mrs. Cohen saying 'Mrs. Cohen, your check bounced and came back.' Mrs. Cohen answered 'So did my arthritis!'" – Henny Youngman

Is a Parisienne with an ileostomy called a baguette?

CHAPTER 49

GREAT SCOTT!

I met Scott Saari in 1995, after performing at his church. He approached me as I was packing up and said, "I'm sorry I missed your show. I do a little magic thing myself here on Wednesday nights for the kids." Scott's a naturally friendly individual with a strong, confident style, who has the spiritual gift of serving others. His hearty laugh that I so easily triggered, combined with my never- ending desire to make people laugh, made for instant rapport. *Before my bus returns for me, I've got to get this guy's phone number,* I thought.

Years later, Scott admitted his motivation to stop and introduce himself to me was to find out who was tromping on his territory as a magician. His concern soon faded as our friendship blossomed. After spending time at one another's places talking about and showing favorite tricks, we decided to attend the national convention of the International Brotherhood of Magicians (IBM). We call it "little blue."

The Twin Cities was hosting this long-running annual convention for the first time. Despite its convenient proximity, we decided to rent a room in the hotel that was hosting the event to attend more of the festivities, some of which ran as late as 2 a.m. As a result, we participated in more workshops and performances while still getting some sleep.

We met magicians from all over the world. Unlike the perception some people have of magicians (that we possess unusual powers), we actually are a group of men and women who enjoy standing on stage, acting silly and pretending to be someone we're not, which is not all that different from many non-magicians (except we get paid for it, sh-h-h-h). Similarly, the interesting reactions Scott and I received by some fellow attendees—that Scott's involvement with me was driven by sympathy—could not have been more untrue.

"I've been observing how you're guiding your friend here and there and I think it's a beautiful thing," sincerely—and almost tearfully—stated some of the magicians we met. It was clear they saw Scott solely as a personal care provider.

"Hey! He's my buddy. I like hanging out with him. He's funny, and we have a good time together," Scott gently pointed out.

Ours is a friendship based on equal contribution in different ways. Many times because of a shared interest, we would go to the same workshops at the convention, so what's the big deal about me grabbing a "wing" (arm)? Other times if we were interested in different workshops, I'd take a sighted guide from someone else.

Scott is a parent of two adult children with special needs. Both were born with their left and right brain hemispheres detached. He and their mother, Cynde, raised them in a way that maximized their capabilities to their fullest. Consequently, Scott considered individuals like me as people (first and foremost) who just so happen to have disabilities.

Scott Saari: distinguished accountant and fellow magician, adventurer, beloved friend, and most of all, a goofball soul-mate.

"A friend loves at all times, and a brother is born for a time of adversity." Proverbs 17:17, TNIV

"A friend is one who knows you and loves you anyway." – Elbert Hubbard

I have excellent night vision; everywhere I look, I see night!

CHAPTER 50

SHOULDERING THE BURDEN OR A TEAR FOR THE TEAR

My sister-in-law Mollie was my PCA (personal care attendant) for the eight years I lived in an apartment, from 1995 until 2002. One of her duties was to prepare and freeze meals for me to reheat as needed. I really welcomed her help in this area but not because I was totally helpless in the kitchen. Maybe it's because I may have a degree of ADHD or something else, but I never have had the patience to prepare anything more elaborate than PB-on-Finger or my specialty, chunk-o-cheese, jaggedly torn from one end of the brick. Admittedly, this would have limited the variety and quality of my meals if it hadn't been for Mollie.

Besides providing well-rounded meals, Mollie assisted with personal care and housekeeping. One day in 2002 while she was vacuuming, the phone rang. It was my brother Mike, Mollies's husband, who needed to talk with her. Since she was going to just talk briefly, she turned off the vacuum, laid it down, and hurried to the phone. As she spoke on the phone she was facing the other direction from me. As a result, she wasn't aware that I headed off to use the bathroom. I tripped over the vacuum, falling hard on my right shoulder. Mollie felt terrible.

I sensed that I had torn the rotator cuff, but when my new girlfriend Devon took me to the ER later that evening, the attending physician said, "No way is your rotator cuff torn. You wouldn't be able to lift your arm as far as you can now."

The following week, I performed my shows with difficulty and in much pain. I made an appointment with Summit Orthopedic, which had begun as St. Anthony Orthopedics where years earlier Dr. Babb, Dr. Thompson, and I had so much fun together. I had an MRI and doctors discovered I had a very large (more than 7 mm) tear in my rotator cuff.

I hadn't had any surgery since 1975, so I had forgotten all that was involved. On the morning of my September surgery, my church sent an elder to the hospital who sat and prayed with me and Devon. I appreciated his prayers, but the possible mishaps he brought up during his petition for my safety began worrying me. One aspect of hospital stays that always gave me the heebie- jeebies, especially as a child, was the excruciating, step-by-step process of preparing for surgery. Building me up with transfusions the day before, prohibiting food or water after a certain time, injecting hypos to relax me, inhaling gas to drift off, all fueled my over-active imagination as I likened it to the steps of a condemned prisoner bound for the chair.

After many years absent of these negative feelings, they returned in force as I was prepared for rotator cuff surgery. In spite of pre-surgery relaxation medication, I was trembling like Don Knotts in *The Shakiest Gun in the West*. Still trembling after being wheeled into the surgical theater, the anesthesiologist said, "Looks like you could use a little more juice!" I didn't argue. Not only did the medication instantly remove all my nervousness, but I began making idle comments such as, "So what are you guys doing this weekend?" or "Seen any good movies lately?"

The surgery was a complete success. I spent the next two weeks in transitional care, and after that six weeks at home regaining strength in my shoulder. This was a financial hardship since I was living pretty much hand-to-mouth, and my bills depended on magic show income. The local magic community generously pitched in and donated a portion of their show receipts to my cause. Moreover, my brothers and sister contributed several hundred dollars to cover expenses until I was back on my feet—or should I say arms? Receiving unexpected income such as this taught me that worrying about financial uncertainties needs to be left in "expert" hands.

"So that your trust may be in the LORD, I teach you today, even you."
Proverbs 22:19

Perseverance is not a long race; it is many short races one after another. – Walter Elliott

Doctors knock you out during surgery so you can't hear phrases like these:
  1. *Darn! Page 47 of the manual is missing!*
  2. *Wait a minute, if this is his spleen, then what's that?*
  3. *FIRE! FIRE! Everyone get out!"*

CHAPTER 51

"LADIES AND GENTLEMAN, INTRODUCING: MRS. AMAZING!"

2002 was a significant year in my life because of the opportunity I had to build a home, but most importantly, 2002 proved to be a year that fulfilled a lifelong dream of mine: to build a future with someone special. God's timing once again put my showbiz timing to shame. Right before meeting my future Mrs. Amazing in March of that year, I had been praying to God, "If you don't want me to get married, then withdraw this sense of urgency where with every single woman I meet I wonder, *Is this the one?*" I had never been so transparent before God.

That very night, I had a fantastic dream. The setting of the dream was in the apartment where I was currently living. The subject of the dream was preparing to be married the next day. The dream was filled with the kind of powerful emotions that I only imagine to be in a place like Heaven. Though it was a dream, I was experiencing the sensations of deep contentedness and the feeling of joy as I had never felt it, awake or asleep. I was flooded with an overwhelming sense of happiness. *So this is what it must really feel like the day before getting married*, I reflected upon waking.

The next day, I headed off to what I imagined to be just another show…but what a show it was! The fulfillment of my prayer and dream materialized on the middle ground between the heavenly and the everyday as my vehicle pulled up to the front doors of a school in Oakdale where Devon McVeigh, the future Mrs. Amazing, was working as a school-age care site manager. Months earlier, one of her co-workers had arranged for Amazing Jeffo to perform for students. By the time the show date rolled around, the event planner was out on maternity leave. Devon had just returned after being out sick and was catching up with paperwork. She wasn't in the mood to host this event on top of her already over- packed schedule. "Who ever heard of a blind magician anyway?" she griped. Ironically, Devon would turn out to be one of my most gracious hosts, from a field of 2,000 previous hosts.

There was a certain *je ne sais quoi* about her. I was impressed by Devon's poise and charm. I also noticed how relaxed she seemed around a person who was blind. I later learned that, in part, Devon's immediate comfort level with me came from growing up next door to a homeowner who was blind. She noticed how he maintained his homestead independently by mowing his lawn, shoveling his snow, cleaning out and painting the gutters, and so forth. Because of his example, Devon's mindset was more along the lines of "show me things that blind people cannot do."

My instant comfort with Devon was based on less objective reasons. Though I didn't know it at this time, I later discovered Devon had once been a member of that rare and select group from my boyhood that had so lifted my spirits: a teenage candy striper.

In retrospect, I believe Devon also had a genetic predisposition to the allure of mystery, part and parcel of magic, since her maternal grandfather had been a professional magician. Unfortunately, he combined his magic with his personal life when he disappeared from the family to seek greener pastures when Devon's mother was a mere toddler.

"Can I get you a soda, Jeff?" We had some time to kill until the room where I was to perform was free.

"Sure, thanks," I responded and thought, *This girl's a class act.* Early on I learned it's not good to mix business with pleasure. I didn't expect my professional contacts to also serve as dating prospects and thus jeopardize possible return engagements. Devon was the irresistible exception to the rule. In retrospect, this leads me to believe she truly was an answer to my prayer.

While setting up for the show, I asked Devon, "Do you mind me asking you a personal question?" I had already determined by a subtle line of questioning that she was single. "How is it that an attractive person like you isn't married?" Caught off guard, she stuttered,

"W-well, I'm married to my career!"

"If you'd ever like to go out for coffee sometime..." I asked. "Uh, I think we're going to need help setting up," Devon said, as she ran off to get her co-worker and friend, Karen.

Following the show, as Devon, her colleague, and I were packing up, I asked Karen, "Are you Devon's boss?"

"Why, no. How come you ask?" Karen responded.

"Well, I just thought if you were her boss, you could order Devon to go out to lunch with me."

"You know, my dad was an electrical engineer," said Devon, desperately trying to change the subject as she wrapped my power cords.

Karen was delighted by Devon's predicament. She had been encouraging Devon to date again after a bad relationship ended years earlier. Flustered, Devon was giving Karen hand-signals to get her to guide me to my awaiting vehicle. But I wasn't the only one with an agenda. Karen announced, "Devon...I'll pop back to the kids and let you escort Jeff to his ride." It was two against one...No...It was infinity against one. Poor Devon.

It just so happened that the previous week Devon had returned from a retreat where she became, at last, at peace about her destiny. She prayed, "Lord, if it's your will that I never marry, I can accept that. But if it's not your will, please make that clear to me." There was some kind of matchmaking force at work here!

As she escorted me out to my Metro Mobility vehicle, I thanked Devon again for hosting the event and, while shaking her hand, slipped a business card into it and said, "If you'd ever like for me to take you out to dinner, give me a call."

Three days later, my phone rang. It was Devon. She agreed to dinner at the Mall of America. Ah-ha! She had been holding out for my best offer! Entrepreneurial shrewdness—yet just another reason I'm crazy about her. Our first date coincided with a major dumping of snow here in the Twin Cities, to the tune of 13 inches! School was canceled. Not even 13 inches of snow was going to stop what might have been the last best chance for a couple of past- the-expiration daters from going out. We had extra time to get to know one another thanks to the snow and Devon's preference of navigating by the "left or right" system. We toured five cities before completing what was meant to be a 10 mile trip.

"Do I go left or right, Jeff?"

"Well, are we facing north or south?" "Is left north?" she asked.

"Well, it depends on which way you're facing, Devon." "I'm facing straight ahead..."

See what I mean? Devon knows she's navigationally challenged. *The blind leading the blind* is not a trite expression in our home.

Devon finally got us back to my apartment but was too nervous to think to mention that the snow had completely covered over the sidewalk. Moreover when I asked, "Can I give you a hug?" the recoil on her super-fast hug almost dumped us both in opposite snow banks. But the hug was good enough for both of us to see each other again.

I wouldn't rank the magic performance on the day I met Devon as one of my best. Perhaps Devon's charms were preoccupying my focus. After we had gone on our second "blind" date, as it were, I asked, "By the way, what did you think of my magic show?" Fortunately, her opinion of me wasn't based on how good my show came off, but rather the irresistible qualities of "love is blind."

"I don't remember anything about it. I was too busy thinking, *Gee. What am I going to say if he asks me out again?*"

"Then the LORD God said, 'It is not good for the man to be alone. I will make a helper who is right for him.'" – Genesis 2:18, GW

"A man is already halfway in love with any woman who listens to him." – Brendan Francis

CHAPTER 52

THE HOUSE THAT MAGIC BUILT OR I'M NOT THE ONLY ONE WITH GOOD TIMING

In 2002, I received a phone call from an old friend after 33 years of no contact. Craig Wagenknecht, whom I last knew as a restaurant chef, and former 6th grade smoke bomb conspirator, had become a building contractor. "How about we get together and do some catching up?" suggested Craig.

Sitting in my apartment reacquainting with one another, Craig said, "Have you ever considered building a home?" One thing led to another, and we began making plans for my house. He spent a lot of time and effort developing an affordable blueprint for me (Too bad the house was more expensive than the blueprint). Once construction began, he spent far more time explaining my options than any other contractor would have because of our history together as childhood friends.

While recovering from rotator cuff surgery at the transition facility, I was accumulating hundreds of dollars of charges on my cell phone because the phone in my room did not work. The accumulated hours of calling came out of my sheer boredom and, as someone who likes to be in control, the need I felt to supervise the last details of my new house, along with the packing at my apartment and unpacking at my new place. One day I was on the phone talking to my brother Mike regarding building details. My four-year-old niece, Mallorie, happened to overhear her dad. "Dad? Can I talk to Uncle Jeff?"

"OK," he responded, handing the receiver over.

"What are you talking about with my dad, Uncle Jeff?"

"We're talking about me building a house," I responded.

"Come on. Really, Uncle Jeff, what are you talking about?"

"Seriously, we're talking about me building a house."

In her disbelief, she turned to her dad and pleaded, "Dad, are you and Uncle Jeff really talking about Uncle Jeff building a house?"

"We sure are, honey," he said.

"But Dad...Hello-o-o?...He's blind!!"

Once again God was placing me in the right place at the right time.

My dad used an ad idea I inspired... I was the before, my brothers were the after.

The street where I decided to build my house just so happened to be in the neighborhood my brother Mike patrolled as a cop. No one in our family would have predicted that our little Boobie Benson would grow up to be a guardian of order and responsibility. In retrospect, he was clearly made to carry out this duty. In almost every case, he can defuse a potentially explosive situation through his genial personality and intimidating physical proportions. My mom's baby had grown to 290 pounds of muscle and power.

I can't tell you the number of times Mike checked (and still checks) on my safety on meal breaks during his patrol. And as long as he was in the neighborhood…he'd refuel in my kitchen to provide the physical wherewithal to continue his unceasing vigilance.

"You, LORD, will keep the needy safe and will protect us forever from the wicked." Psalm 12:7, TNIV

A few years later after I acquired Krypto, my pampered pooch, I couldn't blame him at all for seeing his adored "Uncle" Mike as competition. Once, Officer Mike unknowingly helped himself to doggy treats I kept in stylish tins. The decorative containers only made it more difficult to discern from people food by a hungry patrolman on the beat. "Are these homemade?" Mike asked crunching away.

"Store bought," I answered. "Not very good," Mike said.

"I've never tried them," I responded in all honesty.

"Don't buy any more on my account."

"OK, Mike," I snickered.

As a restless kid, Mike occasionally dabbled into our family dog's kibble bag. I guess once you get a taste for that stuff, it's just hard to give it up!

I know living with, and observing, the hilarious behavior of my little brother has gone a long way in developing how I see and appreciate the humor in everyday situations.

With the anticipation of the completion of my new house, I thought, *Oh boy! I'll have hundreds more square feet for magic tricks!* Little did I realize how all that extra space would soon be used.

"There is more than enough room in my Father's home. If this were not so, would I have told you that I am going to prepare a place for you?" John 14:2, NLT

Superheroes frequently invite me over as they, (1) know I won't discover the location of their secret lair, and, (2) they get to hang out in boxer shorts and a T-shirt.

Immaturity is my fountain of youth! Just ask Devon.

CHAPTER 53

STORY OF COURTSHIP
OR BROKEN PIECES ALL
FALLING IN PLACE

As our courtship progressed, I decided to share my intentions with Devon's mother, Delores. I called her and said, "I want you to know I am planning to ask your daughter to marry me."

"Oh! I've prayed for years someone like you would come into Devon's life!" she exclaimed.

Still unaware that I had shared my plans with her mother, Devon began commenting how thrilled her mom was about our relationship. She related how her mom teased her and after each date asking, "Were you nice to Jeff?"

"Well, yes," Devon would respond, slightly annoyed with her mom's prying.

"Did you give him a little something?" her mom would ask, referring to a kiss. Devon's standard retort frustrated her curious mother,

"Like usual, a Hershey bar and a handshake!"

I'm happy that I chose to share my intentions with Mrs. McVeigh when I did, because one week later she suffered a cerebral hemorrhage that, shortly afterward, led to her death. It was comforting to know that it brought Delores such joy to know that I loved and planned to marry her daughter—and that we had her blessing.

Not long after, I decided it would be a nice date opportunity to visit the Minnesota Zoo after hearing the Saturn Corporation was offering half-price tickets to Saturn owners.

"You own a Saturn, don't you honey?" I asked Devon as innocently as I could sound to hide my tight-fisted nature.

When we got to the admission gate, much to my dismay, I discovered the ticket prices were about seven times more than they had been the last time I was at the zoo—twenty years earlier! Not believing my ears, I asked the ticket seller to repeat that for me. At $14 a ticket, I was seriously reconsidering but knew it wouldn't look good to renege on Devon. As an entertainer, it's important to think quickly on your feet. So rather than being annoyed by the situation, I said to the ticket seller, "I'm blind. Do you let sighted guides in free?" (If you can't take advantage of your disability, then what's the point of having one?)

"I don't know whether we allow a sighted guide to go in free. I'll have to check with my supervisor," the young ticket taker said. "The ticket line is getting long, Honey," Devon pointed out to me.

The ticket seller came back and said, "There's no free admission for sighted guides." I tried another tack.

"Well, don't you abide by the ADA?" I said to the ticket seller. (The ADA is the Americans with Disabilities Act, which is legislation to protect the rights of people with disabilities, and not remotely related to protecting the rights of a cheapskate.) "I'll have to check with my supervisor," repeated the young ticket taker.

"Here, Jeff, I can pay for my own ticket," offered Devon. "It's not the money Honey, it's the principle of the thing," I politely responded.

When the ticket taker finally returned, she said, "The only kind of discount they have is for the developmentally disabled."

"I'll take it!" I said. All pride aside, my desire to save a buck was greater than my dignity and desire to impress a date.

"Save room for lunch," Devon said as we stopped at the homemade fudge table for samples.

"H-m-m, this one is good, not as good as the last one, but better than the first two I tried."

"You should probably choose one, Jeff," encouraged Devon.

"Is there a line behind us?" I asked,

"No, but..." Devon responded.

"OK, OK. It's down to these two." (I'm sure I bought something out of a sense of obligation. I just can't remember how much.)

Some might consider this type of behavior nothing more than "playing the blind card." I like to think of it more as demonstrating my resourcefulness and self-confidence.

Luckily, my brashness impressed Devon. She looks back on that day with amusement and has enjoyed retelling that story to our friends more than once.

"He showed tenacity," Devon recounts.

As frequently as I have unintentionally embarrassed Devon through unfiltered comments and impulsive behavior, in the great cosmic balance of things, she, at the same time, often becomes the amused beneficiary of my escapades. As we rested during the zoo tour, she looked at me and said, "You have a curly mustache hair that's bothering me. Here, let me pluck it."

As she plucked the strand of hair, I felt a "thwank" from between my eyes. She hadn't plucked out a half-inch mustache hair but rather a good two-inch long nasal hair that had somehow escaped detection throughout its (perhaps) decades long journey to daylight. Devon never laughed harder nor longer—and still chuckles today remembering the image of my eyes expanding to the size of saucers.

Over the years, I have developed ways to offset and compensate for my physical deficits. Tom Dosch, a mentor whose considered opinion I respect on many levels, reassures me that this sort of approach is really a form of adaptability and mental agility. I believe this resourcefulness makes me feel less disabled and appear less disabled to others.

For example, one of my helpers took me once to Applebee's to buy my dad a gift certificate. When we arrived, the restaurant hadn't opened yet. She said that she could see staff through the glass door getting ready for the day. I said, "Debbie, I'll knock on the door, and you hold up a piece of paper that says '$20 gift certificate?'"

Embarrassed, Debbie said, "No, no, Jeff—let's go somewhere else."

"Deb, we're already here! Besides, why wouldn't they want to make a quick sale? "Smile now," I coached. I knocked on the window with my cane. "Can they see it, Deb?" I asked out of the corner of my mouth.

"You're terrible!"

"We don't have time to come back later. We've got other stuff to do!"

The cashier saw us, smiled, and came to the door and said, "Oh, come on in!"

This is not just some unethical or huckster approach. In a larger sense, I'm demonstrating adaptability to the situation, given my natural limitations. I also do this kind of thing because I enjoy outrageous humor. In the vein of opposites attract, Devon, being shy, could appreciate my brashness and confidence.

In spite of Devon's busy work schedule that routinely included evening training sessions, and twice weekly meetings with her church group, we were able to see one another regularly.

Since Devon's school was only 10 minutes from my apartment, we lunched together often. Conversation between us came so effortlessly and we continued to share more and more with one another. Then one day, the light bulb went on for Devon: *Oh no! I've fallen in love!* Personally, I knew after our second phone conversation that this was the woman I wanted to marry. What confirmed it in Devon's mind was seeing the tenderness in my face as we listened to a recording of a skit that had been performed by my nieces and nephews. Curiously, this had captured her heart—a romantic checkmate.

Her heart had already been in a state of check ever since I sang to her extended family the lyrics to the *Hercules* cartoon show theme song, a McVeigh favorite. Devon fondly remembers standing on a box as a little girl, singing the theme song, then imitating Hercules jumping off Mount Olympus as she jumped off the box:

Hercules: winner of song and story.
Hercules: hero of ancient glory.
Fighting for the right. Fighting with his might.
With the strength of ten ordinary men.

Hercules: only the evil fear him.
Hercules: people are safe when near him.
Softness in his eyes. Iron in his thighs.
Virtue in his heart. Fire in every part, of the mighty Hercules!"

Surgically fused knee, bent up fingers and all—I had become Devon's Hercules.

Engagement Night

It was Halloween 2002, and we had plans to celebrate my birthday which had occurred the day before. I said to Devon, "Why bother making a cake for me? Let me make it magically appear! From this empty cake pan..." I said as I struck a dramatic pose.

Of course, this was all a ruse to get her to lift the lid and see a ring box inside!

Knowing me, she figured the nice box must contain something scary like a fake spider or spring snake. When she finally opened it, she said, "Jeff! Is it real?"

"It's ¾-carat-diamond real," I responded crassly. Her question later made me wonder that if she couldn't even tell the difference between a fake and a real diamond...hmm...

Genuinely speaking, Devon shows authentic beauty not through the display of her ring but through the clarity of her faith in me.

"...show me your face, let me hear your voice; for your voice is sweet, and your face is lovely." Song of Solomon 2:14

"Laughter is the sun that drives winter from the human face." – Victor Hugo

CHAPTER 54

THE WEDDING OR GET ME TO THE CHURCH ON TIME

When I look back on that wonderful day, I'm just glad I actually made it to my wedding. Everyone knows that on the wedding day, the passage of time compresses itself, making the clock your enemy. Everyone also knows I run habitually late, though I'm much better than I used to be. My best man, Don Dinger, advised me:

"Make your haircut appointment as early as you can. Let's make sure we don't run out of time."

Since we weren't supposed to get to the church until three o'clock for pictures, and the wedding didn't start until six o'clock, I thought an eleven a.m. pick-up time was unnecessarily early. I didn't want to rock the boat, so I agreed.

Well, the day started off fine enough as I got a haircut, and a styling which was thrown in for good measure by my barber, Jerry. Jerry and all my friends tease me about the "over importance" I place on my hair. For Pete's sake! My hair is one of my few body parts that isn't disabled! Besides, shouldn't a magician be known by his hare?

Next, Don and I went back to my South Saint Paul house so he could shower, since the water heater at his house had gone out. And of course we'd fetch the ring before we left. I knew I was in good hands with Don who was keeping everything under control, and the pressure off me. Next stop was the formal wear store (now out of business, and it's no wonder) where we were informed my tux wasn't ready. I still didn't feel any pressure, though, because my old friend

Don was in charge. *His* blood pressure, however, was steadily moving up. After a long delay, my measurements were retaken, and then we waited again for the alterations. Finally they came out with a tux that made no allowance for my one shorter leg and shorter arm. When we pointed this out, the clerk said,

"The tux is fine. It's your arm and leg that are too short."

"Excuse me?" I said incredulously. I wanted to start swinging my cane at this guy, who needed basic lessons in customer service—not to mention diversity awareness.

But Don jumped in and politely said to the insensitive clerk, "Well, if you wouldn't mind, sir, he needs this readjusted as soon as possible for his wedding today."

After three hours, I felt the first pangs of pressure. The pressure mounted when we realized we had to go back to my house for the ring. I thought Don had it; he thought I had it. If Don at that point had been hooked up to a blood pressure cuff, its internal fluid would have had the force to be the next tourist attraction at Yellowstone Park.

We ended up arriving 90 minutes late to the church and there was only about an hour left to finish the remaining photo shots.

In our absence, the photographer wisely snapped the shots that didn't require our presence. We raced through the church doors; Mollie combed and sprayed my "do"; Don borrowed someone's electric razor to shave and changed into his tux; and we presented ourselves to the photographer who snapped the remaining pictures—all in about twenty minutes.

The photos turned out great.

And our story continues, making my life complete and introducing Devon to all kinds of crazy things. As all my friends and family repeatedly remind me, "That Devon...she's a gol-darned saint!"

Photo - courtesy of Jenkin's Photography

As I waited in the foyer to proceed to the altar, I listened to the musicians sing lyrics I had selected to reflect my feelings toward Devon and the circumstances of our relationship.

I chose a song written by contemporary Christian artist Geoff Moore, "If You Could See What I See."

Chorus:
And you would know you have my heart,
if you could see what I see,
that a treasure is what you are,
if you could see what I see. Created to be,
the only one for me.
If you could see what I see.
(Readers can download this piece from iTunes.)

My father and mother escorted me down the aisle, with my mom continuously whispering "Smile, don't be nervous, Jeff."

If she keeps saying that, I will be nervous! I thought. At the altar my dad shook my hand and my mom hugged me. Later I was told two of my burly, rough and tumble, weight-lifter brothers, Mike and Steve, had tears in their eyes.

Three hundred and fifty guests attended our wedding. Expensive? Yes, but considering we had hoped and waited for this event for four decades, definitely worth it! We celebrated in style— a sit down dinner followed by a 16-piece swing band that kept everyone hopping all night long.

Throughout the evening, my parents had many guests tell them that our wedding had been the best one they had ever attended.

Although some had attended more lavish weddings, the remark my parents repeatedly heard was, "Jeff and Devon's wedding had a storybook quality unlike any we've ever attended before."

"That is why a man leaves his father and mother and is united to his wife, and they become one flesh." Genesis 2:24

"To get the full value of joy you must have someone to divide it with."
— Mark Twain

At our wedding reception, the videographer asked my 5 year old niece Mallorie what was special about her Uncle Jeff. She responded, "He does magic twicks. He can't dwive a cah 'cuz he's bwind. And he gots a stiff leg… and bendy fingahs!" To emphasize her point, she held both hands with bended fingers up to the video camera before her mortified mother. Mallorie still jokes with me because she sees me simply as regular-ol' goofy Uncle Jeff.

CHAPTER 55

GREETING CARDS AND CHARM SAVES HARM

Like most newlyweds, we encountered some challenges that first year. Not surprising considering how long we each had been set in our ways. Because Devon was so used to a sighted, able-bodied world, I lost sight (no pun intended) of all the adjustments she had to make committing to our marriage. She really opened my eyes to how much she's had to adapt to my world. In a short period of time, Devon faced a lot: she lost her mother and friend during the first year of our relationship; after our wedding, she sold her childhood home and many treasured possessions to move into my house—half the size of hers; she had to learn a new part of town; and she had to remember to put things back in exactly the same spot for my sake, among others. As an introvert, Devon recharges her batteries with quiet, but I, the performer, am an extrovert and thrive off the energy of others. My personality, business, and physical needs sometimes result in a hurricane of activity buzzing around our home, while Devon tries to maintain her calm being the unwitting eye of the storm.

Devon's wit and appreciation of my humor served her well during the first year of trials as she transitioned into her new world, half the time in tears, the other half laughing. Lucky for me, my special lady appreciates the funny things of everyday life. Even when she's not coming up with a funny quip or observation, she emboldens me to step out of my comfort zone where funny situations can be a result. Just such an opportunity arose on the eve of her birthday when we visited a local card shop.

"Don't peek, Honey! I'll be watching!" I joked as I sorted through the greeting cards. Wanting to convince her how romantic a husband I can be, I insisted on choosing a birthday card for her all by myself. (I also was testing new degrees of personal independence, which Devon always encourages.)

She laughed, but found the idea charming and romantic. She pointed me in the direction of the cards. I felt around a little bit, but since all the cards looked the same to me, I just grabbed one. It was an unusually shaped card, and I had difficulty finding its matching envelope. I ended up taking an envelope that was handy. I figured even if the card had to be folded an extra time or two, Devon would appreciate the gesture just the same. I was really quite proud of myself and even imagined the "x's and 'o's" that might later arise from my gesture.

I went home and asked my assistant (she helps me with the clerical tasks involved with my business) to tell me what card I had chosen. My hand-chosen card turned out to be one of the store's display signs that indicate the category of greeting card, such as Anniversary, Sympathy, and, in this case, Birthday! My intent was to buy Devon a card with a funny message on it. Well, this was as funny a message as I could ever want. My assistant folded it to be shaped like an actual greeting card, and we wrote on it, "I would like to share with you my unique love by giving you a most unique card."

The funniest part of this whole story was the reaction of the store clerk. As I brought the card up to the counter to pay for it, I had instructed Devon to not look at the card. I had unintentionally presented the clerk with an unusual dilemma. I beamed with pride as I asked her, "Have you ever had a blind person pick out a greeting card all by himself?"

With a confused voice, she responded, "No...I can't say we have!" I don't know if it was a desire to spare my feelings, or general nervousness about interacting with a person who is blind that led the clerk to ignore my mistake. Whatever the reason, when I asked:

"How much do I owe?" she hesitated, then I heard her turn the card over a couple of times.

Finally she said, "I guess a couple of dollars." I thought it kind of strange, a clerk not knowing the price of something they were selling.

But it didn't matter that I had chosen the wrong card, because I had just scored big points with my wife.

Speaking of scoring points on birthdays, when Devon turned 40, she expressed a little dissatisfaction with the aging process.

My hand picked, unintentionally unique birthday card to my wife Devon.

To encourage her, I said in all sincerity, "But Honey, for a woman of your age, you're as beautiful as you can be!" (Men, learn a lesson from me: what may seem to you to be a reasonable, reassuring message to your wife can land you in the doghouse for reasons you don't quite understand...)

A few months later, a morning radio show host invited husbands to call in with something they said to their wives intended as a compliment but taken differently. Since my comments were seared in Devon's memory, she encouraged me to call in. Our story was the winner, and we were awarded a 40th anniversary DVD of *Mary Poppins.* As we viewed it sitting together on the couch, I turned to her and said, "Honey, you've never looked younger—really!" Whenever I say something stupid to Devon, I've learned to fall back on the fact of how much school I missed as a result of illness and hospitalization. "I must have missed that year, Honey." On the morning of her 48th birthday, I thought it would be fun to needle her. I cheerfully greeted her by saying, "48...what a grand old age."

"What!" she responded sleepily, *and* annoyed.

"I mean, Honey, being 48 is like finely aged beef."

"Excuse me?" she responded, now totally awake. "Wouldn't it sound better, Jeff, to say something like 'finely aged wine'?"

"Well, I meant it in the good sense that you are well-marbled with no gristle."

"You're digging yourself deeper. How about just a 'Happy Birthday' and leave it at that?" She moved into the bathroom, leaving me in bed wondering if what I had said had been such a great idea after all. For a guy with arthritis, I'm pretty nimble. I can put both feet in my mouth.

"Whoever keeps his mouth and his tongue keeps himself out of trouble." Proverbs 21:23, ESV

"You grow up on the day you have your first real laugh, at yourself."– Ethel Barrymore

"There are three kinds of men who do not understand women: Young, old, and middle-aged." – Anonymous (and with good reason)

PUTTING MY SHOULDER TO THE GRINDSTONE OR I'M A HOSPITAL MAGNET

During a routine physical in 2004, my doctor noticed that I had a high PSA count.

The biopsy cleared me, and I had a clean bill of health, temporarily. But the following spring, I fell while sitting down in a bus, and tore my left rotator cuff.

I wasn't anxious about the surgery since I had successfully healed from surgery on my right rotator cuff two years earlier. But the anesthesiologist whom I was soon to encounter would change that.

To avoid the potentially harmful side-effects of anesthesia, they were going to use a local anesthetic for the surgery. The anesthesiologist's technique was proving to be unsuccessful in deadening the nerves in my shoulder area. Normally able to handle pain, the agony I felt from the continual probing of her needle was too much. "You're going to have to knock me out," I said through gritted teeth. What happened next led me to believe she may have been new to her profession.

Obviously, I don't understand all that's involved with general anesthetic, and I can only speak for myself regarding the experience. Part of the process involves inserting an intubation tube down your throat to allow a respirator to breathe for you since the general anesthetic prevents your lungs from breathing on their own. This anesthesiologist was so slow and clumsy in maneuvering the breathing tube down my throat that I was suffocating. Granted, the effects of RA prevent my neck from bending backward more than a few degrees, but other anesthesiologists have managed despite this limitation. My arms were taped down but my legs were flailing away trying to signal her that I didn't have a spare orifice for breathing and that she'd better be quick about it! Somehow I became unconscious—I assume from medication, not a lack of oxygen.

All said and done, the doctors were happy with their repair job. This time around, I realized that home health care was available in the form of physical and occupational therapists as well as aides trained to help with showering, etc. Medical wisdom says that a patient recovers better at home anyway. Devon stayed home from work my first week back. Recovery from rotator cuff surgery is more problematic for someone like me because of how much I depend on the use of my arms to help me stand and sit down. We investigated the cost of an electric lift chair, but the price was prohibitive. As I called around, I'd ask medical providers if they knew of anyone who had a used lift chair they no longer needed. Surprisingly, one of them said they did. Kindly, my buddies Craig Wagenknecht and Don Dinger picked it up and hauled it into our living room.

Cooking was a great stress reliever to Devon following my shoulder surgery and subsequent staph infection. Some days were more stressful than others.

Recovery was proceeding on schedule, and the stitches were removed. But shortly thereafter, I began feeling dizzy. Devon took my temperature; it was approaching 102 degrees. She called my then internist's office and convinced them I needed to be seen right away. He prescribed a full spectrum antibiotic and told me I instead needed to see the orthopedic doctor who had performed the surgery. We made an appointment to see him the next day. After more blood work, he joined us in his office, obviously upset. "An infection has started within the surgical site, I'm afraid to say."

I didn't understand why he was upset over what seemed to be minor infection. I thought the solution would be to simply take a course of antibiotics, and that would be that! Unfortunately, it was a staph infection, which meant the shoulder would have to be reopened and cleaned out followed by a month of daily intravenous antibiotics. I was readmitted to the hospital and had surgery the next morning.

Surgeons had to remove all the sutures to properly clean out the site. The infection had already eaten away the remaining healthy tissue that would have enabled them to repair the rotator cuff once again.

Devon and me on the deck of our home constructed by our friend Craig Wagenknecht.

I felt sorry for Devon as she fretted about the day-to-day challenges involved with this process, including the later reinsertion of a new intravenous PICC line as the first line had plugged. Once they felt the infection was gone, I began home health physical therapy. I needed to develop compensatory muscles in my shoulder to prevent the arm from being totally useless. I've regained good range of motion, and am able to perform my magic shows with only minor adjustments. The shoulder, however, is about 80% disabled and will always be very weak. The physical limitations of my injury helped me realize that the strength of my professional presentations is less based on what I can do "magically," but rather on the personality and perspective I share.

"You are my hiding place; you will protect me from trouble and surround me with songs of deliverance." Psalm 32:7

"If you can find a path with no obstacles, it probably doesn't lead anywhere." – Frank A. Clark

There are some disadvantages to being blind. The other day I accidentally brushed my teeth with gunpowder. For the rest of the day, I shot my mouth off!

CHAPTER 57

KRYPTO, THE WONDER DOG OR FUR-EVER YOURS

"On lunch break, I stopped at the pet store and saw the cutest Goldendoodle puppy," Devon explained to me hesitantly in January of 2006.

When the subject of buying a dog first came up, I had reservations. "A dog would shed on my tuxedo; I won't be able to play with it on the floor; I might trip over it."

But following my rotator cuff surgery, my physical therapist continually talked about her new Goldendoodle puppy.

"What's a Goldendoodle?" Devon and I asked.

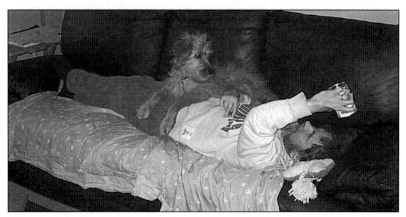

Devon trained Krypto to be a service dog. He decided to also be my rehab coach after my rotator-cuff surgery...or maybe he's more interested in what's inside that can of fruit.

"Goldendoodles are a mix of poodle and golden retriever." Devon quietly researched the breed. "It's supposed to be a gentle dog, and you wouldn't have to worry about it knocking you over, Honey," she pleaded. "They're really smart, so we could train it to pick up things that you drop," she continued. "I'll take full responsibility for its upbringing, Dear." My resistance was crumbling. Oh-h-h, the wiles of a woman. But the final barrier to getting a dog was removed when I noticed the stress Devon was under from a series of difficult transitions occurring at work. Caring for a puppy would help take her mind off work.

"I'll let you name him," she offered.

"OK, OK. How about Krypto?" Krypto was the name of the dog Superman had as a boy.

After more discussion (during a fantastic steak dinner prepared by Devon out of the blue), I agreed to go see him. "Well, he is kind of a cute little guy," I admitted as he nibbled the tip of my cane.

The first night home, Krypto cried for several hours in his crate in the next room until we caught on that he needed to be with us. After corralling him alongside our bed, he immediately fell asleep and didn't make a sound until the next morning, when we stepped out of the room.

Shortly after bringing him home, I fell over him. But I can't really blame Krypto for that. At the time, I was doing my famous impersonation of "husband chasing wife." I'm not fast, but I've got a quick first step. As I lay there assessing whether or not I had broken anything, Krypto curled up tightly against me. I interpreted this behavior as his saying, "I'm here for you, Dad, no matter how long it takes." After this experience, he caught on that I cannot see him. Even if he's asleep, once he senses that I'm approaching and not going to stop, he'll leap out of my way which sometimes I only discover after stepping on the warm spot where he had been. From that point on, he's never left my side; his protective nature keeps him near me wherever I go.

"Hurry up with the kibble or Lincoln gets it!"

253

Unless he's distracted by someone like a delivery person or postal worker, he'll keep alongside me, matching my slower pace as I move about the house.

Doggone it, Devon was right about Krypto's usefulness. He has been a help to me, picking up all kinds of things I drop: my cell phone, tableware, paper, you name it. In fact, he's a downright neatnick! If a stack of DVD's isn't in alignment, he'll growl at them and poke at the offending cases until they meet his standards. Krypto is a self-appointed indoor grounds keeper. It really bothers him to see anything out of place on the floor. Devon will sometimes drop newspaper sections onto the carpet after reading them, and he will pick them up again as if saying, "Here, Mom. You must have dropped this piece of newspaper—let me help." Nothing out of place escapes his scrutiny, except his dozens of stuffed animals strewn about.

His love affair with these toys is complex with overtones of passive-aggressiveness. Krypto relishes disemboweling his "babies," the term we use for his stuffed animals. However, eating too much of this stuffing causes his bowel movements to become bound with material. This results in what Devon has coined "chasers," which describes (to be as discrete as possible) residual matter not separating from Krypto's body after he goes potty outside. Following nature's call, Krypto immediately bursts into a run to shake off his "pursuer," hence the name "chasers".

Hark! Do I hear a bowl of kibble in distress? Up, up, and away!

I'm grateful Krypto has a natural bent toward forgiveness of apparent disloyalty, especially with his old man. One day after letting him out, I was surprised how quickly he was ready to come back in. Petting his head, I said to him after shutting the door, "You came right in like a good boy," while thinking, *His fur is pretty matted; he could really use a shampoo.*

"Hey, what's this black dog doing in here?!" Devon hollered from the office.

Almost simultaneously I heard muffled barks coming from outside the back door. I opened it and as Krypto brushed by me, snorting and huffing, it was clear he was disgusted that his own dad could replace him so cavalierly.

Because of what Krypto means to Devon and me, it was devastating when in January of 2011 we learned that he had lymphoma. Our local vet recommended that he be treated at the University of Minnesota's veterinarian clinic. We made the decision to pursue the recommended, albeit very expensive, course of chemotherapy. We also used a nutritional daily food supplement and prayed and prayed. Some questioned our logic in praying for our dog, telling us it was silly. But I felt that since the Bible says that Jesus will return on a white horse, it might mean animals will exist in heaven. At the least God cares about our feelings.

Krypto's chemo treatment slowed him down and caused him to lose most of his fur. Despite his cancer, he carried on with life as if he didn't feel the discomfort. Through good care at the University and at home with extra love and lots of prayer, at this time (June 2013) much to the amazement of everyone, Krypto is in remission, cancer-free, and has far surpassed the median survival rate of dogs with his type of cancer. He's now referred to as "the miracle dog" by clinicians at the U of M and our local vet. His fan club, including his groomer and assistants along with vets and technicians, showed up at my book launch party—but were disappointed that Krypto couldn't make the event.

His cancer episode reminds us that nothing in life is forever or can be counted on, except God's love.

Krypto and I are comedians and love to show off, particularly low-brow humor. I make funny faces and noises, sometimes ones that are even intelligible, to get a reaction out of Devon. In the same vein, Krypto hops up on the couch, turns his back to us and pretends he doesn't realize he's swatting us in the face with his tail. He gives himself away, however, when we see him look back over his shoulder to see our reaction.

But what is most similar about Krypto and I, according to Devon, is that we have each traveled a bumpy road and have come through with our tails wagging.

"Good people are good to their animals..."
Proverbs 12:10, MSG

"With the exception of women, there is nothing on earth so agreeable or necessary to the comfort of man as the dog." – Edward Jesse, *Anecdote of Dogs*

"A door is what a dog is perpetually on the wrong side of." – Ogden Nash

Chapter 58

Surprise 50th Birthday Party or Tricking the Trickster

As a professional trickster, I never imagined I'd be so bamboozled as a result of a scheme from my very own wife, of all people! The fact I had no idea that I was in the dead center of the whirlwind preparations for my own surprise party qualifies me as having a whole new degree of blindness.

Two months before my actual 50th birthday, Devon threw the ultimate surprise party. To ensure the surprise, and to get me out of the house, she arranged with a friend to hire me for a bogus birthday party. She then worked with the DARTS transportation service to drive me around in circles for a while and drop me back home at a designated time.

Earlier that week, as Devon was working at the stove, I innocently asked "Weren't you making sloppy joes just yesterday?" not realizing Devon had actually been making vats of sloppy joes for days.

"Well, uh, yes I was, but they had a great sale on hamburger and I wanted to stock up on meals for the winter," she answered coolly enough to keep my radar from going off.

On the day of the big event, friends and family worked in the garage preparing for the party. The planners were confident I would not stumble upon their true mission because of yet another misdirection Devon had ready in her back pocket.

"My sisters-in-law and I are going to have a garage sale this weekend at our house. It might be a little noisy; just ignore us," Devon said nonchalantly.

Upon arrival at my supposed show, I couldn't understand why all of the guests at my "client's" birthday party were yelling, "Happy Birthday, Jeff!" Once I recognized Devon's voice among all the well-wishers, I said, "What are YOU doing here?" "I live here!" she replied. "And you do, too! Surprise!"

I forgive all the deception perpetrated by my trusted wife, not only because of her well-intentioned purpose, but because of the sacrifice she made to earn the $600 to pay for the party. Months earlier she agreed to drive me on a three-day tour of libraries in northern Minnesota. July 2007 turned out to be the hottest month on record for northern MN. Air conditioning was non-existent or not adequate because temperatures rarely exceed 85, let alone 100 degrees.

"For by me your days will be multiplied, and years will be added to your life." Proverbs 9:11, ESV

Here I am walking up my own driveway, thinking I am at a client's home and asking the driver, 'So, is this a pretty nice house?"

My Super 50th cake.

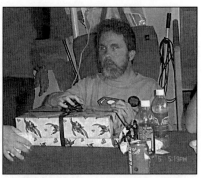

Commencing with the most important part of the party – I opened the loot!

My nieces and nephews were surprised how my cherished presents were the same kind of gifts they received a decade earlier. They sure do bring out the kid in me.

Don't you just hate it when you go to a party and someone shows up in the exact same outfit?

CHAPTER 59

SELDOM IS HEARD A DISCOURAGING WORD OR I'M RIGHT BEHIND YOU, JEFFO!

Throughout the first 18 years of my career, I had two or three inquiries about out-of-state opportunities, but nothing ever panned out. It was only after I received a phone call from the TV show *America's Got Talent* in 2006, with an invitation to audition in Chicago, that the framework for future trips began falling in place. The possibilities that might come out of winning this contest were almost too much to comprehend: a $1,000,000 prize was at stake! Since I've always relied on the Biblical maxim of "wisdom comes from the counsel of many," I once again reached out to those whose opinions I respected in these areas. Magician friends Geoff Williams, Scott Franz, and Norm Barnhart shared with me their experience in the areas of comedy, magic technique, and showmanship, and a ninety-second audition was created.

"Jeff, the only way you are even going to have a chance to impress the judges is by being yourself and playing off your natural strengths," Geoff advised. "There are more talented magicians around than you… And there are funnier comedians around than you…And there are better looking presenters around than you…" "You aren't doing much for my confidence at the moment," I interjected.

"My point is, there aren't a lot of guys who have all these things in one package like you do…"

"And besides, they're not blind!" Scott chirped in.

Conjuring up a group of supportive people to accompany me to Chicago was a cinch: Devon, Craig and Scott Saari. Team Jeffo was born.

In this endeavor, Devon was my rock, comforter, dresser, and hair fluffer. She knows better than anyone how fussy I am preparing myself for a show. "The hair! The hair! Watch the hair!" I don't even mind friends giving me a hard time about my vanity as long as the hair looks good. Scott encouraged my creative juices and kept me loose; Craig shared in the driving and was my designated grunt and food-runner.

After checking in at the convention center and being directed to the waiting area, the producer who had called to invite me to audition greeted us. "I've really looked forward to meeting you, Jeff. You look fantastic!" he said.

Whew...the hair must be looking ok, I thought in relief.

An NBC crew filmed my audition, which took place in front of a team of assistant producers. Following the filming, one of them said, "Almost everyone has done two takes, but you were so good, one is all we need."

Another producer said, "Hold on, Jeffo, I'm going to get the supervising director. I want my boss to see this film."

"You're really funny," a crew member added while we were waiting.

I was thrilled with their feedback, but I hadn't considered that the novelty of being a blind magician could work against me. In the process of narrowing down 4,000 acts, I imagined the producers having a conversation like, "Well, he's good, but if we advance him, we might be accused of doing it out of tokenism, not because he earned it. On the other hand, if and when he is eliminated, people might accuse us of being unfair and biased against a person with disabilities."

Although overall I presented an appealing package, my individual components did not match the judges' criteria. I wasn't Hollywood flashy; I wasn't entertainingly bad; I just wasn't their cup of tea. In spite of not advancing beyond the audition, it was fun putting together an act with my friends and exciting preparing for and traveling to the audition with Team Jeffo. The greatest benefit that came out of this experience was learning I could take my act on the road—even if it was just overnight. Once these beloved encouragers showed me it could be done, it gave me the confidence to accept future invitations to travel professionally.

We brought along a video camera and filmed as much of this adventure as we were allowed. Devon dubbed this type of video production as "Jeffreality," which also serves as the title of my blog. We took the camera into the Billy Goat restaurant made famous by the Saturday Night Live skit ...

"Cheezborger! Cheezborger! No fries, cheeps! No Pepsi, Coke!"

Members of the Greek family working the counter were extremely gracious and re-enacted with us the skit from the show, exaggerated accents and all.

"One who has unreliable friends soon comes to ruin, but there is a friend who sticks closer than a brother." Proverbs 18:24, TNIV

Did you know I can parallel park as well as the average driver?

CHAPTER 60

THE UNSINKABLE JEFF AND DEVON OR CRUISING FOR A BRUISING

⁓

The first four years of marriage, punctuated by three surgeries, six months of collective home rehab, and stress from Devon's department downsizing left us ready for our first vacation. At the suggestion of many friends, we booked a one-week cruise to the Caribbean on a cruise line whose name shall remain anonymous. Devon and I were proud on two accounts: first, we got the cruise at a great price. Second, we had compiled an exhaustive file that contained information on every possible contingency: itinerary, cruise line reviews, seasonal discounts and promotions, packing tips, airline and cruise assistive services, airport security regulations, etc. We put everything on a credit card (knowing we couldn't pay it off the next month), which may have been our first step in pulling the proverbial finger out of the hole in the dike.

Our second questionable step came from my desire to make a quick buck. In spite of the repeated advice in our two-inch thick travel portfolio recommending we arrive twenty-four hours ahead of the ship's departure, I squeezed in one last show. I cringe when I remember saying to Devon, "It's fine! Don't worry!"

"But Jeff, the research I've done strongly advises we leave a day ahead."

"We'll arrive five hours before the ship leaves. We'll have plenty of time," I reassured her. I did the show and beamed over the extra

$200 in my pocket, "Now, Honey, we're ready!" But I didn't consider one contingency: Twin Cities' weather.

On the morning of our March 2007 departure, the fog that encased the Twin Cities equaled anything London could produce. The Minneapolis-St. Paul International Airport was shut down indefinitely. Sitting in the departure gate waiting area, we stewed as hour after hour passed, wondering, "Are we going to make it in time to catch the ship in Miami?" A black cloud had already settled over us; Laurie Dinger had to cancel last minute due to illness but insisted her husband, Don, continue on without her. Devon and I consoled him as best we could during our wait. It was clear he was there on behalf of his wife's wishes, and out of a sense of wanting to assist us on our first cruise, more than for his own pleasure.

Finally, after a five-hour delay, our plane departed. The representative from our travel agency reassured us (the group of 30 or so who had booked a flight and cruise package with them) they had contacted the cruise line and requested the ship to be held in the event we were late. During the flight, I kept checking my Braille watch. We landed, grabbed our bags, and met the cruise line representative, who stopped us dead in our tracks. Ignoring the request, our ship, the only one to do so, left right on time. Everyone else on our plane made it to their awaiting ships. Our group was left sitting in the Miami airport because our captain took pride in being punctual. Mulling over our situation, Devon asked, "Was that extra $200 really that important?"

My silence spoke volumes. To her credit, Devon just hugged me and said, "You lovable knucklehead! Compared to working, this is still great!"

Our travel agency scrambled to find accommodations for the 30 of us until a flight could be arranged to catch up with the ship at the first port of call: San Juan, Puerto Rico. But alas, Miami's convention business was booming, and vacancies were nonexistent. Once again we stewed, waiting hour after hour for plan B. The only option turned out to be a midnight flight to San Juan, where a single hotel could accommodate a group of our size. We were informed of this at 11:45 p.m. We embarked on our march through Miami's deserted and sprawling airport toward our gate on its opposite end.

Don was an experienced traveler. The entirety of his luggage consisted of a carry-on and a garment bag. Conversely, our "covering every contingency" mentality left Devon and me with no less than seven pieces of luggage. Without asking, Don came to our aid and grabbed three of our bags. He looked like a luggage rack had fallen on him. Devon and I were left with the other four suitcases.

Devon put two on my shoulders and said, "Walk fast. We have a long way to go." I couldn't even use Devon for a sighted guide because her luggage was in the way. She needed to keep looking back, yelling directions, "More to the left!" or "More to the right, Honey!" Neither my arthritic frame nor heart were accustomed to such physical demands. I hit the wall, my energy totally spent. "I can't go anymore!" I shouted as I dropped the bags off my shoulders in total frustration and exhaustion.

I stopped, not caring whether or not I made the flight. Devon suddenly spotted an empty wheelchair. I fell into it, limp as a wet noodle. Devon piled three of our four cases on my lap, and we continued our weary way. With Devon in tears, we made it to the plane just in time, though we had to wait another hour aboard the plane, without air conditioning, until the pilot had flown in from another location.

Arriving at our San Juan hotel at 3 a.m., we slowly moved with the line to the check-in counter feeling fortunate that, unlike some in our tour group, we had all our luggage. If we couldn't be on the ship, we were at least looking forward to the next two days in this upscale hotel (which the travel agent in Miami told us they had arranged) as well

Here I am in San Juan, Puerto Rico, in the crow's nest of our hotel balcony, searching for our missing cruise ship.

as sight-seeing in this beautiful and historic city. Devon, Don and I were the last three to check-in and were informed there was only one room remaining. Knowing we three would be sharing a room, we adopted our 50-year-old friend Don and referred to him as "Little Donny." "I've been on a cruise before, and it's nothing like this!" Don said sympathetically.

Our hopeful expectations were dashed when we were then informed the hotel could accommodate us only until 11:00 that morning and arrangements had been made with a second hotel to house us until our ship arrived.

With only airline snacks in our bellies and having been awake for 27 hours, we fell into bed. After four hours of sleep, we hurried to get ready so we could squeeze in some breakfast before check-out time.

Hotel officials told us a van would be sent and the hotel manager added, "We're expecting new guests any minute and need to clear the lobby. Can you please wait outside for your transportation?"

We sat in the hot sun on our luggage all afternoon, hope rising with each approaching bus, none of which were intended for our group. Finally, we were picked up and were transported to the second hotel.

Everyone was exhausted and went to bed immediately. I don't know if anyone actually slept; I know I didn't. I couldn't find the control to adjust the sleep number on my concrete slab.

The next morning, with another check out time at 11, we had nowhere to go but the Port of San Juan to wait for the arrival of our ship, scheduled for 5 PM. As Devon and I exited the hotel, we heard the theme from the movie Titanic playing over the hotel speakers. Somehow, it seemed strangely appropriate.

Don put on an optimistic face, "When we get to the pier, we'll have six hours to shop and lounge at different cafes. I can't wait for my first mojito," he added.

After the hotel van dropped us off, we discovered everything on the pier was locked down. Even the check-in building was locked. To add insult to injury, the black cloud that had formed in the Twin Cities had traveled with us and now began to literally rain down.

The 30 of us sought shelter under the one-foot overhang of the front gate. Plastered against the brick, I felt like one of the victims of the St. Valentine's Day Massacre waiting in dread to see what would happen next. *At least those doomed gangsters stayed dry to their end,* I thought.

An occasional cab drove by. "Let's take a cab to a fantastic restaurant I've been to that has the world's greatest mojitos," suggested Don, who had previously vacationed in Puerto Rico. Taking turns watching one another's luggage, clusters of people from the group alternated going into old San Juan for lunch.

Reaching this noted location, I managed to climb several dozen non-ADA compliant ancient steps before arriving at the restaurant.

Looking around, we didn't see anyone. Seeing our confusion, someone nearby approached us and said, "Sorry folks. They're closed on Mondays."

"I've been on a cruise before, and it's nothing like this!" Don mumbled.

After traversing back down the veritable mountainside of steps, we stopped at the first restaurant available. The three of us didn't even look at the menu; we asked what was good—and fast—and ordered Cuban sandwiches. Don and I tried to relax with a drink and Devon had her customary diet soda.

"I feel so bad about how everything has turned out for your first cruise, so I'd like to take care of the check," Don announced.

"Great!" I jumped in.

"Honey, we shouldn't take advantage of the situation," Devon pointed out.

"Please! Can't we be gracious about Don's kind offer?" I asked. "Whatever..." Devon said, rolling her eyes at Don.

When the bill arrived, Don looked at it and said to the server, "There must be a mistake on our bill."

The server examined the slip for a few seconds and said, "No, everything's correct." Don blanched.

The server continued, "$15 appetizer; 3 sandwiches, $20 each; 3 drinks, $30...it all adds up, Senor!"

Wet and frustrated, we took the cab back to the pier. After standing at attention for more than five hours, everyone was delirious as we saw our ship approach.

An official under a large umbrella warmly greeted us on the pier. "The captain has decided to let the passengers disembark before you people board."

"How long is that going to take?" several of us asked, almost in unison.

"Not long…about an hour." This news was greeted with muffled profanity.

Once 2,000 passengers left the ship, our sodden, rag-tag group stumbled aboard. Devon and I made it to our cabin. Bladders and bowels bursting, we fought over who would use the bathroom first. "The toilet won't flush, Honey!" Devon alerted me from the bathroom.

With an overloaded ileostomy bag, images of the Hindenburg disaster flashed in my mind. Our steward called maintenance, and fortunately our toilet was put back into business.

"Man! Listen to the clarity of these walkie-talkies. It's like you're right here, Don!" As always, Don patiently endures.

The next five days were filled with dark clouds and rain, except for the one day of sunshine we had on the beaches of St. Maarten. Devon and I spent the entire day under a giant umbrella, protecting our rice-cake complexions. Like rice, I cooked, ending up with heat exhaustion. Heading back to the ship in a taxi driven by a Cuban cabby who launched into a profanity- laced tirade espousing Castro's mani-festo, I fought off dizziness and nausea. He left us at the pier, several blocks from the ship. After weaving my way for about a half a block I said to no one in particular, "How much longer until the ship?" "We still have a ways to go, Honey," Devon said calmly. I kept thinking, *Left foot forward, followed by the right.*

"Are we almost there?" I mumbled.

"Only a few more blocks," Devon responded. "I can't go anymore!"

"Hang in there, Honey." "I need a wheelchair!"

"I'm sorry, there's none around." "Don, can you carry me?"

"Honey, Don's got his arms full of our stuff."

My feet felt like anvils; my breathing sounded like Darth Vader; my head spun like a tilt-a-whirl. "I can't do it! I can't do it!"

"We're almost there," Devon encouraged.

"I think I'm going to need a doctor," I slurred.

"Well, remember, if the ship's doctor thinks you're infectious, he'll quarantine you for the rest of the trip," Devon said, reiterating what she had read online. After an hour in our cabin with ice on my head and Devon's portable fan blowing on me, I felt better.

We sailed to our following day's destination, St. Thomas Island.

We hired a cab to take us to the highest point on the island, a popular vista overlooking the bay. Arriving at the mountain top, I said "Don, tell me what it looks like."

"Well, I see a deck railing and a bunch of fog," Don said dryly. "Come on. What else?"

"That's about it. It's even thicker than the fog in Minneapolis!" he added. We finished our piña coladas and asked our driver for his recommendation for a good lunch place.

The restaurant was crowded, so we gave our names and stood, waiting for a table. After 45 minutes of seeing many others seated, we began hearing, "Jones family, table of four." Every five minutes for the next half hour, our frustration grew as we continued hearing, "Jones family, table for four." Our normally reserved friend Don went up to complain, and convinced them the Jones family was obviously not there, but three paying customers were. Relieved, we sat down, and before the server could say his first word, someone came out of the kitchen announcing, "The water main is broken, and we cannot serve until it is repaired."

"I don't believe this!" we said, almost simultaneously. Don dusted off his well-rehearsed harangue:

"I've been on a cruise before, and it's nothing like this!" After about 20 minutes, they resumed service.

Throughout the five days aboard the ship, high winds and six- to eight-foot waves caused everyone aboard to have the appearance of drunkenness as they made their way through the corridors. The chilliness and rain kept us mostly inside, but an announcement was made one day that a reggae band would be playing on the aft deck. As the three of us made our way there, I asked Devon, "Honey, could you get me a piña colada?" She disappeared among the crowd while

Don scoped out a quiet corner for us to veg out. "Jeff, I found the perfect spot, let's go." He escorted me to a crowd-free corner where only a sleeping, bikini-clad woman lay. Devon returned and carefully set down my icy piña colada and looked for a chair. As Don was lowering me into a lounge, a powerful gust of wind picked up the heavy lounge and blew it behind us. It reminded me of those old slapstick movies where a chair moves itself just before being sat on. Don quickly reversed my downward momentum and turned around to look for the lounge chair. Instead he noticed the dozing bikini-clad woman, now fully awake, plucking icy chunks of my piña colada from her top. "Sorry," Don said, stifling a smile. The woman grunted, got up, and left. "I guess I don't need to look for a chair," said Don. We listened to the band for half an hour until Devon and Don succumbed to my whining about being cold (in spite of wearing a jacket), and we retreated from the elements into the warmth of a snack bar.

Devon and I have never walked so much in our lives, not because of the size of the ship, but because of its flawed design. Most ships have corridors that go straight through to the other end of the ship, especially on heavily traveled decks, but our ship's main decks had bulkheads (solid, impassable walls) smack in the middle of their corridors. This presented great challenges to my already directionally impaired wife. To get from one end of the ship to the other, we routinely walked half the ship's length, only to be stopped cold by an impenetrable wall. (Obviously the architect was over budget and cut out the doors from the design to save money.) Therefore, we needed to locate the elevator, find a deck free of a bulkhead, make our way to that end of the ship, find another elevator, and go to the desired deck and area. As a result, we were late for the start of every ship event. After many futile steps and tears of frustration, by the fifth day (our last), Devon and I had figured out how to navigate the ship.

We occasionally marvel that we made it through all the trials and tribulations encountered in such a short period of time. Instead of these events souring us, we look back on them warmly because of how the experience bonded us. In fact, at this writing, we are planning another sea excursion, only this time with a different cruise line.

"So I commend the enjoyment of life, because there is nothing better for a person under the sun than to eat and drink and be glad. Then joy will accompany them in their toil all the days of the life God has given them under the sun." – Ecclesiastes 8:15, TNIV

"The most successful people are those who are good at plan 'B.'"
—James York

"Laughter is an instant vacation." – Milton Berle

CHAPTER 61

EXITS AND ENTRANCES: ONTO THE NEXT STAGE

I received a call from Norm Barnhart, a local magician (whose last name I feel is indicative of his having a heart the size of a barn). "Things have been looking up for me," he said, "I'm about to enter a clown contest. I hope it turns out as well as last year's award."

"What award was that, Norm?"

"Last year I won the *America's Funniest Magician* contest."

"Congratulations, man!"

"You should enter it, Jeff. It's going to be held this year in Minneapolis."

I contacted Steve Kissell, the event organizer, and registered for the summer 2008 event. I decided to use the bit I had put together for the *America's Got Talent* audition. Out of a field of ten performers, I came in first. (Pictures and details are on my website: www.amazing-jeffo.com.) At the conclusion of this thrilling evening, Steve Kissell invited me to perform at one of his events in Virginia. "I can pay for the expense of your flight to Virginia," Kissell said.

"Flying is out of the question, Steve. I'm afraid it would be too difficult logistically to fly with all my equipment, plus I'd be a little nervous about the airline losing my stuff."

Steve is a wonderful supporter and bent over backward to raise funds to enable Scott Saari to drive me to the east coast. I performed two school shows, another at Steve's church, and once again presented my *America's Got Talent* bit as part of Steve's evening program. Our personalities and mutual love of adventure (along with a warped sense of humor) make Scott and me perfect travel mates. Only true adventurers could drive 15 hours in one day—especially with me doing most of the talking—and arrive without one of us suffering bodily harm at the hands of the other. I guess I should consider myself lucky.

I think of Scott Saari as a true "roads scholar." Besides, our partnership sounds so good on a bill: *"Amazing Jeffo and Great Scott! Coming soon to a theater near you."*

God has placed encouragers in the right place at the right time to nudge me forward into the next phase of my personal and professional development. I can systematically trace how every subsequent challenge has been a little greater than the one before. My *America's Got Talent* experience taught me that auditioning in a high pressure situation is possible with the right people at hand, namely Devon. My award as *America's Funniest Magician* proved to me that I can win an award competing against a field of non-disabled magicians. My invitation to perform at a national family entertainers' workshop in Virginia showed me I could travel long distances and be away from home for an extended period in spite of medical needs. So when I was invited in early spring to present an act the following July at the 2009 International Fellowship of Christian Magicians convention in Marion, Indiana, I was confident I could handle it.

But shortly after accepting the invitation to Indiana, I suddenly experienced regular and increasing pain in my left hip. Years earlier, my internist recommended a diet low in calcium to combat the regular passing of kidney stones I was experiencing. Unfortunately, years on a low calcium diet led to the condition my orthopedist described to me in the spring of 2009, "Both your left and right hips are very deteriorated."

"Does the left hip look worse?" My right hip had periodically bothered me over the years, but the occasional pain was nothing like the now constant ache in my left hip.

"They look equally in need of replacing," the doctor said matter-of-factly. "I recommend scheduling surgery right away."

"I've got too many magic show commitments and can't turn them down," I argued. "Can you squirt some cortisone or something into the hip to postpone the surgery until November?"

I suggested this timeline knowing that November typically is my slowest month of the year. The shot did me wonders. Within a week it felt like a new hip. But the doctor cautioned that the effects of the cortisone would last a few months at most before the pain would return. The question began looming in my mind, "Is this the week the pain returns?"

As the convention approached, I began experiencing bouts of severe pain again in my left hip. I said to Devon, "I don't know if I'm going to be able to make it."

"I'll go along with whatever you think." Devon said, supportively.

"I've got to go to the convention. I've worked on this new routine and I'd be so disappointed if I couldn't do it. I'll up my anti-inflammatory medication—even though I know my rheumatologist won't like it."

Mike Stenberg, editor of *The Voice of FCM*, an internationally distributed magazine for Christian illusionists, and his wife Donna graciously drove Devon and me to the July convention.

I hobbled around the campus, snagging golf cart rides when possible. Carrying around our backpack of stuff made me stand more upright and actually reduced the pain, somehow.

The tricks I performed for *America's Got Talent* were tricks I could do with my eyes closed (no pun intended...o.k., maybe just a little one). So I decided to introduce a new trick for the Indiana audience: "The Lie Detector Helmet." This is a comedy routine where a volunteer wears a dolled-up noodle strainer on his head. I worked with someone at the local hardware store and hobby shop to add lights and other gizmos to the "helmet" to make it look more "scientific." Basically, in this routine I ask a series of questions that have been customized to specific types of audiences and volunteers. No matter how they answer, the loaded questions make the volunteers look bad and result in an obnoxious buzzing sound. This gives me an opportunity to make follow-up snarky comments. (See the trick on YouTube.)

Timing and delivery are so important in a successful magic routine. Because this was an entirely new and basically untested trick, I spent hours each day practicing in our dorm suite at Wesleyan College, the site and host of the 5-day convention. I give endless thanks to my ever-patient Devon who gave me valuable feedback as she endured countless rehearsals and, to this day, could care less if she ever saw the dang trick again. Mike stopped by our dormitory to see my last rehearsal and said, "Are you sure you want to go ahead with this trick, Jeff?"

"I've worked too long and hard to give up on it now, Mike," I responded.

He didn't realize that I feed on the adrenaline that comes with the uncertainty of performing a new trick.

After my well-received performance, he said, "Jeff, what I just saw was totally different from what I watched in your dorm room. You really had me worried, but you pulled it off. You must like living on the edge!"

He was right, I do. Intentional or not, I've lived my entire life on the edge.

"Do not let your hearts be troubled. Trust in God; trust also in me." John 14:1

"There's no business like show business, like no business I know!"
- Irving Berlin

As a blind driver, safety comes first for Jeff Smith. For every increase of 20 MPH, I add an additional foot of white cane.

CHAPTER 62

ABANDON HIP!

That fall, as the Doctor predicted, my left hip suddenly began throbbing with pain. Because of the difficulty I had with the anesthesiologist during my second rotator cuff repair, I wanted to make sure I didn't get her again. I contacted the records department at the hospital to discover her name.

After several weeks of waiting for a response, they finally contacted me and said their policies did not permit them to divulge such information. The memory of my pain and fear gave me the resolve to assiduously avoid this particular anesthesiologist—even if it meant refusing surgery at the last minute if I had the unfortunate luck to encounter her again. Given the transitional nature of the job market, the three year time span since my last surgery, and the sheer number of rotating hospital staff, what would be the chances of getting the same anesthesiologist anyway? *Don't worry. Be happy,* I reminded myself.

I went into surgical prep armed with only a sketchy recollection of her first name. Memory is a funny thing. We can recognize tons more than we can recall. I was asking the prep team if they knew who my anesthesiologist was going to be. "I had a really bad experience with the last anesthesiologist," I said loudly enough for anyone in the room to hear. "I'm pretty sure her first name is—" "Yes, that's me, Jeffrey," uttered a voice from the foot of my bed. All the relaxing effects from the pre-surgical medication instantly disappeared. She made her identity official when she then said her full name.

My mind was reeling. For someone who makes his living dependent on having a keen sense of timing, mine at the moment stunk! I didn't know which was the greater challenge: having this woman again as my anesthesiologist or wriggling out of what I had just said. After 20 minutes of silence (or so it seemed), I said with a sheepish smile, "Oh! Hi, doctor. I hope you didn't take anything I said personally. It's just that the peculiarities of my body aren't compatible with your skills." (Whatever that means! Come on, I was drugged up.)

She graciously responded, "That's okay, Jeff. I want you to feel comfortable." She left the room and 15 minutes later a different anesthesiologist appeared, and the surgery proceeded without further drama. Following the surgery what amazed me most was the instant pain relief. Two days after surgery I was up walking the hospital halls with absolutely no pain. Pain is something a person can adjust to, and even get used to. You don't realize how uncomfortable you have been until the pain is gone.

It's like when I was a child before going blind. I was fitted for glasses because of nearsightedness. When the doctor placed the prescription lenses on me, the sudden clarity was remarkable. I hadn't realized how blurry my vision had been.

Good as she knew they may be, rather than depending exclusively on pain dampening narcotics, Devon brought relief to my hospital room on four legs—Krypto! Devon knew his *je ne sais quoi* would help me heal. As they made their way down the hall to use the elevator, old-school hospital staff shot them funny looks. Once arriving on my floor after embarrassing Devon amidst several elevator passengers by hitting the deck, spread eagle, as the elevator began moving, Krypto instantly knew his place, next to his old man in bed, just like home. He carefully maneuvered around tubes, cables and other hospital bed paraphernalia before settling down snug against me. Devon noticed how quickly we fell asleep.

Though I was out of work for two months, one of the unexpected benefits of having a new hip installed was an increase in the length of my leg. I didn't realize it until during one of my post-surgical walks when Devon exclaimed, "Honey! You're not limping!" In everyday terms this meant I would not have to pay the orthotics technician as much for building up my left shoe, since he charges by the inch. In emotional terms, Devon's observation exorcised the painful memory of watching myself in the reflection of the plate glass window as I limped up the sidewalk to my elementary school each day.

"In this world, you will have trouble. But take heart; I have overcome the world." John 16:33

My hip replacement went so well, I recommend it to everyone, whether they need it or not!

CHAPTER 63

UP, UP AND AWAY, AMAZING JEFFO!

I n the fall of 2010, my phone rang.
"Hello. I'd like to talk with the Amazing Jeffo." "Yes, that's me."

"My name is Denise Wycherley, and I'm calling from West Virginia Northern Community College. I don't know how it got here, but I have a copy of the Minneapolis-St. Paul Star Tribune sitting here on my desk. It has a story about you."

"Now, that's amazing!" I commented.

"We'd like you to come out and perform shows for October Disability Awareness month." As with every new challenge, I hesitated, thinking about the logistics of a trip to the east coast.

"Would there be funding to pay my assistant Scott for his time and mileage?" I asked, knowing we had already successfully accomplished this method.

"I'm sorry. We would only have enough to pay airfare and shipping costs for your equipment," she responded.

I could already hear the sounds of stretching begin: a new challenge that, again, was moving me outside of my comfort zone. The first hurdle was figuring out how to ship my gear ahead and pack efficiently to bring the rest of it onboard a plane in as few bags as possible.

Before tackling this challenge, I needed to research and secure additional shows in that tri-state area to make the trip profitable. After more planning than ever before, Scott and I left the Minneapolis-St. Paul International Airport and headed to Pittsburgh.

We presented five shows with three different themes in four days, in three states, including shows for college students, school children, church families, and retirees. (Nothing like driving 100 mph in the dark!) Everyone loved it.

"...there is nothing better for people than to enjoy their work, because that is their lot." Ecclesiastes 3:22, TNIV

"Whenever you are asked if you can do a job, tell 'em, 'Certainly, I can!' Then get busy and find out how to do it." –Theodore Roosevelt

Good Old Southern Hospitality

Our first 23-hour drive to present my show in Norfolk, Virginia had been a lot of fun. Ever since then, Scott Saari has tried his best to arrange his schedule to accommodate my travel invitations. Even though I have been performing for 20 years and presented over 3,000 shows, new kinds of opportunities are still popping up.

I can't explain it, but just in the last two years I have been invited to perform in six states: Indiana, Pennsylvania, West Virginia, Virginia, Louisiana, and Ohio. Early in 2011, I was invited as a keynote presenter at the Shreveport, Louisiana Regional Arts Council Conference. After the fun Scott and I had driving to Virginia, I obviously turned to Scott again to be my driver/assistant. "I'd love to drive you to Louisiana!" Scott boomed. Just like me, Scott thrives on adrenaline, which naturally occurs when he tries to balance his schedule as a self-employed accountant with driving me to perform around the country. Well, as it turned out, funding was available to fly us to the event.

During the five-day event in Louisiana, we presented eight shows, some at the Shreveport Convention Center, the rest at local schools. Up against constantly changing client demands, we naturally encountered some challenging moments. Before one show, there was some difficulty linking my sound effects system to the in-house system. As hundreds of people sat before me waiting for the show to begin, it became an unwelcomed opportunity for me to develop my ability to ad lib to the audience during the 15-minute technical delay. Since scrambling was the theme of the day, the audience assumed my ad libs were all part of the show. Notwithstanding Scott's coolness under pressure and his ability as a driver and assistant, the *greatest* gratitude and appreciation I have for Scott is what he means to me as a friend. His ability to listen and know how to encourage me are his greatest gifts.

With all but one show scheduled during the day, Scott and I were left with free time in the evening. Our hotel was just blocks away from two casinos. I had never played blackjack before and decided to try it out since it was readily accessible. I got caught up in the excitement of potential easy money. Not knowing the strategies involved with this game of chance, I took advice from the dealers and somehow won a couple hundred dollars over the course of the week. (Call it blind luck.) Feeling good about my winnings, I chatted with the dealer. "Would your patrons have any problem with a blind dealer?" I asked.

"Uhhh…no…"

"He or she would have to use braille playing cards, of course," I said.

He laughed and continued dealing. "There'd be no arguments from the house," he added.

"Scott, this is easy!" I exclaimed as I started to get the hang of this game.

"Let's just see what happens."

"But Scootie, I got a system."

"Right, Jeff, a system."

"Have some faith, baby—I can't lose."

"Calm down, big fella," Scott said as he patted me on the shoulder.

On the very last day of the event, I said, "Scott, let's try my luck one more time at the casino."

"I don't think you should push a good thing, Jeffrey." Because I'm basically a salesman, I eventually won out. Scott shrugged and, against his better judgment, said, "OK. It's your money. I warned you." We went to the casino. I foolishly lost everything I had made — plus an additional $80. If Scott hadn't given me the rope to hang myself, I might have at a later time risked, and lost, more. I learned a valuable lesson: you can't beat the house odds. Note to the reader: Consider where the funds came from to lavishly appoint and festoon these casinos—right out of the pockets of those thinking they have figured out a winning system.

God's blessings are not limited to filling my life with good friends. Sometimes the Lord just takes the wheel, literally. Later that year, en route home from another magic show, the Metro Mobility driver suddenly realized he had no brakes. We were on a five-lane highway at rush hour moving along at 55 mph. This is not a good place to lose one's brakes...but is there really any good place? "I think this would be a good time to pray," I suggested. (Talk about God opening a window to evangelize.... *"Rise up and help us; rescue us because of your unfailing love."* Ps. 44:26) Being a by-the-book driver, he picked up the mic and said,

"403 to base, brakes have gone out."

"Base to 403, can you pull over?"

"Negative. I'm three lanes from the shoulder."

I knew I should have memorized that 23rd Psalm! I brooded.

"Do the best you can. Get back to us if you're able," said the dispatcher. The driver pulled the emergency brakes, hit the hazards, and adeptly wove through the heavy traffic to the shoulder.

"Base, send a new vehicle, over." Another close call, another answered prayer.

"For in the day of trouble he will keep me safe in his dwelling; he will hide me in the shelter of his sacred tent and set me high upon a rock." Psalm 27:5

You've heard about that trick where the magician is blindfolded but is still able to drive his car around? I bought the secret to it and let me tell ya right now...it doesn't work! I borrowed my wife's car...and now it's being dredged up from the lake...

CHAPTER 64

WHAT GOES AROUND COMES AROUND

In the summer of 2011, Devon and I took a trip down to Rochester specifically to stay at the Kahler Hotel and tour the Mayo Clinic. For several years, I had wanted to go back to this former battleground where I had fought so many personal wars with illness. En route, I felt like a victorious Caesar revisiting his conquered territory. As we walked through Mayo's vast subway system connecting one medical building to another, each represented different limitations that my doctors had forecast and my parents feared for my future. Their voices echoed through my mind as I retraced my childhood footsteps:

"Jeffrey, we are going to do everything possible to keep you out of a wheelchair."

"Jeffrey, we have no other choice but to give you an ileostomy. You'll be the second youngest person ever to have one."

"Jeffrey, the blindness in your right eye is from iritis. The chance of that happening to your other eye is extremely unlikely."

"Jeffrey, ever since your dad and I brought you here, I've noticed you're having a harder time saying your words."

"Honey, why are you so quiet?" Devon asked, interrupting my thoughts.

"I'm trying to imagine little Jeffrey's feelings and I want to tell him it's gonna all work out."

"It has," she said, smiling.

I started writing these memoirs, so to speak, at five and a half years old. Having more than enough time throughout my childhood to reflect while separated from the preoccupation of the everyday, I clung to, and stored up in my heart, memories of the good and funny things instead of the all-too-frequent unpleasant moments. I was an anachronism. Though I moved forward, my eyes were often fixed on what was behind me, focused on the good times of the past to keep me from seeing the uncertainty ahead. But maybe, not seeing what's ahead should feel right to someone who's blind. The trials of the past and how God led me through each one have been the foundation upon which was built the hope and optimism to move forward.

What have been the long-term side effects of arthritis, blindness, colitis and stuttering? Lasting friendships, the blessings of a marriage, and the knowledge of the love of God through His Son, Jesus Christ. Without these conditions, physically I'd be well-built but unaware of how God's strength has sustained me. My medical conditions and life experiences have illustrated God's complex but perfect plan that He has woven into a magnificent tapestry.

Though I wouldn't have wished it on myself, in retrospect, I wouldn't have had it any other way.

"Our mouths were filled with laughter, our tongues with songs of joy. Then it was said among the nations, 'The LORD has done great things for them.'" Psalm 126:2

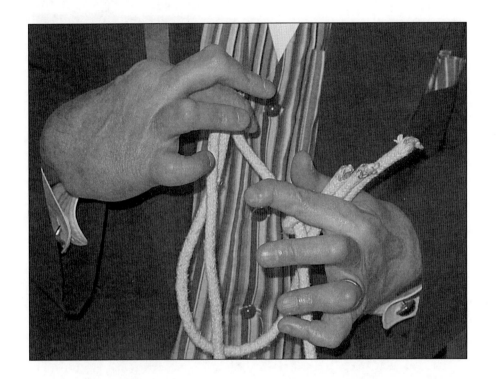

"I CAN DO ALL THIS THROUGH HIM WHO GIVES ME STRENGTH."

PHILIPPIANS 4:13

"DON'T STOP
NOW, YOU'VE
WALKED WITH
ME THIS FAR;
COME SEE WHAT
HAPPENS NEXT!"

Epilogue
Reflections, Observations, and Adventures

Chapter 1 – Where Would I be Without the Kids?

Though to date I have presented more than 3,000 shows (hundreds of which have been for adult audiences), the programs I have presented for children stand out most in my mind. The reason for this, I imagine, is because of the purity and unwashed innocence of their comments. Here are just a few of their letters that can also be found on my website:

"Mr. Spawl was turning red because he was laughing too much. I love when people make me laugh...you are great!" — Marissa

"You really opened my eyes that people like you can do the same things as us, just differently. Does it get darker when the lights go out?"
—Rebecca

"Even if you're blind and have arthritis, you're still the funniest man on the face of the earth. I'll always miss you and your corny jokes. Bye!"
—Josh

"You were amazinger than ever. P.S., Thanks for the sticker that says I am special."
—Jonathon

"You were great! You really expire (sic) my world!"
—Ben

I enjoy performing for adults and children for different reasons. Shows for adults give me more intellectual satisfaction and a greater sense of accomplishment, especially when I ad lib and the audience has the good sense to find me hilarious! On the other hand, with children, it may at times be challenging to keep their attention focused, but their unbridled enthusiasm and spontaneity more than makes up for my efforts. As much as this is shown in the "thank you" letters, it's also reflected in personal encounters with the kids. You just never know what surprises will come out of their mouths. Here are some incidents from before, during, and after shows that illustrate my point.

One of my magical routines for children involves changing someone into a rabbit. As a magician, naturally, I'm an expert on rabbits. So part of the routine also includes a little lesson about the different names that are given to this furry creature. On one particular day, I asked the elementary school children, "What's another name for a rabbit or bunny?" I'm trying to get one of the kids to answer with the word "hare." The audience roared with laughter this day as one of the wittier kids answered, "Dinner!"

Depending on what's happening in the magic show at the moment, I might pick up my harmonica and play something familiar that adds humor to the situation. At an intergenerational family party, I began playing the theme from *The Godfather* because someone had said "I've got a deal you can't refuse." After playing the recognizable first 12 notes, I paused and asked, "Anyone know where that comes from?" A little guy, who was being totally sincere, piped up, "From your harmonica!" Everyone laughed, and all I could respond with was, "You're right!"

After another show, a child of about five bellied up to my magic stand, proudly holding an Amazing Jeffo business card. In a mischievous voice, he announced, "I've got one of your cards!" I said, "That's great!" He continued, "Now I'll be able to remember who you are." He paused and said, "So, what's your name again?"

Once at an out-of-town venue, my wife was busy providing little magic tricks to children after the show. A boy of about seven approached her table and picked up one of the available tricks called "Multiplying Rabbits," wherein a mommy and daddy rabbit suddenly multiply into a family with four baby rabbits. As Devon was helping other children, she overheard the boy carefully reading the package label to himself: "1+1=4." She heard him reread the label, "One plus one equals four?" In a tone that was clearly questioning the very foundations of what he thought he understood, he turned to my wife with a look of desperation and said, "One plus one doesn't equal four, does it? Does it?!!!" My wife reassured him that one plus one does not equal four and that it was just a joke. He let out an overwhelming sigh of relief.

Following a show for the Cub Scouts, a seven-year-old boy who had achieved the scouting rank of Wolf approached my magic stand and asked me, "Can you tell me the secrets of your tricks?" I thought I'd have a little fun with him and answered, "The magic rules say you are not supposed to tell anyone your secrets except for your wife and your dog." The young Cub Scout wasn't going to be outwitted by a mere magician and responded, "Well, you tell me the secrets and then I can tell my dog!"

After every show, I encourage questions from the children. I think preschoolers have the most amusing and out-of-left-field type comments, such as, "Are you married to a dinosaur?"

When preschoolers eagerly raise their hands with questions for me, they typically enjoy telling me all kinds of things about their own life experiences, rather than actually asking a question. After hearing them ramble for a while, I gently explain to them, "A question is when you say things like 'how' or 'why' or 'when' or 'who' or 'where.'" Feeling confident they understood, I asked if anyone had a question for me. A hand shot up. "Yes," the teacher acknowledged, "What's your question?" The preschooler said proudly and simply, "Where?" Laughing, the teacher asked, "Are there any other questions?" Taking the lead from the previous child, a different child asked also in a sincere tone, "Why?" So much for my teaching career.

I often teach magic classes for community education departments, park and recreation departments, and other such groups. As I was demonstrating a trick by slowly and magically unfolding a previously torn up napkin and now revealing it to be fully restored, I overheard one of the children saying to another, "OK, I know this one. Watch. It's going to change colors." He was so caught up in the whole magic experience, he couldn't see the tree for the forest.

After performing at a family party, the grandma who had hired me related the following story regarding Casey, her three-year-old granddaughter. While snuggling with her mother, Casey said, "Wait a minute! I'm going to get Princess to snuggle with us." Princess is the name of her large wooden-spring hobbyhorse. Her mother responded, "Princess is too big to snuggle with us." The precocious three year old answered, "Then we need Jeffo!" Her mother, who was not able to attend the magic show, asked, "Who's Jeffo?" "He's real, Mom! He's not on TV! I saw him in Grandma's living room! He can use his magic to make Princess small so we can snuggle with her."

At a Q&A session following a magic show performed for mostly kindergartners, a little boy asked me, "How old are you?" When I told him I was 50 years old, he was startled and responded, "50?! You should be dead by now!"

Years ago, when I was still single, I was smitten with a charming and lovely teacher who had been my hostess at a school magic show. As I waited for my ride following the performance, I was pondering how I might find out whether she was single without having to ask her. My reverie was broken by a second-grade boy who was just then entering the office and saw me sitting there. He said, "Great show, Jeffo!" I asked him to come over so I could quietly ask him, "Is your teacher a single lady?" The busy din of the office was silenced when he loudly responded, "Are you in love with Miss Jones?! Do you want to marry her?!"

His answer caused me to decide then and there to keep personal interests and business interests separate.

I was taking a variety of questions from an intergenerational audience following a church show in St. Joseph, MN. I always enjoy this opportunity to speak off-the-cuff as myself and share things about my life that people might find interesting. Naturally, as a stand-up comedian in disguise, whenever the chance arises I throw humor into the mix. On this day, after getting a good laugh from what I thought was a pretty good comeback on my part, the chuckling died out. The silence was broken by a boy of about eight. In an obviously disappointed voice, he said, "And I thought you called yourself a man of comedy."

One young Cub Scout volunteer whom I used during my show approached me afterward and said he thought he knew the secret of one of my tricks. I complimented him by saying, "That doesn't surprise me. When you were helping me with a trick during the show, I thought to myself, *This boy is smarter than the average bear*." He quickly responded, "That's cuz I'm not a Bear. I'm a Webelo."

As I was descending the stairs for a birthday party show, I overheard the birthday boy tell his buddies, "I seen him; he's really good! He can do tricks without even lookin' at them—that's cuz he's blind."

While putting together the final touches before a magic show at a preschool child care, one of the little ones in the front row asked a nearby classmate, "Did his parents name him that?"

Recently I received a letter from a parent who attended a Valentine's Day magic show for first-grade children. Her letter had many kind words about how much the children enjoyed the show. The part of the letter that really made my day said, "There were several kids that were not convinced you were really blind; they had the wildest theories about how you may have painted your pupils to fool us. They just could not believe you could do all these things without being able to see."

Magic transcends sight itself, as I regularly demonstrate. In our visually-oriented society, this can be an overwhelming concept to grasp, especially from the viewpoint of a child. Following one show, a second-grade boy approached me and said, "You're not really blind." I answered, "I certainly am! Do these look like the eyes of a truck driver?" The still unsatisfied boy responded, "If you're really blind, then tell me how many fingers I am holding up." For the heck of it, I picked a number. He shot back in a triumphant voice, "Wrong!" Oh, the logic of kids. You've got to love it.

My motivation has always been foremost to educate people about using their abilities to the fullest and recognizing the ability in others. My ability to entertain people and create laughter serves as an effective vehicle for teaching. I hope my magic, music, and comedy gently help people think beyond conventional stereotyping. During my magic show, I have a routine in which I deliberately remove my sunglasses. Aside from the comedy that is generated from the routine,

I am teaching that all persons who are blind do not necessarily wear sunglasses. I was reminded of this fact following a recent school performance. Aside from the ooh's, aah's, and laughter I hear throughout the show, my favorite part of the whole performing experience is when audience members, young and old, come up in front of my magic stand to talk with me after the show. After talking and teasing with children following a couple of shows at an elementary school in Austin, Minnesota, one boy wanted to thank me one more time. As he walked through the auditorium doors he yelled back, "Thanks again for the show, Jeffo! Don't forget your glasses."

Once, a seven-year-old birthday boy concerned about my blindness asked, "Maybe you should eat more carrots!"

A preschool girl once said, "You're the best magic guy I ever saw." "How many magic guys have you seen?" I asked. She excitedly said, "You're the first one!"

After passing out complimentary magic tricks at a private family party, I suddenly realized the presence of a young boy, somewhere around four years of age, standing in front of me. He proceeded to drop two pennies and a nickel on my magic stand, explaining they were for the trick he had been given. I thanked and reassured him the trick was free. He insisted I take the money. After trying to convince him he could use the money more than I could, he said, "Don't worry. There's plenty more where that came from."

When my fiancé (and now wife) told her elementary-aged class she was marrying Amazing Jeffo, whom they knew well from his performances and magic classes, a group of them asked her what her new name would be. A little girl said in exasperation, "Don't you know, sillies? She'll be Mrs. Amazing!"

A kindergarten student, whom I awarded with a little magic trick but who had yet to read the instructions, came up and asked with some frustration, "I can't make the trick work right. What are the magic words again?"

Following another performance, a little Girl Scout came up to me and whispered, "I know you really can see, but don't worry, I'm not going to tell."

During a Sunday School performance, a little guy with a rather healthy self-image wandered up to me behind my stand, right in the midst of my performance. He kept repeating, "Amazing Jeffo? Amazing Jeffo?" I initially tried ignoring him until realizing that he was obviously more determined than I was. I stopped the trick and turned to him asking, "What do you want?" He answered, "My big brother is here now. I'm sorry, but I'm going to be leaving." I told him, "That's okay. I'll try to finish the show without you."

Once at a childcare center, after flicking a magic wand and causing a loud bang, a preschool boy yelled out, "What was that? If you try that again, I'm leaving!" As it turned out, later in the show I needed to use a magic wand which shot out confetti. Immediately I heard the same boy slap his lap, hop off the chair, and say, "OK that's it! I'm out of here." He ran out the door with teachers eagerly chasing after him.

At one school-age care assembly, I had a teacher take back to her chair a sound effect box, and upon hearing a joke that's "not too funny," she was instructed to press the "bomb" sound effect. Following one of her "bomb" critiques, a child, unaware of the ruse, stood up and came to my defense by saying, "Come on! That joke was funny!"

Another time I was teaching magic to several families at a church retreat. No matter what new trick I was introducing at the time, I was interrupted by an eight-year-old boy who would yell out, "Oh, I know that trick!" Likely, of course, he didn't—but he was craving attention and recognition. Being professional, I moved right along while trying not to show annoyance with his disruptions. Late in the program, I was explaining the secret behind a trick and once again was interrupted by the boy. This time, however, he said, "Now that one I can't figure out." I was so relieved upon hearing it that I yelled out, "Thank you, Jesus!!! I'm now ready to come home!" This broke the tension among the parents and got the biggest laugh of the day.

Once, a Cub Scout, not realizing the "not-too-funny" criticism is done intentionally, told me after the show, "I like the magic tricks, but maybe you should buy a joke book to help with your bad jokes."

I was explaining to a group of school-aged childcare kids about how blind people go about doing everyday activities. I'd just finished telling them about how some blind people use seeing eye dogs to help them get around. In all seriousness, a little girl asked me, "Does a seeing eye dog drive you to your shows?"

Not all the comments are innocent...

"Hello?" I answered after picking up the phone.

"I'm calling to have you come out and do a birthday party magic show," responded the high-pitched voice of a child.

"Well, sure," I answered. "What's your name?"

"Tony," came the reply.

"Let me talk to your mom or dad so we can work out the details, Tony."

"I am the dad," he said, now with an affected deeper register in his voice.

"Excuse me?"

"I said 'I'm the dad,' and I want you to come out and do a magic show at my house."

I quickly assessed that this kid was a combination of initiative and larceny. He wanted to have me perform a show for him and only realize afterward that there wasn't any money with which to pay me. Playing the situation out a little, I asked, "Do you mind my asking how old you are?"

"Forty," he said without hesitation.

"Can I ask you another personal question?" "Sure."

"I'm just wondering why, if you're forty years old, does your voice sounds like a ten-year-old?"

"I was in a terrible car accident. My neck got caught in the car motor. That's why I sound like a ten-year-old."

I didn't want to hang up on the kid; besides, I wasn't going to have a ten year old outwit me. Then I heard a woman's voice in the background.

"Tony? Are you on the phone again?"

"I just heard your mom," I responded. "Let me talk to her." "Uh, you can't talk to her because she died in the same car crash that wrecked my voice."

"Well, then who was that woman I just heard?" "That was my grandmother."

"She sounds pretty young to be a grandmother, Tony. Did your dad die in the car crash as well?"

"Well, uh...no, I'm the dad." And on and on we went. I think I finally told him that I was pretty booked up.

Following a show for preschool kids, I mentioned that I'll be leaving business cards if they want to take one to their parents because I do birthday party shows. A little one in the front row coyly said, "My birthday is this month!"

I responded, "Well, tell your mom and dad…"
"They already know that."

At an event attended by seniors and kindergarteners, I held up my autobiography and asked the kids if they see anything wrong about the photograph on the cover of the book. One of them proudly said, beaming, "You only have one hand on the wheel!"
"Maybe I need to go back to blind driving school," I retorted.

"May the LORD cause you to flourish, both you and your children."
Psalm 115:14

> *"If I were a wiggly worm*
> *I'd thank you, Lord, that I could squirm.*
> *If I were a fuzzy, wuzzy bear*
> *I'd thank you, Lord, for my fuzzy, wuzzy hair.*
> *If I were a crocodile*
> *I'd thank you, Lord, for my great smile.*
> *But I just thank you, Father,*
> *for Making me, me."*
> —Words and music by Brian M. Howard

As with many young children, it was difficult for John Arehart's little girl Debbie to fully comprehend blindness. When she was 4 years old, she began asking me on a weekly basis at church, in a most compassionate, hopeful voice, "Does (sic) your eyes work today, Jeffo?

CHAPTER 2–A MOTHER'S POINT OF VIEW

Martha Smith's 10 Commandments of Parenting a Child with Disabilities:

1. Thou shalt not pity your child.
2. Thou shalt talk to your support when your child isn't present and shalt not cry in front of your child.
3. Thou shalt not pamper nor make allowances for your child who isn't as hale or hardy as your other children.
4. Thy child must live up to the regulations of the household to the best of his ability.
5. Thou shalt give your child total encouragement but shalt not spoil your child.
6. Thou shalt take one day at a time, or it will be overwhelming and discouraging.
7. Thou shalt believe a bad diagnosis is never the end—there's always hope.
8. Thou shalt laugh at yourself so your child learns how to laugh at himself.
9. Thou shalt approach physical challenges head on and say, "OK. What's the next step?"
10. Thou shalt pray every day.

My mom and I doing a Disability Awareness Training Seminar Presentation for parents who have children with disabilities.

An Interview with Martha Smith

Q. What were your greatest challenges raising a child with multiple disabilities?

A. To successfully attempt to raise a mature, productive, socially acceptable human being who could go into the world and do for himself, be educated, and be a good person. That's what I wanted for all my children.

Q. What was one of your biggest triumphs concerning Jeff going to college?

A. Convincing the State Services for the Blind to support Jeff while in college. I was dead set against him getting vocational training. He was too intelligent and articulate to settle for anything other than college. I didn't get a chance to go myself, so I was determined to give Jeff the chance. I felt like a lone voice up against the system. I had become totally frustrated with the negative thinking from many officials who were working with Jeff. I felt extremely upset because I knew my son had the ability to handle higher education. With the support of a high school counselor and teachers who had worked with him, I requested a meeting of the powers that be. By the end of the meeting, officials begrudgingly agreed to support Jeff attending college as long as he maintained a B average.

Q. How did you come to the conclusion Jeff would be better off living independently?

A. After he graduated from college, I came to the realization I had to push my baby robin out of the nest. He had to get on his own. Jeff was leaning on me too much. He was at a point where there was no more personal development. So I said to him, "Mr. Jeff, I think the time has come that you find your way. You've been trained well, and we'll all be behind you." It wasn't easy, but I encouraged him to find an apartment. I had a lot of guilt at first but not enough to stop him. I knew it was the right thing.

Q. How do you see Jeff's physical circumstances playing a part in how his personality has developed?

A. It made Jeff a much more mature person as a young person. As a child, even because of what he had been through, it had made him an extremely strong human being, a particularly determined human being, and a compassionate human being with a big heart."

Q. What about mentoring or support groups? How did you get through?

A. I had a father who instilled determination in me. He gave me advice when Jeffrey was first diagnosed in how he thought Jeff should be handled. He had great compassion for me, the mother, but he brought my sister and me up with an iron hand with high expectations. We engaged in no monkey business because we knew the consequences. That's how I tried to raise my family. My father emphasized how I had to be strong and teach Jeffrey to hold his head up and move forward, and it would all work out. "Accept any help that would come your way. Any help you can get, grab it," was my father's advice. Besides my father, my support came from my sister, the nurse, and so many wonderful friends who got me through heck and high water. Those were the people I could cry with...and I did.

Q. Did you go to any support groups?

A. I did a tremendous amount of reading. I went to therapists.

Q. How did Jeff surprise you in his adult life?

A. I knew he'd always be physically and medically covered, but I never thought there would be a possibility of a wonderful woman stepping into his life.

Q. What were some of the worries you had while raising Jeff?

A. I wasn't sure we had the financial wherewithal while fighting through seemingly hopeless medical circumstances. I worried about keeping the family intact when it would have been easier to be spared the grief of marital upheaval. I worried about keeping the other children from feeling not cared for while I was in Rochester for weeks at a time.

Q. Who was one of your greatest influences growing up?

A. My father. He always said, "Do what you can where you are with what you have." He only had an eighth-grade education, but he possessed more common sense than most. When he was sixteen, he became the head of the household when his mother died. He was the man of the house and took responsibility for raising his brothers and sisters. He taught me what it meant to be responsible and not give up. Later on, he died a hero's death. He was working as a desk clerk at a senior high-rise, and a deranged man came in and wanted to rob residents in the living area. My father fought the assailant, but he was severely beaten—the attacker was in his twenties, and my dad was in his mid-seventies. My father died later that night from that beating. He gave his life to protect those people.

Q. If you had a chance to do it over again, what would you do?

A. Acquire a great deal more patience. Not worry about things in Jeff's life that didn't really matter, but concentrate on smelling the roses. I was at times extremely high strung and impatient, and he would get on my nerves. He would put up with my leaping up and down in frustration. I'd tell him his meal was on the table and to come eat. I'd leave the house for a while and come home, and it would still be there. I'd be so angry; I'd go berserk."

Q. In retrospect, Martha, what advice could you share?

A. First, I would never think of, call the child, or speak of him using the term "disabled." I don't think it's necessary. I don't think it's good for them. What is…is. I absolutely say, no matter how brokenhearted you might be, resist feeling pity for your child. Never, never, never pity them, or that will reflect on your child. When your heart is breaking and you need to talk to your support—do it when your child's not there. You don't cry in front of your child. Hide your tears. I spilled my fair share of tears in private, but I didn't want to let Jeff see me down. If your child starts to feel self-pity, he will never move on and do things for himself. I often told Jeff, "If I could take the physical difficulties away from you and put them on to myself, I gladly would." But since I couldn't, I had to show him the right attitude. I knew if I kept back the tears, Jeff would too.

Do not pamper your child, as difficult as that may be. You must not make allowances for your child who isn't as hale or hardy as your other children. That child must know the rules and regulations of the household and live up to those regulations to the best of his ability, just as his siblings are expected to do. Give him total encouragement. A bad diagnosis is never the end. There's always hope. Support and encourage your child, nurture him, but don't ever spoil him for heaven's sake; don't do that, or you will raise a human being who one day will have to go out into the real world and won't be accepted. People don't want someone like that. They want someone who knows how to laugh at themselves, and Jeff is good at that. We've had a lot of fun together laughing about terrible things that happened to him while he was learning how to function as a blind person, like walking down the middle of Dupont Avenue—cars going on either side of him, and him thinking he was on the sidewalk.

"As a mother comforts her child, so will I comfort you; and you will be comforted over Jerusalem." Isaiah 66:13

"It doesn't matter if you try and try and try again and fail. It does matter if you try and fail and never try again." – Charles Kattering, American engineer and inventor

With today's emphasis on environmentally friendly products, I can't figure out why my new company that manufactures paper ileostomy bags isn't taking off!

CHAPTER 3 – THE ROAD TO RELEVANCE

My career as a magician came about not out of a great master plan of mine that strategically utilized my natural gifts and abilities; no, it came as a result of being desperate because nothing better had come along. The circuitous route to where I am today, however, is exactly what a non-linear type like myself should expect. Not only was the route indirect, but where I ended up was anything but expected. In short, you wouldn't believe the doors of opportunity that have been opened through Amazing Jeffo, such as giving me a purpose in life, the chance to meet my wife, the ability to build a home, and a way to make an impact on peoples' lives. And keep in mind this magic thing is not just a job that accommodates my physical limitations. It's an ideal career that fits who I am as a person: a hopeless ham and a terrible showoff! Or a blind teacher opening the eyes of sighted people.

Once I decided to dedicate myself to seeing where magic would take me, the sheer novelty of a blind magician gave my career the jumpstart it needed. Granted, I didn't start my working career until several years after graduating from college in 1985 at the age of 29, but I had been preparing for my career my entire life without realizing it. Ultimately, time and circumstances had to run their courses to culminate into the persona of Amazing Jeffo. Amazing Jeffo is a response to the events in my life. The first decades of my life, I saw myself as a patient: someone always being cared for beyond the standard care parents can provide. My need for extraordinary care stunted my personal development. I was preoccupied with reacting to life's circumstances rather than having a chance to be proactive as a contributor in the affairs of living.

As time and events moved along, I began seeing more and more a purpose for it all. Ironically or divinely, the myriad events of my life provided for me a unique platform in which to share lessons learned. Amazing Jeffo has given me the chance to present within the public arena some strategies and perspectives for overcoming challenges. Before this opportunity, there was always internal tension because of my desire to play the role of teacher while not being able to, because I was preoccupied with being the object of care. That's probably why the making and preparation of Amazing Jeffo required decades of life training that only time and circumstances could make possible.

Besides external circumstances delaying the start of any kind of career, my own self-defeating attitudes created roadblocks. *A magician?* I thought. *No way! How can I be a magician? Magic is so visual, and I'm so blind. Doesn't magic require agility and tremendous dexterity? My hands are all bent up from arthritis. And what about my stuttering? I mean, magicians have to talk, at least sometimes!* But these obstacles helped me develop social and emotional skills (that I'm still developing, just ask my wife). Before even imagining the words "blind," "arthritis," and "stuttering" in the same sentence as "magician," I had to use creativity, imagination, and curiosity to develop adaptability and make this vision a reality.

Many encouragers have continually given me a vision for helping people needing encouragement themselves. Through trusting friends and being open to what I believe were God's promptings, I now realize that no matter what the challenges, success begins with having a dream. These individuals, many times unknowingly, have been tools of God that have enabled me to build this amazing and fulfilling career. They gave, and continue to give, me the confidence I need to take each new step toward overcoming the barriers before me. They have enabled me to become comfortable pursuing a career that requires being silly, having outrageous and provocative behavior, public speaking, the appearance of having vision, and the highest levels of dexterity—all without formal training and all of which I once thought was impossible for me!

Truth be told though, it hasn't taken a lot of convincing for me to be silly, outrageous, and provocative on a regular basis. I believe, unbeknownst to some of them, that God was whispering in their ears what His plans were for me. Thank God that I'm also a little offbeat! It took some off the wall imagination to see this vision…or maybe it was beer (just kidding). Otherwise, I would have never realized how naturally qualified I am for this career that teaches while entertaining. Instead, I'd be pounding my head on the wall somewhere, still trying to fit the mold of other people's expectations.

I'm someone who in many ways doesn't fit the traditional nine- to-five mold. One of the ways I'm different is that I don't like convention. I'd describe myself as a non-conformist as opposed to a subversive. I've consciously made the decision to express myself in creative ways to help enable me to explode myths that John Q. Public has about the abilities and capabilities of people with disabilities. If I can do this in an entertaining and disarming way, all the better!

Letting nature take its course also applies to the creation and origin of the name *Amazing Jeffo*. It wasn't a carefully thought-out title, but rather came about as a result of a summer camp director unexpectedly inviting me on stage to show a trick and asking tongue-in-cheek how he should refer to me. I blurted out, "How about Amazing Jeffo!"

The irony of all this was that through Amazing Jeffo, I have found my place in the world after trying so hard to follow every customary avenue recommended to me, when all along I just needed to be myself! I can see, though, that it was all part of God's master plan.

Today, I still use the conventional training I received, such as the advertising and copywriting skills I acquired from earning a journalism degree, and use it to market my magic and speaking career. Moreover, all my efforts and job skills training that I hoped would lead to employment taught me that being employed cannot be an assumed thing, but that it takes even greater skills to *secure* a job than the skills necessary to perform the job, at least in my experience. *If I'm going to all this work to find a job, I might as well use my energies to explore self-employment,* I thought idly, not realizing how this seed would ultimately germinate. In the meantime, this kind of mindset became critical in carving out new methods and adaptations required for success as a self-employed blind magician and presenter.

Most importantly, I need to remind myself how God has taken challenging circumstances in my life and used encouragers along the way to help me discover and reinforce my God-given talents and abilities. As I perform sleight-of-hand tricks requiring dexterity, it reminds me that He is the potter and I am the clay.

Creativity, humor, salesmanship, and teaching have been the essential elements enabling me to do what I believe He wanted me to do all along. Creativity has helped me fit square pegs into round holes, as you might imagine to be the case for a magician who's blind and arthritic. A successful performer may be considered the ultimate outcome-based profession around. It doesn't matter how complicated the magic trick technique is that elicits the best "ooh's" and "aah's" from the audience. It comes down to tying in the right message with the right trick to get the best audience response. I basically choose tricks that are easy to perform for my bent up fingers and stiff wrists, then develop a message that reflects my personality and history to ultimately share a take-away point. For example, there's a trick called "The Coloring Book." This comes in many versions, such as a coloring book, a stamp book, a Bible, etc. By repeatedly flipping through the pages, the magician can make the pages go from blank to a black-and-white sketch, to a full-color image. This is an extremely easy trick to perform, but to a crowd, it gives me an opportunity to briefly explain how I became blind.

"Boys and girls, let me use this book, *The Adventures of Amazing Jeffo*, to explain how I went blind. I was born at a very young age—I think it was around zero—with perfect eyesight." (Flip through the pages to show full-colored images.) "Then, because of an eye disease called iritis that comes from having rheumatoid arthritis, I began to gradually lose my eyesight." (Flip through the pages to show the black and white sketches.) "Eventually, after several years, I became totally blind!" (Flip through the pages to show they're all blank.) "But the pictures and the thoughts in my mind - in other words, my imagination, hopes and dreams—are as colorful as anything you can see!" (Flip through the pages to show full colored images.) Thank God I needn't worry that by detailing this routine it will be stolen by a magician without scruples, because of how it specifically fits my unique personality and circumstances. To my knowledge, there aren't a whole lot of blind, arthritic magicians out there.

As I've mentioned earlier, my humor, that I believe arose in part as a defense mechanism against the teasing from other children and continued to develop because of the positive feedback I received, has been pivotal in modeling to audiences a positive attitude despite challenges. God has put me in a position as a presenter who affects people in ways I certainly couldn't have planned myself. More than once after a performance, someone dealing with disabilities or a senior adjusting to the challenges with aging will hug me saying, "Here I am, complaining to God and others about losing some of my independence, and then I see you cracking jokes about your situation despite obvious challenges."

I've become aware through these incidents that the things you say, do, or the way you react can have a life-changing effect on someone else. While listening to comments like these, it makes me feel good that I can be an encourager to someone. It also inspires me to formally develop that area of my presentation that touched someone in a special way.

"We make a living by what we get, we make a life by what we give." – Winston Churchill

On the other hand, I sometimes feel awkward receiving this kind of feedback from those whose hearts and emotions were moved because, depending on my current financial situation, I might be focusing on how well this presentation is paying the mortgage.

Recently, Devon and I watched the well-known musical *The Music Man*. (Incidentally, phrases I use such as "I watched" or "I see" are not given a second thought in my household or by anyone who knows me. These terms are expressions or figures of speech everyone uses, sighted or not.) Anyway, I saw some of myself in the lead character, Professor Harold Hill. Though his aim was to make a quick buck by selling cheap uniforms and instruments to the citizens living in a small town, he unintentionally provided them with hope and, ultimately, a reason for optimism and feeling good about themselves. Although Professor Hill and I differ in our motives in the method of providing ourselves with a living, we share in achieving positive results. I, along with my friends and family, have always seen myself as a salesman.

Everyone in my circle is well aware of how, in spite of my lack of physical ability, I have attained things important to me by possessing a quality of natural salesmanship when persuasion is called for. Humor, charm—whatever you wish to call it—has enabled me to gather around myself the strength and support of others to maintain a sense of control amidst circumstances I have no power over. I admit that sometimes my salesmanship has gone to the extreme and moved into the area of being a "ringmaster," trying to control people. Focusing on the blessings in my life has helped me to maintain a healthy emotional balance between feeling helpless amidst the uncertainty of a situation vs. using people just to make myself feel good. This has enabled me to stay positive and continue doing what I so love: going outside myself to teach important truths and lessons about life.

How I have ultimately applied my natural gifts with what I learned from my degree in advertising and marketing has been serendipitous to say the least. It has enabled me to use the salesmanship, so to speak, to sell a trick or message to an audience and, by the same token, use a different version of salesmanship to book shows. Because I am offering something out of the ordinary, it sometimes requires a special kind of salesmanship helping people realize that this is more than just a magic show.

There is much for me about which to have a sense of accomplishment, and, more so, gratitude. I've been fortunate to get publicity regarding Amazing Jeffo on local and national TV, newspapers, and magazines. It also makes me feel good when I am able to tailor one of my shows to a requested theme. I'm both amused and proud of the times that children come up to me after a show and, on the sly, say to me, "Come on! I know you're not *really* blind." What I'm most proud of is the feedback I sometimes get regarding the hope and encouragement a particular person got from my show, especially when they were going through a difficult time in their life.

I look back and see how much my attitude has changed about blindness. When I still had my vision in fifth grade, I remember watching the movie *The Miracle Worker*, the story of Helen Keller. I imagined how terrible it would be to go blind, one of the worst things my mind could conceive. Since having gone blind, my perspective is totally different. I now see that my fear of blindness was rooted in not knowing all the resources that would be available to me in the event of losing my vision. I've discovered among other blind friends and acquaintances a similar point of view: the reality of having gone blind is more manageable than a fear of the unknown.

"'For I know the plans I have for you,' says the Lord, 'plans of good and not disaster, to give you a future and a hope.'"
Jeremiah 29:11, NLT

308

"The best and most beautiful things in the world cannot be seen or even touched – they must be felt with the heart" – Helen Keller

I use a cane with a rabbit head for a handle to make every step a hare-raising experience.

CHAPTER 4–IN THE PRESENT AND MOVING INTO THE FUTURE

Devon

As I complete my memoir, I have reviewed the stages of my life with a glow of nostalgia and measure of perspective. Perhaps the most dynamic of these stages has been and continues to be my marriage. Today, a common question I am asked following a show is "How long did you date before getting married?" I must admit, when I met her, it wasn't love at first sight. All kidding aside, I'd respond, "I knew after our third conversation that this was a woman I'd be comfortable with always." To an adult crowd asking the same question, I might answer, "I hardly knew her then, but now that we're married, I read her like a book...make that a Braille book."

In my travels as Amazing Jeffo, another question I'm commonly asked is "does your wife accompany you to your shows?" Originally, Devon somehow managed to accompany me to several shows. This was in addition to her separate full-time job. She was burning the candle at both ends.

"Devon," quipped one of her little charges one day, "Why are you all of a sudden playing so much basketball with us kids?"

"I don't know. I just feel good," Devon responded.

"You're also smiling more," added the second grader. Given that this was during the infatuation stage of our relationship, Devon and I had surplus energy to burn. But after a while, having a full-time job and spending hours on end with me, routinely making for a 16- to18-hour day, wasn't good for her health or our relationship.

Being more aware of her physical limitations nowadays, as she watches me buzz around the house getting ready for my ride which is due to arrive in sheer seconds, she says, "You'd better be ready for your ride, Mister. I ain't taking you." That's okay with me. I have to save her energy for her important role as my behind-the- scenes joke writer instead of merely my roadie. She'll polish up a funny but rough idea I have and turn it into a funny line I use in the show. If she begins taking too much credit for my comedic success, I remind her, "It's not *what* you say, it's *how* you say it!" Seriously, though she may not now accompany me to my shows, she is my indispensable partner.

Devon is full of helpful ideas to someone like me living with arthritis. One of her tips is to immerse hands into warm water while washing dishes. "I've read somewhere it's excellent for loosening up stiff fingers," she explains. For improved range of motion, she suggests folding laundry, then putting it away. She hasn't yet explained the therapeutic benefits of putting the laundry away. "I'll get back to you on that," she reassures. Lastly, she suggests on those days when it's too painful to do just about anything, take your wife out to eat.

One of the challenges of being blind is living with sighted people. Devon, who's a fantastic cook, likes to keep the refrigerator filled to the brim with all kinds of interesting foods and ingredients. When I lived as a single guy, I kept just the essentials in my refrigerator, which made everything really easy to find. I wasn't denying myself anything though, because I'm one of those people who, for the most part, eats to live, not lives to eat.

Recently, Devon suggested I try something new. "I bought this chocolate, almond, and coconut flavored creamer. See what you think." I tried it in my coffee. It was delicious! The next day I called her at her work and asked, "Honey, where do you keep that creamer?"

"It's on the top shelf in the refrigerator, on the right side. You'll find it in a bottle that's wider at the bottom and narrows as it goes to the top. It also has a flip top."

While Devon was taking great care to describe these little details, I was standing at the open refrigerator verifying her facts. "Oh yeah, I see it."

"You feel the ridges on the bottle, Jeff?"

"Well they could be better described as little shoulders ascending upward."

"Shoulders? They're more like ridges," asserted Devon.

Ridges...Shoulders...It's all semantics, I thought. "Oh, and be careful, Jeff. It really pours out quickly." "Well, not that quickly. I feel the little opening." "It's not that little," Devon insisted.

Big opening...little opening...It's all relative, I thought. My eagerness to pour a fresh, hot cup of coffee ended our de facto conversation regarding semantics and relativity. Having taken matters into my own hands, I took my first gulp of coffee... liberally flavored with tabasco sauce. A hot cup of coffee, indeed. *Ay carumba!*

Our nightly routine often includes watching a movie. Devon has described so many movies to me that she can hardly watch one all by herself without narrating it. It's not uncommon for my eyelids to grow heavy during her narration, especially after a busy day of work. But they spring right open when I hear, "Are you sleeping?" Devon, understandably, does not want to waste her energy on someone who's not awake. Because my pride does not allow me to admit such a thing, I always respond, "No, of course not!" "O.K. What was the last thing that was said in the movie?" she will say in frustration.

I'm a light sleeper with the uncanny ability to snore away but still be able to instantly wake up and tell my accuser what was last said. But upon further questioning, my ruse becomes exposed and I fall on the mercy of the domestic court.

After pausing the DVD a couple more times to ask me whether I'm awake, she typically suggests that maybe it's time for bed. "I'm not tired," I'll insist. Krypto usually takes the lead so off to bed we go.

I don't know why, but the instant my head hits the pillow, I wake right up and begin gabbing away while Devon tries to sleep. "Here I am, trying to get to sleep and here you are, Mr. Chatty Kathy, who's been sleeping all night and now wants to chit-chat. Your pillow must be a charger cradle and your head the battery," Devon sighs.

Some of Devon's work as a school-age care coordinator has involved going to professional development conferences, sometimes even on the weekends. One such conference not that long ago had her returning home later in the evening and she was totally exhausted. She had already gone through an action-packed workweek then sat through and listened to lectures all day Saturday.

As you may have sensed by now, I am a very chatty guy who likes sharing insights with anyone who will listen. Whereas my wife is one of those quiet, introverted, processing types. So, on our way home from church the morning following her day-long conference, Devon commented, "Although the sermon was really good, I had a hard time staying awake. It's probably because of the conference yesterday."

I said, "It must be really tiring sitting and listening to someone talk all day."

She responded, with a twinkle in her voice and extra emphasis for my benefit, with the following simple utterance which said it all, "Uh-*huh!*"

Boy, I wish Devon didn't talk so much.

Devon and I have an ongoing debate that surfaces every time we bump into one another. Who defers to the higher law? "Ladies first," or "Blind guys have the right of way"?

Don Dinger

Of all my friends who have physically been there to assist in the development of Amazing Jeffo, it's Don Dinger, whom I met in 9th grade, to whom I owe the most. Don and I first met when the teacher noticed he and I were the only ones left in the room following the immediate evacuation by the rest of the class upon hearing the lunch bell.

In the early years of Amazing Jeffo, Don was invaluable critiquing my shows to prevent me from creating additional self- inflicted challenges. Don coached me on everything from the dangers of going off script to pointing out my misguided jokes that resulted in unintentionally insulting an audience member.

Besides his observational and analytical strengths that have helped perfect my routines, he has been available on the spur of the moment to take me to shows when regular transportation had failed or I forgot I had a show. (Note to prospective client: Today, I have an effective method for remembering my schedule.) For a period of several years, Don drove me to all my out-of-town shows—I estimate 300 all together. I've been fortunate to have been with Don during the most harrowing times; his cool, quick thinking always came in handy.

I remember one time Don and I were furiously packing up my magic equipment after the audience had safely retreated to an underground shelter because a tornado was heading our direction. This was based on the logic that if I got killed, my gear wouldn't mind, but if my gear got blown away, then where would I be without my stuff?

On one of the busiest days of my career, Don and I performed five shows in five cities while I was suffering through the worst laryngitis of my life.

Last winter after a fifteen-inch snowfall, my normal means of transportation, Metro Mobility, was running three hours behind. The snowstorm had already been going strong for about six hours. When I could wait no longer, I called Don and asked him if he could get me to my show. "I can't believe they haven't canceled it," he responded. "Chalk it up to Cub Scouts resourcefulness, I guess." Yammering all the way there, Don and I slid and fishtailed in his four-wheel drive but arrived safely. During the two-and-a-half hours at the VFW, the snowfall only increased in ferocity. As we were about to leave, a patron who had been in the upstairs bar was also exiting. "Did it snow?" we overheard him mumbling in surprise as he looked out.

I consider Don to be a hot-and-cold friend. Don has always been there for me whether my problems arose as a result of the cold winter or the hot summer. On one occasion, I had made arrangements with Don and his wife Laurie to drive me home after my show, which I had been invited to perform at our twenty-year high school reunion. Before arriving there, I had just completed two long outdoor shows in exhausting 90-degree heat with high humidity levels. I was bordering on heat stroke. The hotel caterer, a fellow classmate, served me a pitcher of ice water. I drank that pitcher right down but still felt drained. *I guess I need to drink another pitcher to feel better*, I thought.

Instead, I began feeling worse; my body seemed like it could not absorb any more water. A classmate suggested I try to sleep in a room they had reserved. In my tux shirt and pants, I lay there for a half hour, unable to relax my overwrought body. *I can't let my classmates down*, I thought. Besides, I wanted to show them I was no longer a figure to be pitied as they might have once remembered me back in high school. So I decided I would go on with the show. I was so weak and dizzy that I had to hang on to my table as I shifted over to each volunteer joining me on stage.

My showmanship somehow hid my dire condition from the audience, so I was later told. Although we had all been looking forward to reacquainting with old friends, immediately following the show, I asked Don to take me home.

"I can't leave you alone at your townhouse," Don said, concerned. "You're having a hard time breathing; I should really take you to your folks."

"You can't do that. I don't want them to think I can't handle it on my own." I was so saturated with water, I felt like I was drowning from the inside out!

"You can stay at our house tonight," Don offered.

In retrospect, we should have gone to the hospital. Finally, following several hours of difficulty in breathing, I fell asleep. Upon waking, my body, though still weak, felt 100% better.

"You can always tell a real friend: When you make a fool of yourself, he doesn't feel you've done a permanent job." – Laurence Peter

John Arehart

With the onset of writing my memoirs with John Arehart, new and unexpected professional opportunities have presented themselves to us. John, always the visionary, seeing the episodes of my life revealed before him, has been inspired with ideas and compelled to encourage me to explore new avenues to educate the public about disabilities.

A few years back, John and I had developed a basic disabilities awareness presentation at the request of the Mayo Clinic, Prudential Insurance, and Lockheed Martin. Both of us were excited at the prospect of developing this concept, but John's sudden employment at Northwestern College and subsequent doctoral research put our plans on hold. I was crushed. The prospect of presenting a deeper message to a wider audience was simply not possible as Amazing Jeffo, but presenting as Jeff Smith would enable me to really make a difference in peoples' lives. Without the assistance of John and his bigger-picture mentality, my prospects seemed to vanish. I called John frequently, but he was rarely available because of the demands of his new job. I almost gave up, but once again God was working behind the scenes. I had only to be patient while He unfolded His perfect tapestry of timing. The Lord used John's absence from my life to give him the academic background and the expertise from which we would both benefit.

He came back to work with me as an experienced forensics professor who's assisted me, and continues to assist me, with public presentations. He now has contacts and resources previously unavailable to us. As a result, we currently have many projects on the table, which include a dedicated website devoted to training; nationally marketing customized programs for colleges, service organizations, and professional development. Our willingness to fully commit to this new venture has been blessed by the Lord and resulted in presentations throughout the country.

"Two are better than one, because they have a good return for their work: If one falls down, his friend can help him up." Ecclesiastes 4:9-11

A Knockout Performance

2012 started on as high a note as I've ever experienced before with my memoir ready for its first printing. However, the following year would prove to be the most challenging year of my life, physically and emotionally.

In March of 2012 while waiting for a return flight home from Newark airport after presenting a corporate show, I checked my voicemail. I listened to a message from a representative of the Kiwanis Club about the possibility of presenting at their international convention that summer in New Orleans. Soon arrangements were made with the Kiwanis to perform a magic show and present a workshop to one of their groups, the Aktion Club, made up of adults with disabilities.

As the days hastened toward departing for the "Big Easy," I continued my performances and a whole new activity, promoting the autobiography that you are holding in your hands.

A natural venue for promoting my memoirs has been educational conferences where my assistant and I man a booth and also market Amazing Jeffo and workshops on overcoming adversity. While a friend was helping me pack for one such conference, I asked her, "Would you please open the window in the living room?" Realizing how warm I was getting, I thought, I could really use a glass of water. Then I evidently stood up from my desk and moved toward the kitchen.

Out of necessity, my helper had packed the suitcase in the doorway between my office and the living room. Devon and I live in a palatial home – that is, only if our names were Barbie and Ken. Our house is so small, if we order a large pizza we have to eat it outside. My request to have her open the window had interrupted her process of closing and moving the case out of the way. I carelessly assumed the task had been completed. I ended up flat on my face, unconscious for about three to four minutes. The next thing I realized, paramedics and police were lifting me up and placing me on a kitchen stool. As I was assisted to the ambulance, I was later told I kept asking my helper the same question: "Now what happened and where did I land?"

The timing of my accident coincided with Devon turning up our block on her way home from work. She saw a squad car pull over and an officer cross the street. Devon figured he was perhaps investigating something having gone awry at our next door neighbor's garage sale. But when the cop instead walked up our driveway, Devon's heart began pounding. She stopped her car right there and tried to call out to the cop who had already entered our front door. Providing momentary relief was the appearance of my helper who gave Devon the o.k. sign with her hands and lips.

We were at United Hospital for five hours, mostly waiting to have a CT scan done on my head. After lots of paperwork and exams, the results of the scan were in. The nurse said, "We're happy to report that the CT scan of your head showed nothing!" (I apologize for this corny joke…uh, no, actually I don't.)

The emergency room doctor diagnosed me with a mild concussion and advised me to rest for a couple of weeks. Not very practical for someone self-employed. Against the better judgment of Devon and my mom, the next day a driver took me to Ettrick, Wisconsin to do a show at a church for their Strawberry Ice Cream Social. There's nothing like the sincerity of people in a small town. After the show, the host came out to the car, thanked us for the umpteenth time, and said through the passenger window, "That was the most inspiring thing I ever saw!" My driver said afterward he had tears in his eyes as he spoke.

A week later, with expectations of absorbing as much atmosphere as possible, John Arehart and I took off for New Orleans to the Kiwanis gig. My well-planned magic show didn't come across as perfectly as I expected due to circumstances outside my control. A technician had rearranged some power cables after we had set up the evening before. Moreover, during the show one of my tricks broke in my hands. In spite of these unexpected snafus, how I handled them gave authenticity and power to my workshop message of "Overcoming Challenges." The most encouraging development from my presentation was that for the first time, after having done approximately 25 workshops as Jeff Smith, everything clicked. John, my writing and speech coach, had been working with me to have the same energy, confidence and stage presence when I'm Jeff Smith as I do in my role as Amazing Jeffo, but prior to this trip it just wasn't happening. My "eureka" moment came when we realized I had been taking myself too seriously and was trying to come off as a typical talking head. John pointed out to me there's nothing typical about a blind magician so it should follow when speaking as Jeff Smith. What makes Amazing Jeffo entertaining, I believe, are my mostly unscripted comments that hit audiences as refreshing instead of something sounding over-rehearsed.

Unfortunately, because of a limited budget, our only absorption of New Orleans atmosphere was satisfying John's craving for local cuisine—frog legs, crawfish tails, and alligator—which caused me to shudder and fight the urge to think of it as "swamp food."

"This calamari is delicious," John said, stuffing it in. "How can you tell?" I asked.

"The suckers stick to your tongue," teased John, fully aware of my reservations. I still enjoyed the overall experience and hope to continue receiving professional opportunities nationally.

Once home, I continued performing and presenting. Unbeknownst to me was that my fall, now nearly three weeks ago, had caused a brain bleed that was developing pressure within my cranium. Following a great show at an out-of-town child care center, while en route home I suddenly began feeling faint and said to my driver friend, "Turn on the air-conditioning full blast and open all the windows." We were still several miles from home. Then, my driver realized I had started seizing and called 911.

"Should I drive him to a hospital?" he asked the 911 operator. "No. Pull over as soon as you can," instructed the operator.

"We'll send an ambulance to you." By now we were at the highway exit to my neighborhood.

The part of the city where Devon and I live happens to be on my brother Mike's police beat and he took the call. He met the fire department paramedics and EMTs and stayed inside the ambulance with me until I was stabilized.

After blacking out, 45 minutes later, I awoke to Devon crying alongside my emergency room gurney. Never generally pleased hearing sharp tones from my lips, Devon felt joy wash over her when I responded to her sobbing with, "What are you crying for? You don't need to cry!"

My brother Mike, who stayed with us in the ER, said to me, "Jeepers, Jeff! You look like a professional wrestler with fake blood on your beard, except your blood is real!" (I had bitten my tongue during the seizure.) I chuckled at the time, although the next day I did feel as if I had been in a wrestling match: my shoulders and backs of my arms ached from straining against the interior of the car.

It seemed only minutes until my mom and dad appeared. *Just like old times*, I thought.

As we all waited for the results of the CT scan, my mom asked, "Do you want to hear something strange, Mr. Jeff?"

"Sure," I mumbled.

"With everything we've gone through together over the years, this was the first time I ever broke down hearing bad news about you. When your brother called, I lost it."

"That's okay, Mom," I reassured her.

My mom felt her reaction to my incident needed to be somehow justified. "Maybe I'm just tired from the move into our new apartment," she apologized. *Maybe there's a little more soft and spongy inside Martha Smith than she's willing to admit,* I thought.

I'm currently on a medication to prevent seizures while the blood around my brain reabsorbs. One of the side effects of the trauma and this medication is irritation and a loss of inhibition, which I must admit I'm kind of enjoying.

"Don't think I can't tell when it's the medication talking and when it's you taking advantage of the situation!" Devon has reminded me more than once.

A Step of Faith

In fall 2012, I was diagnosed with a stress fracture in my left leg. (So to all of those who have said to me before a show, "Break a leg, Jeff!" let me say...thanks a lot!) The orthopedic doctor said it was likely due to softened bones from the arthritis compounded by the side effects of the very medication I had taken for many years to strengthen my bones. This side effect turned out to be a propensity for brittle bones, leading to stress fractures. Ironic, isn't it?

When my old friend Mark Roesler heard about my accident from his wife Laura, he exclaimed, "How's Jeff supposed to pay his bills now that he's handicapped?" Laura laughed. Mark looked confused, then laughed at himself because he realized what he had said.

"He's been doing all right so far," said Laura.

The doctor instructed me to use a walker and not bear weight on the leg for four to six weeks. Devon and I were concerned about how this might interfere with our upcoming mid-winter cruise. But we were encouraged when the pain had greatly diminished by the end of the first month of healing. However, one afternoon while carefully taking a shower with Devon's assistance, I shifted my weight in such a way that sudden sharp pain radiated from my leg. I had had spasms occur previously, but nothing as intense and this time it wasn't going away.

Weakness came over me and I clung to the safety bar on the shower wall. "Carl! I need you right away!" Devon shouted to my PCA who was in the other room.

As Carl wrapped his arms around me from behind, he carefully began to lift me out of the shower. Crrraaaack! No one said a word, but we understood instantly what had happened. The silence was broken by my best impersonation of a soprano hitting a high C.

As the lower portion of my left leg dangled freely, the six to eight feet transfer to lay me down on the carpet felt like the longest mile. We were by now on a first name basis with the paramedics as they had been frequent visitors at our house in recent months. Surgery ensued the following morning and a titanium plate was screwed in along my femur.

Trying to make the best of the situation, I thought the newfound time could give me more opportunity to blog, revise and market my book during my weeks away from performing. The "break" also gave me time to reflect and better understand that God is the author of all things and knows what is best for me in the big picture.

I have come to realize that if not for the physical challenges throughout my life—which as a result, irresistibly draw me to seek God's help—the destructive voice inside me that says *I don't need God; I can do it through my own resources,* would tragically prevail. Instead, I can rest knowing God gives me exactly what I need without giving me enough rope to hang myself. Being blessed with an ability to see the big picture has enabled me to deal with ongoing challenges; yet, I often struggle with focusing on details essential to maintaining a big picture outlook whenever I do not consciously cultivate a deeper relationship with Him. Knowing I am tethered to a bungee cord with the other end affixed to eternal life provides me safety traversing over the perilous crevasses of life. Instead of becoming a cynical and bitter man, dreading what my future may hold, my struggles ironically give me hope as I look forward to the joy and unexpected thrills that He brings to each new day. Despite all, God being faithful to me and gifting me with a positive approach to problems is proof to me of His grace.

The prospect of a long recovery and the corresponding loss of income seriously jeopardized a cruise that we had planned for years, and for which we had pre-paid in full. It was to be a special 10 year anniversary celebration as well as an Extreme Makeover from the ridiculous mishaps from our first cruise. But why should these events cause us to be any less dependent on God's tender mercies? The rollercoaster events of summer/fall, needless to say, proved to be an emotional hardship and added workload on Devon. I owe her so much.

A few days prior to our cruise, my dad had a severe reaction to the anesthesia used in a surgery on his cervical spine. Although Devon and I were ready to cancel our travel plans, Mom and Dad wouldn't hear of it and demanded we go. With a wheelchair, leg immobilizer, and a reduced activity schedule, we left with trepidation.

Upon our return, we were devastated to hear that Dad had experienced catastrophic setbacks that had caused him to rapidly decline. After a much delayed recovery from the anesthesia and a cardiac arrest, Dad was left unable to swallow. There was no hope for recovery. After much deliberation, he decided to invoke his living will directives. He passed away peacefully on January 21, 2013, surrounded by his family. I was honored to give a eulogy at my dad's funeral. I feel so blessed that our relationship had become close after he achieved sobriety. Thank you, Dad, for letting me know I was loved every day of my life.

What doctors expected to be a four to five month recovery period for my femur has become many months longer, complicated by a hospital stay due to a GI infection and an unexpected stress fracture in that same leg. Mindful that the unexpected has been my norm and with my greatest challenge at hand – dealing with the personal and professional impact of whether I'll walk again – I have to put my faith where my mouth is, truly walk the spiritual talk and, in real world terms, test my belief that God is the maestro of my life. If the use of a wheelchair is in my future, so be it; I'll develop a new program and presentation style. With trust in His enduring love, the help of His many encouragers, and most of all, in prayer, I continue to take steps of faith in embracing His plan for my life.

"Shouts of joy and victory resound in the tents of the righteous: 'The LORD's right hand has done mighty things!'" Psalm 118:15

CHAPTER 5–MYTHS AND FACTS ABOUT DISABILITIES – A QUICK GUIDE TO FEELING COMFORTABLE AROUND DIFFERENCES

In spite of shared interests, the depth and breadth of opinion within the blind and disabled community is vast. Therefore, the views expressed in the following are those of Jeffrey Smith solely, and not those of the blind and disabled community at large.

Currently the whole disability movement is under great transition. Labels are being used and changed daily. Just as some of us struggle to use the correct racial terms at times, I too struggle with using the correct "disabled term" at times, even though I am the epicenter of this subject. Essentially I am comfortable with words such as "differently abled," "a person with a disability," "disabled," "handicapped," "crippled," but I struggle with connotation. If someone calls me "crippled," I don't blanch as long as the word is used in the right context. That I have a crippled body is a fact, but I am not "crippled" because that word defines my essence as being broken. I am anything but broken. The essence of my being is adaptable, entrepreneurial, innovative, creative, curious, imaginative, critically thinking, and problem solving. Call me what you wish, but don't define me by my "disability." Labeling is just one idea among many to consider within the context of engaging people with disabilities. We hope in this section to improve communication with this major and underutilized segment of the population.

1. **MYTH:** My disability defines who I am.
   "I just can't believe you would marry someone like that," Devon's acquaintance remarked, ignoring the majority of who I am and what I can offer the marriage.
   FACT: A person's disability is merely a characteristic, not a defining feature, of who they are. To other people, my blindness and other disabilities may appear to be my dominant feature, but I see it as just another part of me and rarely even think of it; personhood trumps disability.

2. **MYTH:** People need to be sensitive about word choice to accommodate a person's disability. In the case of blindness, someone might say, "Oh! I'm so embarrassed that I asked you if you watched the Vikings game yesterday."
   FACT: Altering language use is not needed. Using normal figures of speech makes people with disabilities feel included. People who are blind "watch" things on TV, and people who use wheelchairs "run to the store."

3. **MYTH:** People who are blind have better hearing than the sighted. "You and the superhero Daredevil hear just about everything... right?"
   FACT: People who are blind have normal hearing. The blind simply use more of their other senses to take in information since they are not preoccupied by the visual, which within the sighted world accounts for an estimated 90% of the information taken in.

4. **MYTH:** People with disabilities are courageous and inspiring. "Oh Jeff, I just don't know how you can handle all this day after day."
   FACT: People with disabilities are like anyone else. Attitude is the common denominator, regardless of circumstances. I have just as many good days mixed with the bad as anyone else.

5. **MYTH:** People with disabilities need pity.
   "Here, let me help you make that sandwich. It will be easier."
   FACT: We want empathy, not sympathy. Empathy tears down communication barriers and promotes equality. Sympathy is a counterproductive enabler. Pity is a form of prejudice.

6. **MYTH:** Politically correct language is expected when speaking to a person with a disability.
   "How long have you been... uh, you know... 'sight impaired?'"
   FACT: State the obvious by saying, "How long have you been blind?" It would be like calling a Swede "Norwegian impaired."

7. **MYTH:** People with the same type of disabilities are the same types of people. I call this thinking "Blind Sage Syndrome"—Homer,

Milton, and Master Po (the teacher in the TV show *Kung-Fu*)—all transcendentally wise without sight.

FACT: People with disabilities have their own personalities, character, and perspectives like anyone else.

8. **MYTH:** All blind people know one another.

"I know a blind guy from college; he lives in Salt Lake – Bob Johnson, you know him?"

FACT: All blind people know each other to the extent that all Microsoft employees know one another. Common interests are what attract people together (e.g., hobbies, sports, types of movies) instead of the fact of being blind. It would be like saying, "You're sighted! No way! So am I! Let's go have coffee."

9. **MYTH:** People who are blind are poor navigators. "Ma'am, can you please take me into the men's room?"

FACT: The blind have learned navigational skills based on recognizing landmarks and using recall. In our family, I am the human GPS for my intelligent but directionally-challenged sighted wife!

10. **MYTH:** Several people have mentioned I look like opera singer Andrea Bocelli, named in 1998 as one of People Magazine's 50 Most Beautiful People.

FACT: No myth here, as far as I can see. Seriously, other than being blind, there's absolutely nothing he and I have in common. In contrast to Bocelli, I am a "jailhouse singer." In other words, behind a few bars and I can't find the key.

11. **MYTH:** People with disabilities are more apt to be irritable, demanding, and complaining.

"Now look what you've done! Your face broke my white cane."

FACT: It's not personal circumstances that necessarily make someone antisocial. For example Al Pacino in Scent of a Woman portrays an iconoclastic blind person who is embittered, rude, and manipulative. His personality traits were inherent and not because he was blind.

12. MYTH: People with disabilities do not laugh about their situations.

"This is no laughing matter…"

FACT: Laughing at my disability is therapeutic. It provides a healthy element of control over things I cannot control. For example, recently while I was still in bed my ileostomy bag blew, waking my wife Devon in the process. My arthritis was miraculously gone as I quickly made my way to the bathroom. Devon called it the "adrenaline cure."

13. MYTH: All people with disabilities have the same capacity to deal with his/her life's circumstances.

"How do you expect me to accomplish that with my disability?"

FACT: Some people are more adept at dealing with difficult circumstances than others based on their desire to excel. Their capacity to deal with adversity is dependent on the use of creative compensatory strategies, community, and consistency. Helen Keller said, "You will find a joy in overcoming obstacles." Blind doesn't mean helpless. Disability can be a strength.

Blind doesn't mean helpless. Disability can be a strength.

14. MYTH: People with a disability cannot attain personal success because they need help.

"Jeff, how good can you be, really, as a blind magician?"

FACT: Success comes from being the master of your disability. Being blind is beneficial to my magic presentation because my eyes don't play tricks on me. Kids approach me after shows and tell me I'm the best magician they ever saw with or without sight. When you listen to Ray Charles singing "Georgia," do you think he is the best among blind R&B singers, or is he simply one of the best R&B artists ever? Was Beethoven one of the best deaf composers, or simply one of the best composers of all time? When you hear FDR reassuring the nation, "We have nothing to fear but fear itself," do you think of him as one of the best presidents who used a wheelchair or as one of the best orators of a generation?

15. **MYTH:** A person with a disability struggles against an unaccommodating world.
"Hi, I'm blind. What's your name?"
FACT: How people with disabilities view themselves determines how they fit in. "Self-pity is our worst enemy and if we yield to it, we can never do anything good in the world." – Helen Keller.

16. **MYTH:** People with a disability naturally dwell on what they have lost.
"Man, I wish I could see what you see, run like you run, and speak effortlessly like you speak."
FACT: People with a disability are focused on what they *can* do. Like all people, I have unique abilities. I have health imbuing humor, vivid imagination, and the tenacity of a pit bull. So throw me a bone!

17. **MYTH:** It's polite to help people with disabilities without asking them first.
Once, despite my protests, I was helped/dragged across the street by someone hard of hearing when I had no intent to cross.
FACT: People with disabilities, like anyone else, strive for independence. Give them dignity by treating them like people instead of a problem to be solved. You wouldn't ask a commercial pilot if he or she needed help flying a plane, so don't assume a person with a disability needs or wants help with a given task; they want independence like anyone else.

18. **MYTH:** People with disabilities are more transparent about personal affairs than non-disabled people.

A woman, out of the blue, approached Devon and me while shopping and said, "Let me pray for you now." She assumed I was ready to discuss deeply personal aspects of my life right in the grocery aisle. First, how could anyone assume our marriage is going to be any more challenging than others? Second, I'm more than willing to share great intimacies of my life for the bigger goal of helping educate the populace about disability awareness, but there is a time and place for everything.

FACT: Personal space is personal regardless of who owns it. Violations of personal space are never okay.

19. **MYTH:** Interacting with people with disabilities is potentially embarrassing.

    While waiting for a bus, someone approached me and asked, "Do you have the time?" "Sure," I responded checking my Braille watch. "Oh, Man! Sorry! I had no idea you were blind! I'm really sorry!" the man said backing away from me.

    FACT: It's potentially embarrassing to interact with anyone, but interaction is the spice of life. Statistics show that foot-in-mouth disease ravages the entire human population.

20. **MYTH:** People who are blind naturally avoid sighted activities.

    "Hey Jeff, let's go see a Twins game! Oh, that's right...you wouldn't be interested."

    FACT: Activities transcend vision and are built on camaraderie, conversation, laughter, and sharing. People who are blind like to browse, explore, and, yes, go to the movies. I live and die with the Minnesota Twins. Any person who is blind can determine the play- by-play by listening to the nuances of crowd reaction. Just because I experience shared activities in a different way doesn't mean I don't get as much out of them.

21. **MYTH:** People with disabilities are more likely to be self-employed so they can work at their own pace.

    "I made six telemarketing calls today. That's got to be a record!"

    FACT: Self-employment is the purest form of capitalism. If I don't book shows, I lose the house. My clients dictate my hours.

I've prepped for shows at 5:00 a.m. and performed at midnight. Self-employment in the entertainment industry is not 9-5.

22. **MYTH:** People who are blind only see black. "Mister Jeffo, do you see dark black or just kinda black?"
    FACT: A question like this is a sort of mixed metaphor. I see what my index finger sees: nothing, rather than black. I see nothing, but I imagine in vivid colors which leaves no room for black.

23. **MYTH:** People with disabilities can never feel comfortable with their own disabilities.
    "If I feel awkward around you, I can imagine how you must feel."
    FACT: The perception that being a blind magician must be totally outside of my comfort zone piques the curiosity of people and gives me a uniquely marketable niche as a presenter. Any difficulties I have as a magician are the same as those of a sighted, able-bodied performer: learning tricks, showmanship, and stage presence. Amazing Jeffo has provided great comforts, meaningful employment, a wife, a home, and the ability to touch people's lives.

24. **MYTH:** Parents of children with disabilities treat them differently than their non-disabled children.
    "Must be nice not having to do chores, huh Jeff?"
    FACT: Informed parents encourage *all* their children to use their abilities to their fullest. Despite my protests, my mom made me walk a long, steep hill each day to the bus stop. I emptied the dishwasher, made my bed, cleaned the toilet, and kept my side of the bedroom clean. My chores were different but not less important than those of my siblings.

25. **MYTH:** People who stutter are stupid. "Spit it out, you stammering fool!"
    FACT: People who stutter have IQ scores 14 points higher than the national average, according to researchers. One of the causes of stuttering is the mind having too many thoughts at the same time rather than the absence of thought. Hence, the brain-speech pipeline becomes jammed.

26. MYTH: People with disabilities socialize primarily with other people who have disabilities.

"Most of your friends are blind, right?"

FACT: Getting together on a social basis with a group of people only because they have disabilities is not socializing—that is a support group. I socialize with people who share similar interests like sports, politics, and religion—and if they happen to have a disability, that is secondary.

27. MYTH: Most people upon meeting a person with multiple disabilities should be perfectly comfortable with the initial contact.

"Quit staring at that little boy, Johnny. It's impolite."

FACT: Most people do react at an emotional level when first meeting or seeing someone with multiple disabilities. Once a relationship is established, the prominence of the disabilities diminishes and the personality dominates. Natural curiosity is to be expected and is OK, but please don't stare. It makes no difference to me, but it bugs my wife.

28. MYTH: With the passage of The Americans with Disabilities Act (ADA), people with disabilities no longer face discrimination or access issues.

"Come on, ADA is the law. Look at all those ramps and elevators."

FACT: Workplace and societal discrimination are still present today. According to the Office of Disability Employment Policy (ODEP), the unemployment rate for people with disabilities is double the national average.

29. MYTH: People with disabilities cannot enjoy marital sexual intimacy.

"I guess there won't be any little Jeffies running around, huh?"

FACT: God blesses marital intimacy, no matter the physical condition of the participants; besides, where there is a will, there is a way.

30. MYTH: People who are blind can't use the technology of today.

"Dang It! I'm all about touch but how am I supposed to use a touch screen?

FACT: Technology is neutral and serves the needs of everyone without bias. In truth, technology creates opportunities for people with disabilities.

Just as all people who are blind don't naturally play the harmonica, learning new technology takes time, patience and perseverance.

I walked into a shopping mall, and someone yelled out, "Isn't that the world famous Amazing Jeffo?" Everyone turned and looked at me. I was so embarrassed! I wish I hadn't yelled it out in the first place!

Here are Jeff Smith's
Top 10 Benefits of Being Blind:

#10 – He was voted "Most Popular Snack Table Monitor" at the Weight Watchers Convention!

#9 – He saves BIG money on bed sheets by NOT needing to cut eye holes for his Halloween costume!

#8 – He's a popular house guest since the hostess doesn't have to tidy up first!

#7 – He's never lonely. He's running into people ALL the time!

#6 – He's qualified as a car parking valet at the demolition derby!

#5 – He's loved by co-workers because he doesn't compete for the office with the window!

#4 – He's still using the original flashlight batteries, 25 years later!

#3 – If you invite him over for the 4th of July, instead of buying expensive fireworks, you can just pop bubble wrap!

#2 – He can hold the tape dispenser for you while you wrap his Christmas presents!

And Jeff's NUMBER ONE benefit to being blind:

He's never had to answer that most dangerous of all questions: "Honey, does this outfit make me look fat?"

If you're interested in keeping up with personal and professional events in Jeff Smith's life, please check out his frequent amusing musings at: Amazingjeffo.com/blog, or by linking through his website: www.amazingjeffo.com

If you would like to have Jeffrey Smith speak at your event, or Amazing Jeffo perform for your group, please contact him at: jeffo@amazingjeffo.com. Or for more information: www.amazingjeffo.com, or www.jeff-speaks.com

Seeing Light in the Darkness
Discussion Questions

1. As outlined in chapter 2 and on, do you feel young Smith's cool exterior aided or harmed his ability to deal with the onset of his various diseases? How did Smith's childhood innocence help or hinder him in facing challenges during his early years?

2. As portrayed in chapter 4, discuss young Smith's ethereal vision in his hospital room. Do you feel it was a hallucination or a spiritual phenomenon?

3. At the time Smith was a child, parents sometimes still institutionalized children with disabilities. Did you know anyone with a child like Jeff? What choice did the parents make for their child and how did that decision play out in their lives?

4. It's evident in the book that Jeff's parents did not have an easy marriage because of his disabilities and other factors. How might it have impacted his physical and social development? What positives and negatives came from his family's dynamics?

5. Talk about the book's humor. What did you find funny, and is Smith's use of humor helpful or appropriate in dealing with serious disabilities?

6. "Different" kids like young Smith are often teased or bullied at school. Does his story give you any ideas on preventing or stopping that behavior?

7. When young Smith was growing up, his mother didn't pamper him, or wait on him hand and foot. She had the same requirements and expectations for him as she did for his siblings. If you have (or were to have) a child with special needs, how similar or different is your approach from that of Smith's mother? Do (would) you have fewer or greater expectations for your child?

8. Medical staff and teachers broke rules for Smith: allowing him to shoot socks up the hospital mail tube and allowing him to repeatedly skip high school health class. When is it appropriate for professionals to go against official policy?

9. Talk about Smith's upbringing: socio/economically, family size, relationships among family members, etc. What privileges and disadvantages did he have unrelated to his disabilities?

10. Outside of your immediate family, has someone made an impact on you as Tom Dosch made on Smith? If so, who? And what was that impact?

11. Two major themes in *Seeing Light in the Darkness* are friendship and faith. What role did Smith's friends play in his personal development and spiritual journey? Do you have friends who play a similarly important role in your life?

12. Smith's challenges early in life both helped and hindered his personal and professional growth as an adult. What have you learned about your challenges after reading this book? Has it broadened or changed your perspective about a difficult issue— personal or societal?

13. Despite Smith's life-threatening illnesses, multiple disabilities, and seemingly impossible challenges, *Seeing Light in the Darkness* is not a tragic memoir. Instead, it is encouraging and uplifting. How does Smith accomplish this?

14. Consider the people you know who are living with disabilities. Did the experiences of Smith change or shed light on your understanding of them?

15. What other new insights, if any, did you gain? What struck you as significant—profound, amusing, sad, illuminating, disturbing?